NF

INTERNATIONAL PROBLEMS OF ECONOMIC INTERDEPENDENCE

CENTRAL ISSUES IN CONTEMPORARY ECONOMIC THEORY
AND POLICY

General Editor: **Mario Baldassarri**, *Professor of Economics, University of Rome
'La Sapienza', Italy*

Published titles

Mario Baldassarri (*editor*)
INDUSTRIAL POLICY IN ITALY, 1945-90

Mario Baldassarri (*editor*)
KEYNES AND THE ECONOMIC POLICIES OF THE 1980s

Mario Baldassarri (*editor*)
OLIGOPOLY AND DYNAMIC COMPETITION

Mario Baldassarri (*editor*)
THE ITALIAN ECONOMY: HEAVEN OR HELL?

Mario Baldassarri and Paolo Annunziato (*editors*)
IS THE ECONOMIC CYCLE STILL ALIVE?: THEORY, EVIDENCE
AND POLICIES

Mario Baldassarri, Massimo Di Matteo and Robert Mundell (*editors*)
INTERNATIONAL PROBLEMS OF ECONOMIC INTERDEPENDENCE

Mario Baldassarri, John McCallum and Robert Mundell (*editors*)
DEBT, DEFICIT AND ECONOMIC PERFORMANCE

Mario Baldassarri, John McCallum and Robert Mundell (*editors*)
GLOBAL DISEQUILIBRIUM IN THE WORLD ECONOMY

Mario Baldassarri and Robert Mundell (*editors*)
BUILDING THE NEW EUROPE
Volume 1: The Single Market and Monetary Unification
Volume 2: Eastern Europe's Transition to a Market Economy

Mario Baldassarri, Luigi Paganetto and Edmund S. Phelps (*editors*)
INTERNATIONAL ECONOMIC INTERDEPENDENCE,
PATTERNS OF TRADE BALANCES AND ECONOMIC POLICY
COORDINATION

Mario Baldassarri, Luigi Paganetto and Edmund S. Phelps (*editors*)
PRIVATIZATION PROCESSES IN EASTERN EUROPE: THEORETICAL
FOUNDATIONS AND EMPIRICAL RESULTS

Mario Baldassarri, Luigi Paganetto and Edmund S. Phelps (*editors*)
WORLD SAVING, PROSPERITY AND GROWTH

Mario Baldassarri, Luigi Paganetto and Edmund S. Phelps (*editors*)
INTERNATIONAL DIFFERENCES IN GROWTH RATES: Market
Globalization and Economic Areas

Mario Baldassarri and Paolo Roberti (*editors*)
FISCAL PROBLEMS IN THE SINGLE-MARKET EUROPE

International Problems of Economic Interdependence

Edited by

Mario Baldassarri

Professor of Economics
University of Rome 'La Sapienza'
Italy

Massimo Di Matteo

Associate Professor of Economics
University of Siena
Italy

and

Robert Mundell

Professor of Economics
Columbia University, New York

St. Martin's Press

in association with
Rivista di Politica Economica, SIPI, Rome
and
CEIS, University 'Tor Vergata', Rome

337
I615

First published in Great Britain 1994 by
THE MACMILLAN PRESS LTD
Houndmills, Basingstoke, Hampshire RG21 2XS
and London
Companies and representatives
throughout the world

A catalogue record for this book is available
from the British Library.

ISBN 0–333–62297–9

Printed and bound in Great Britain by
Antony Rowe Ltd
Chippenham, Wiltshire

First published in the United States of America 1994 by
Scholarly and Reference Division,
ST. MARTIN'S PRESS, INC.,
175 Fifth Avenue,
New York, N.Y. 10010

ISBN 0–312–12126–1

Library of Congress Cataloging-in-Publication Data
International problems of economic interdependence / edited by Mario
Baldassarri, Massimo Di Matteo and Robert Mundell.
p.   cm. — (Central issues in contemporary economic theory and
policy)
Includes index.
ISBN 0–312–12126–1
1. International economic relations.   2. International trade.
I. Baldassarri, Mario, 1946–   .   II. Di Matteo, Massimo.
III. Mundell, Robert.   IV. Series.
HF1359. I5863   1994
337—dc20   94–20703
                                                      CIP

Contents

v

PART III: THE COMPLEX CONNECTIONS BETWEEN NORTH
AND SOUTH

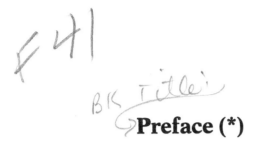

Preface (*)

Massimo Di Matteo
Università di Siena

The three main topics dealt with in the volume are the problems arising from interdependence between countries, the difficulties of real and financial integration processes and the stormy relations between North and South.

1. - On the first point, traditional analysis has long maintained that the adoption of flexible exchange rates, able to isolate an economy from external perturbations, is a way of reducing the effects of strong interdependence between countries. However, this theoretical position has been the subject of increasingly severe criticism, beginning with Laursen and Metzler and culminating in Dornbusch's (1) treatment of the Mundell-Fleming analysis. The emerging idea is that with flexible exchange rates, for example expansive fiscal policy in the USA benefits both Europe and the USA, whereas expansive monetary policy in the USA is still to the advantage of the USA but not Europe.

The implications do not seem to agree with events in the eighties, when unemployment stabilized in Europe at a high level despite expansive fiscal and restrictive monetary policy in the US. Phelps and Fitoussi (2) have devised a model of imperfect competi-

(*) The papers published here are revised versions of some of the lectures delivered in July 1992 at the International School of Economic Research (ISER) held, as it has been each year since 1987, at the Certosa di Pontignano (Siena), and organized by the Dipartimento di economia politica of Siena University with the financial contributions of CNR.

(1) See DORNBUSCH R. [4].
(2) See FITOUSSI J.P. - PHELPS E.[5].

tion to explain these events, according to which expansive US fiscal policy, such as that implemented in the Reagan era, was a beggar-my-neighbour policy, whereas the expansive monetary policy had beneficial effects in the USA and Europe. In his paper, Frisch criticises this model as being based among other things on the hypothesis that in Europe the aim of monetary policy was to stabilize the nominal income. He shows that conclusions qualitatively similar to those reached by Phelps and Fitoussi follow from a version of their model that allows ample space for the fact that in European econ-omies (3) there is a strong trend towards stabilization of the real wage.

Still with an eye to the relations between the USA and Europe in the eighties, the problem of the interdependence between countries is analysed with a different type of model by van der Ploeg and Alogoskoufis. In their paper they propose a two-country, overlapping generation model in which the growth rate, endogenously determined, is equal in the two countries (in the absence of adjust-ment costs of investment): this follows from the fact that, with perfect mobility of capital, it is necessary to keep the real interest rate equal in the two countries. The differences between the two countries lie essentially in their different productive efficiency (which explains why incomes in the two countries do not converge) and in their different fiscal policy. The two authors examine the effects of a different repartition of the public debt (which is constant at a world level) between two countries and find that the country with the higher debt/GDP ratio also has a higher foreign debt (as in the case of the USA). Furthermore an average increase in the overall debt/GDP ratio decreases the rate of growth: the reason for this is clear, the model being of the neoclassical type in which savings determine investments and unemployment settles at its natural level. The latter implication is in contrast with the situation in the eighties when unemployment rose in Europe. However I think that a variable level of unemployment could easily be inserted in the model on the basis, for example, of the theoretical (and empirically verified) economic analysis of Layard-Nickell-Jackman (4).

---

(3) See BRUNO M. - SACHS J. [1].
(4) See LAYARD R. - NICKELL S. - JACKMAN R. [8].

The phenomena of unemployment and inflation, and the increasing interdependence of the industrialized world, in terms of movement of both goods and capital, have been among the causes of one of the hottest debates on the coordination of macroeconomic policy since the famous dispute on locomotives in the second half of the seventies. In actual fact, coordination has only occasionally been achieved and with limited objectives such as the Plaza (1986) and the Louvre (1987) agreements on exchange rates. Obstacles to the achievement of this aim have increased over the years, and we recently saw Germany increase the rate of interest in 1991, despite the stagnant-recessive condition of the world economy.

The benefits deriving from coordination depend on what public good is lacking in the "spontaneous" world equilibrium: a satisfactory level of employment or stable currency. In their contribution, Frankel and Funke underline three of the many economic reasons (ignoring ideological and political motives) that make coordination difficult: the fact that defection is possible (and also convenient), lack of credibility in the struggle against inflation, and uncertainty. The latter can in turn be divided into three main categories: uncertainty about the model to choose, uncertainty as to the value of the "multiplier" and uncertainty about how to divide the benefits of coordination between the various countries and/or objectives.

Frankel and Funke suggest that these difficulties could be reduced if the countries involved chose a single, clear, precise, easily measurable objective such as monetary income. On the basis of a two-country model, they show that such an objective is nearly always better than others such as constant growth of money supply, corroborating this with the results of simulation using the McKibbin-Sachs model.

2. - The case of Germany's economic policy mentioned above brings us to the second subject discussed, namely the effect of endeavouring to increase real and financial integration within Europe. The transition from a customs union to a genuine common market (i.e. one with free circulation of production factors) and the forecast of economic union in the near future have stimulated lively discussion (see for example the interesting article by Spaventa (5)) that the events of September 1992 will surely reinforce.

The paper by Gandolfo and Padoan is aimed at explaining the instability of the Italian economy and the lira. They stress that a fixed exchange rate is incompatible with perfect mobility of capital as soon as the economic agents perceive divergence on the fundamentals. Spaventa, among others, sustained that the change of regime brought about by EMS membership enabled Italy to hold a position in which the influx of capital financed the trade balance deficit that it was no longer necessary to correct with restrictions on demand; in other words, capital would have continued coming in because the country had earned credibility by keeping its exchange rate rigidly fixed. In the light of recent events, this position seems correct in the medium but not in the long term.

The results of Gandolfo and Padoan are obtained with a macroeconomic disequilibrium model of the Italian economy, estimated in continuous time and based on an eclectic approach in which great importance is given to realistic hypotheses reflecting the institutional idiosyncrasies of the country (6). In the framework of their model, that uses different types of expectations, the authors note that although the exchange rate may be the subject of expectations based on the fundamentals, they are unable to avoid the destabilizing effects of the liberalization of capital movement. Gandolfo and Padoan also examine the effects of policies aimed at counteracting this instability, ranging from Tobin's tax on capital movement to further liberalization of the movement of goods: all have the effect of delaying but not changing the final result.

The paper of McKinnon also contributes to the debate, concisely but effectively casting doubts on the possibility of a transition to a single currency in the present European situation in which several countries have a high public debt/GDP ratio. The latent instability implied by this situation can be eliminated or rendered harmless if investors consider there is a lender of last resort, such as the Central Bank of the country in question. Hence under such conditions in

(5) See SPAVENTA L. [10].
(6) See GANDOLFO G. - PADOAN P.C. [6].

these countries, the transition to a single currency and the accompanying institution of the Central European Bank would make it impossible to use inflation (even as an extreme measure) to solve the public debt problem (as has often been done in the past and in countries in other situations).

McKinnon's argument counters the position of those who sustained that monetary coordination would lead to fiscal coordination, an event that has not occurred (at least in Italy). His argument also runs counter to the idea of instituting a true single currency in order to eliminate speculative movements of capital.

Among other things, McKinnon observes that after the violent fluctuations of exchange rates in the seventies, there was a trend to create new regional blocs and to reinforce those already existing, within which it is easier to establish fixed exchange rates that facilitate trade and reduce the risk of the investor.

Clearly there are many reasons for this phenomenon, and in her paper, Chichilnisky recalls several discussed in occasion of the recent NAFTA. The main question posed by Chichilnisky is whether this regionalization leads to greater or less liberalization of world trade. According to the traditional approach, the creation of customs unions does not necessarily bring advantages, as trade creation can be counterbalanced by trade diversion which is as wide as the customs union is small with respect to the rest of the world. Moreover, it is well known that a single (group of) country(ies) can improve its(their) welfare by imposing the optimum tariff. This presupposes a certain market power leading to a favourable change in the terms of trade (more accentuated in the Metzler case) and to restriction of trade. It follows that a sufficiently large group of countries (e.g. the EC) will tend to impose duty on goods from outside.

However it should not be forgotten that the greatest advantages of customs unions come from widening of the market, that according to the old proposition of Adam Smith leads to an increase in the division of labour, namely increased productivity and efficiency. Chichilnisky builds a general equilibrium model with increasing returns to scale generated by economies external to the firms (in order to conserve competition) and shows that in such a case it does not benefit a group of countries to restrict trade as it would prevent the exploitation of the scale economies on which the union is based. Hence, to the extent that a union is based on the exploitation of scale economies, it should be in favour of increased rather than restricted trade.

A clue that NAFTA could be based on comparative advantages rather than the exploitation of scale economies is suggested by the fact that it is hoped, among other things, that it leads to a decrease in the emigration of labour from Mexico to the USA. This conclusion is based on the traditional H-O-S theory according to which movements of goods and factors are substitutes (7) so that liberalization of trade reduces flows of factors induced by wage and interest differentials.

3 - This leads us to North-South relations, the third topic discussed. One of the most controversial questions of this vast topic are the patterns of the terms of trade between manufactured and primary goods. On one hand it was considered (since the work of Prebisch and Singer) that there was a secular trend for the ratio to increase and hence for the situation of the South to deteriorate. On the other hand, the exports of the South were considered to be instable so that the South could not count on them for building a coherent development policy.

On the first point, recent studies have found that although the phenomenon exists, it is not as severe as was thought (8). Attention has also been focused on the variability of primary commodity prices as source of instability of exports. Kaldor recently called attention to the deflationary effects in the North and South of a fall in primary commodity prices (reflecting the thesis of Lewis (9) on the thirties) and to the stagflationary effects of an increase in these prices. He hoped for stabilization of primary commodity prices in the interests of both groups of countries.

---

(7) For a discussion of the basis of this theory, see CHICHILNISKY G. - DI MATTEO M. [2].

(8) See GRILLI E - YANG M.C. [7].

(9) See LEWIS A.W. [9].

In his paper, Newbery concentrates on the causes of the particular type of variability and persistence shown by time series of prices of primary commodities. He identifies two main causes: the fact that these commodities are stocked by economic agents who have expectations of future prices and the fact that storage cannot be negative. Moreover, the economic cycle of the North can cause fluctuations in demand, particularly for intermediate goods.

How can this instability be reduced? Newbery proposes several sophisticated financial instruments that cannot, however, be used easily when producer countries are in heavy deficit and cannot freely obtain loans. Moreover, large scale storage has high costs and low marginal benefits. Hence stabilization is useful for avoiding attempts by the South to increase exports to settle its deficit, leading to deterioration of its initial situation via a decrease in the terms of trade, but it is not easy to find efficient and economical stabilization schemes, given the type of price fluctuations and deficit of the South.

This leads to the last paper, by Di Matteo, that rather dampens enthusiasm for recommending export enhancement policies to countries of the South. The starting point of his analysis is that the South should be modelled in a manner compatible with certain of its empirical characteristics, not only that of a supply of labour highly elastic to the real wage, but also the fact that the South exports highly labour-intensive goods and has dualistic technology (unlike the North). If these assumptions are made, Chichilnisky, using a static model of general equilibrium, has shown (10) that the welfare of the South, unlike that of the North, is negatively correlated with an increase in exports.

This implication has been the subject of much criticism, because since Nurkse's analysis, exports were generally regarded as the prime mover of growth in neoclassical and neokeynesian models. Di Matteo recalls these facts in his paper, dedicated to a dynamic extension of Chichilnisky's original model. The main results obtained are that accumulation (decumulation) of capital in the South is accompanied by a decrease (increase) in exports, and that beyond

---

(10) See CHICHILNISKY G. [3].

*a certain limit, the South ceases to accumulate, even if the North
continues to do so. Accumulation in the South can continue if
technical progress slows the fall of prices of services of capital
associated with the dynamic process described, and/or if demand for
industrial goods keeps pace with the process of accumulation.*

BIBLIOGRAPHY

[1] BRUNO M. - SACHS J.: *Economics of Worldwide Stagflation*, Cambridge, Harvard University Press, 1985.

[2] CHICHILNISKY G. - DI MATTEO M.: *Migration of Labour and Capital in a General Equilibrium Model of North-South Trade*, mimeo, 1992.

[3] CHICHILNISKY G.: «Terms of Trade and Domestic Distribution: Export-led Growth with Abundant Labour», *Journal of Development Economics*, 1981, pp. 163-92.

[4] DORNBUSCH R.: *Open Economy Macroeconomics*, New York, Basic Books, 1980.

[5] FITOUSSI J.P. - PHELPS E.: *The Slump in Europe*, Oxford, B. Blackwell, 1988.

[6] GANDOLFO G. - PADOAN P.C.: «The Mark V Version of the Italian Continuous Time Model», Università di Siena, *Quaderni dell'istituto di economia*, n. 70, 1990.

[7] GRILLI E. - YANG M.C.: «Primary Commodity Prices, Manufactured Geods Prices, and the Terms of Trade of Developing Countries: What the Long Run Shows», World Bank, *Economic Review*, 1988, pp. 1-48.

[8] LAYARD R. - NICKELL S. - JACKMAN R.: *Unemployment*, Oxford, Oxford University Press, 1991.

[9] LEWIS A.W.: *Economic Survey*, 1919-1939, London, G. Allen & Unwin, 1949.

[10] SPAVENTA L.: «From the European Monetary System to the European Monetary Union: An Uneasy Transition», *Economie Appliquee*, n. 3, 1991.

I - INTERDEPENDENCE BETWEEN COUNTRIES

Fiscal and Monetary Interdependency in the Fitoussi-Phelps Two-Country World

F36

F41

Helmut Frisch
University of Technology, Vienna

Introduction

Assume a two-country world with flexible exchange rates. Associate the foreign country with the "USA" and the home country with "Europe". Does a fiscal expansion in the USA stimulate the economy in Europe? Does a monetary expansion in the US stimulate or contract the output level in Europe? The two-country version of the Mundell-Fleming model offers the following proposition in this context (Dornbusch [4] (*)): a foreign fiscal expansion raises the output level of both countries, while a foreign monetary expansion increases the output level in the foreign country but contracts the output level in the home country.

This familiar proposition was rejected in a recent essay by Fitoussi-Phelps [7].

In contrast, they offer the provocative proposition that in a two-country world with flexible exchange rates a fiscal expansion in the foreign country would contract output in the home country while a monetary expansion in the foreign country leads to an increase in the output levels of both countries. This is exactly the opposite prediction of the Mundell-Fleming model.

(*) *N.B.:* the numbers in square brackets refer to the Bibliography at the end of the paper.

Fitoussi and Phelps argue that the empirical evidence supports their proposition. The US-policy mix of fiscal expansion and monetary contraction in the first half of the 1980's was accompanied by a prolonged "slump" in Europe and was a major factor in the rise in European unemployment.

According to the predictions of the Mundell-Fleming model, the "orthodox view" in terms of the authors, both elements of the US-policy mix — fiscal expansion and monetary contraction — should have been expansionary for Europe.

In this paper I show that the discrepancy between the Fitoussi-Phelps and the Mundell-Fleming model follows from the fact the former imposes a set of new assumptions not found in the latter. I demonstrate that in a more general version of the two-country model of the Fitoussi-Phelps type the effects of a fiscal and monetary expansion in the USA on the output level in Europe are in principle ambiguous (Section 2). It is further shown that Fitoussi and Phelps derive their result exclusively from a specific assumption about supply in Europe which the authors term "liberal monetarism" (Section 3).

According to this rule the monetary authorities "accommodate" a rise in the money demand due to a fall in the interest rate by expanding money supply and "offset" a fall in money demand due to an increase in the interest rate by reducing money supply. Finally I show that "liberal monetarism" is not the only assumption which leads to the Fitoussi-Phelps proposition: The assumption of Real Wage Targetting in the domestic economy (Europe) also yields qualitatively the same conclusion (Section 4).

1. - The Fitoussi-Phelps Open Economy Model

The Fitoussi-Phelps model [7] is from the Mundell-Fleming type but augmented by imperfect competitive markets and a direct influence of the real interest and real exchange rate on the price setting behavior of the firms. A linearized and generalized version can be represented by the following nine equations:

(1) $z = \psi S - \alpha R + g$ *IS*-curve

(2) $m - q = (z + p - q) - \beta i$ *LM*-curve

(3) $c = w + \gamma (z - \bar{k}) + \delta R$ marginal costs

(4) $p = \lambda c + (1 - \lambda)(p^* + e)$ price setting equation

(5) $w = \theta q$ wage indexation

(6) $q = a p + (1 - a)(p^* + e)$ consumer price index

(7) $i = R + \dot{p}^e$ nominal interest rate

(8) $s = p^* + e - p$ real exchange rate

(9) $R = R^* + \dot{s}^e$ real interest rate

These nine equations determine nine endogenous variables: z, e, p, R, q, c, w, i and s, all variables are in logarithm, except interest rates.

1.1 *List of Variables*

z denotes real domestic output, q the consumer price index, e the nominal exchange rate ($-$ domestic price of foreign exchange), i the nominal rate of interest, c nominal marginal costs, R the real interest rate, w nominal wages, p the price of domestic output and s the real exchange rate.

The following variables are exogenous for the domestic economy: p^* the price of foreign output, R^* the foreign real interest rate, $\dot{s}^e$ the expected rate of real depreciation ($= \dot{e}^e + \dot{p}^{*e} - \dot{p}^e$), $\dot{p}^e$ the expected rate of inflation, m the domestic nominal money supply and g the domestic government expenditures (measured in units of domestic output).

Equation *(1)* describes an *IS*-curve for an open economy with the real exchange rate, the real interest rate and government expenditure. This familiar *IS*-curve contrasts with the Fitoussi-Phelps model in which the demand for domestic output is independent of the real exchange rate. They justify the exclusion of any relative price effect by assuming domestic customers buy only domestic goods and foreign consumers only foreign goods.

Equation *(2)* is a standard *LM*-curve. This contrasts with the Fitoussi-Phelps assumption of liberal monetarism, «which makes the supply of money the same function of the interest rate as the demand for money» (Fitoussi-Phelps [7], p 58). This assumption implies the following money supply rule: $dm = -\beta di$. Inserting this money supply rule into the *LM*-curve yields $dz + dp = 0$; i.e. that nominal income is constant. The assumption of liberal monetarism therefore, is equivalent with a policy of nominal income targetting. (Taylor [9]).

Equation *(3)* specifies the marginal cost function. The term $\gamma (z - \hat{k})$ denotes increasing marginal costs. It is assumed that the desired mark-up over marginal costs is positively related with the real interest rate R.

Firms increase prices in response to a rise in R because the future profit is more heavily discounted. Firms, therefore, become less interested in "investing" in low prices today to increase their market share in the future.

According to equation *(4)* the authors suppose that imperfect competitive firms set prices as a weighted average of their own price c and the foreign competitors price ($p^* + e$). This implies price followership of the domestic firms.

Nominal wages are indexed with the consumer price index q; the indexation parameter θ is between zero and one, the case $\theta = 1$ is excluded in the Fitoussi-Phelps model. Equation *(6)* defines the consumer price index.

(7) defines the nominal interest rate, *(8)* the real exchange rate and *(9)* specifies the real interest parity condition (1). For the two-country analysis we assume an identical structure of the foreign economy. The model of the foreign economy is therefore given by equations *(1)* - *(7)* with unstarred variables being replaced by starred variables and vice versa.

In the two-country world $s = -s^*$; i.e. a real depreciation of the domestic currency implies a real appreciation of the foreign currency.

---

(1) It might be useful to derive the real interest parity equation *(7)* by starting with the definition of the real interest rate:

$$R = i - \dot{p}^e = i^* + \dot{e}^e - \dot{p}^e = i^* - \dot{p}^{*e} + (\dot{p}^{*e} + \dot{e}^e - \dot{p}^e) = R^* + \dot{s}^e$$

This model can be converted into two equations:

IS-curve:

(10) $$z - \psi s = g - \alpha (R^* + \dot{s}^e)$$

LL-curve:

(11) $$\lambda [1 + \gamma - \theta] z + [1 - \lambda + \lambda \theta (1 - a)] s =$$
$$= \lambda (1 - \theta) m + \lambda [(1 - \theta) \beta - \delta] (R^* + \dot{s}^e) + \lambda (1 - \theta) \beta \dot{p}^e + \lambda \gamma \bar{k}$$

The endogenous variables are domestic real output z and the real exchange rate s. Equation *(10)* is a familiar open economy *IS*-curve; while the *LL*-curve can be interpreted as a supply curve given equilibrium in the money market.

2. - The Generalized Two-Country Model

The two-country model consists of a pair of *IS-LL*-curves for the domestic economy and a pair of *IS*-LL**-curves for the foreign economy. We assume that both economies have the same size and associate the domestic submodel with «Europe» and the foreign submodel with the "USA". Putting the four equations into a system we obtain:

(12) $$z + \alpha R^* - \psi s = - \alpha \dot{s}^e + g$$

(13) $$Az - BR^* + Cs = \dot{B}s^e + \lambda (1 - \theta) m + \lambda (1 - \theta) \beta \dot{p}^e + \lambda \gamma \bar{k}$$

(14) $$z^* + \alpha^* R^* + \psi^* s = g^*$$

(15) $$A^* z^* - B^* R^* - C^* s = \lambda^* (1 - \theta^*) m^* + \lambda^* (1 - \theta^*) \beta^* \dot{p}^* + \lambda^* \gamma^* \bar{k}^*$$

$$A = \lambda [1 + \gamma - \theta] > 0 \qquad A^*, B^*, C^* \quad \text{correspondingly}$$

$$B = \lambda [\beta (1 - \theta) - \delta] \gtrless 0$$

$$C = [1 - \lambda + \lambda \theta (1 - a)] > 0$$

The endogenous variables are z, z^*, R^* and s, the domestic and foreign output, the foreign real interest rate and the real exchange rate.

While the coefficients A and C are clearly positive the sign of B is not determined. For low values of θ the coefficient B might be positive; if θ approaches one the sign of B becomes negative, assuming $\delta > 0$.

Now we examine the effects of an expansive fiscal and monetary policy in the foreign economy (the US), on the exogenous variables of the two-country world. The results can be obtained from the reduced form equations in Table 1 and Table 2.

TABLE 1

EFFECTS OF AN EXPANSIVE FISCAL POLICY IN THE US

$$(16) \quad \frac{dx}{dg^*} = \frac{\lambda^* (1+\gamma^* - \theta^*) \{\alpha [1-\lambda+\lambda\theta (1-a)] - \psi\lambda [\beta (1-\theta)-\delta]\}}{\Delta}$$

$$(17) \quad \frac{dz^*}{dg^*} = \frac{-\{[\lambda^*(\beta^*(1-\theta^*)-\delta^*) [\psi \lambda (1-\gamma-\theta)+1-\lambda+\lambda\theta (1-a)] +}{\Delta}$$

$$\frac{+ [1-\lambda^*+\lambda^*\theta^* (1-a^*)] [\alpha\lambda (1+\gamma-\theta)+\lambda (\beta (1-\theta)-\delta)]\}}{\Delta}$$

$$(18) \quad \frac{ds}{dg^*} = \frac{\{-\lambda^*(1+\gamma^*-\theta^*) [\alpha\lambda(1+\gamma-\theta)+\lambda (\beta (1-\theta)-\delta)]\}}{\Delta}$$

$$(19) \quad \frac{dR^*}{dg^*} = \frac{-\lambda^* (1+\gamma^*-\theta^*) [\psi\lambda (1+\gamma-\theta) + 1-\lambda+\lambda\theta (1-a)]}{\Delta}$$

$$\Delta = (-1) \{[\alpha\lambda (1+\gamma-\theta)+\lambda (\beta (1-\theta)-\delta)] [\psi^*\lambda^* (1+\gamma^*-\theta^*)+$$
$$+1-\lambda^*+\lambda^*\theta^* (1-a^*)] + [\alpha^*\lambda^* (1+\gamma^*-\theta^*)-\lambda^* (\beta^* (1-\theta^*)+$$
$$-\delta^*)] [\psi\lambda (1+\gamma-\theta)+1-\lambda+\lambda\theta (1-a)]\}$$

TABLE 2

EFFECTS OF AN EXPANSIVE MONETARY POLICY IN THE US

$$(20) \quad \frac{dz}{dm^*} = \frac{-\lambda^* (1-\theta^*) \left[\alpha \left(1-\lambda+\lambda\theta \left(1-a\right)\right) - \psi\lambda \left(\beta \left(1-\theta\right) - \delta\right)\right]}{\Delta}$$

$$(21) \quad \frac{dz^*}{dm^*} = \frac{-\lambda^* (1-\theta^*) \{\alpha^* \left[\psi\lambda \left(1+\gamma-\theta\right)+1-\lambda+\lambda\theta \left(1-a\right)\right] +}{\Delta}$$

$$+ \frac{-\psi^* \left[\alpha\lambda \left(1+\gamma-\theta\right)+\lambda \left(\beta \left(1-\theta\right)-\delta\right)\right]\}}{\Delta}$$

$$(22) \quad \frac{ds}{dm^*} = \frac{\lambda^* (1-\theta^*) \left[\alpha\lambda \left(1+\gamma-\theta\right)+\lambda \left(\beta \left(1-\theta\right)-\delta\right)\right]}{\Delta}$$

$$(23) \quad \frac{dR^*}{dm^*} = \frac{\lambda^* (1-\theta^*) \left[\psi\lambda \left(1+\gamma-\theta\right)+1-\lambda+\lambda\theta \left(1-a\right)\right]}{\Delta}$$

Inspection of Table 1 and Table 2 shows that the signs of the determinant Δ and the reduced form coefficients are indeterminate. The effects of an increase in government expenditure or in the money supply in the US on s, R^*, z and z^* cannot be determined.

It is necessary to distinguish three different cases:

Case 1: $B > 0$ and $B^* > 0$

i.e. $\beta (1-\theta)-\delta>0$,

and: $\beta^* (1-\theta^*) - \delta^* > 0$

This case corresponds to a two-country world, in which the indexation of nominal wages is rather low and the interest elasticity β on the demand for money is sufficiently high.

With these assumptions it follows that:

$$\Delta < 0, \quad \frac{ds}{dg^*} > 0, \quad \frac{dR^*}{dg^*} > 0 \quad \frac{ds}{dm^*} < 0, \quad \frac{dR^*}{dm^*} < 0$$

A fiscal expansion in the US leads to an increase in R^* and in s, implying a real depreciation of the European currency and a real appreciation in the US.

An increase in the foreign money supply leads to a decrease of the foreign interest rate R^* and causes a decrease of the real exchange rate s, implying an appreciation in Europe and a depreciation in the US.

For the fiscal multipliers it follows from *(16)* and *(17)* that:

$$\frac{dz}{dg^*} \gtrless 0 \quad \text{and:} \quad \frac{dz^*}{dg^*} > 0$$

The ambiguous output reaction in Europe is due to various conflicting forces: the rise in R^* reduces the demand for European output while the rise in s stimulates the latter by improving the competitiveness of the European economy. On the other hand, the rise in R^* and the real depreciation generate a cost-push effect through wage indexation, price followership of domestic firms and the interest effect in the marginal cost function. These factors tend to reduce Europe's gain in competitiveness and make it possible for the negative supply effects to dominate.

The unambiguous increase in z^* is due to the positive effect of the real appreciation of the foreign currency on the supply side. On the demand side the direct impact of an increase in g^* is only partially offset by a "crowding out" through a rise in R^* and the real appreciation.

It follows from *(20)* and *(21)* that the money multiplier of the foreign economy is unambiguously positive but the sign of the European money multiplier is undeterminate:

$$\frac{dz}{dm^*} \gtrless 0 \quad \text{and:} \quad \frac{dz^*}{dm^*} > 0$$

The fall in R^* and s has ambiguous effects on the demand and supply side of the European economy. By reason of those offsetting effects the sign of dz / dm^* is ambiguous.

The expansive demand effects on z^* due to the fall in R^* and a rise in s^* are only partially offset by the cost-push effect caused by the real depreciation overseas.

Case 2: $B < 0$ and $B^* < 0$;

i.e. $\beta (1 - \theta) - \delta < 0$,

and: $\beta^* (1 - \theta^*) - \delta^* < 0$.

This case corresponds to a two-country world in which the wage indexation parameters θ, θ^* approach one and $\delta > 0$.

In this case the sign of the determinant becomes ambiguous and the signs of all reduced form coefficients in Table 1 and Table 2 cannot be determined unambiguously without further knowledge of parameter values.

The assumption $(\alpha\gamma - \delta) > 0$ and $(\alpha^*\gamma^* - \delta^*) > 0$ is a sufficient condition that, for all $\theta \in [0,1]$ and $\theta^* \in [0,1]$ and for all $\beta \geq 0$ the following statement holds:

$$\Delta < 0 \qquad \frac{ds}{dg^*} > 0 \qquad \frac{dR^*}{dg^*} > 0 \qquad \frac{ds}{dm^*} < 0 \qquad \frac{dR^*}{dm^*} < 0$$

The effects of an expansive fiscal or monetary policy in the US on the interest rate R^* and the real exchange rate s are the same as in the previous case and for the same reasons.

However, from the coefficients of Table 1 it follows that the signs of the fiscal multipliers switch compared with the above case.

$$\frac{dz}{dg^*} < 0 \qquad \frac{dz^*}{dg^*} \gtrless 0$$

An inspection of Table 2 shows that both money multipliers of the domestic economy and of the foreign economy are unambiguously positive, i.e. $dz / dm^* > 0$ and $dz^*/ dm^* > 0$.

Helmut Frisch

What about the economic reason behind the sufficient condition $(\alpha\gamma - \delta) > 0$? The model assumes monopolistic competition and increasing marginal costs. Monopolistic firms operate in the increasing part of their marginal costs, γ larger than one is therefore a plausible assumption. Given empirical estimates of α (between 0.5 and larger than one) and assuming δ to be very small ($\delta = 0$ in standard models), the above condition is a plausibile assumption.

Case 3: $B < 0$ and $B^* > 0$;

i.e. $\beta (1 - \theta) - \delta < 0$

and: $\beta^* (1 - \theta^*) - \delta^* > 0$.

This asymmetric case corresponds to a two-country world in which indexation of wages in the foreign economy is rather low and β^* sufficiently high. The domestic economy is characterized by a high degree of wage indexation and/or a rather low value of β . We assume again the sufficient condition $(\alpha\gamma - \delta) > 0$ and $(\alpha^*\gamma^* - \delta^*) > 0$. Therefore the statement of case 2 holds. From Table 1 it follows that:

$$\frac{dz}{dg^*} < 0, \qquad \frac{dz^*}{dg^*} > 0$$

$$\frac{dz}{dm^*} > 0, \qquad \frac{dz^*}{dm^*} > 0$$

In the following two Sections we illustrate the asymmetric case by means of two examples, namely liberal monetarism (Section 3) and real wage targetting (Section 4).

3. - Liberal Monetarism

The hypothesis of Fitoussi-Phelps can be expressed in terms of this model by assuming $B^* > 0$ (indicating a low indexation in the US) and setting $\beta = 0$ (i.e. introducing liberal monetarism into the European submodel). The fiscal multipliers become:

$(16.1)\quad \dfrac{dz}{dg^*} = \dfrac{[\lambda^*(1+\gamma^*-\theta^*)]\,[\alpha(1-\lambda+\lambda\theta(1-a))+\psi\lambda\delta]}{\Delta|_{\beta=0}} < 0$

$(17.1)\quad \dfrac{dz^*}{dg^*} = \dfrac{-\{[\lambda^*(\beta^*(1-\theta^*)-\delta^*)]\,[\psi\lambda(1+\gamma-\theta)+1-\lambda+\lambda\theta(1-a)]+}{\Delta|_{\beta=0}}$

$$\dfrac{+[1-\lambda^*+\lambda^*\theta^*(1-a^*)]\,[\lambda(a(1-\theta)+\alpha\gamma-\delta)]\}}{\Delta|_{\beta=0}} > 0$$

$$\Delta|_{\beta=0} = (-1)\,\{\lambda[\alpha(1-\theta)+\alpha\gamma-\delta]\,[\psi^*\lambda^*(1+\gamma^*-\theta^*)+$$

$$+1-\lambda^*+\lambda^*\theta^*(1-a^*)]+$$

$$+[\alpha^*\lambda^*(1+\gamma^*-\theta^*)+\lambda^*(\beta^*(1-\theta^*)-\delta^*)]\,[\psi\lambda(1+\gamma-\theta)+$$

$$+1-\lambda+\lambda\theta(1-a)]\} < 0$$

From equations *(20)* and *(21)* it follows by setting $\beta = 0$ that:

$(20.1)\quad \dfrac{dz}{dm^*} = \dfrac{-\lambda^*(1-\theta^*)\,[\alpha(1-\lambda+\lambda\theta(1-a))+\psi\lambda\delta]}{\Delta|_{\beta=0}} > 0$

$(21.1)\quad \dfrac{dz^*}{dm^*} = \dfrac{-\lambda^*(1-\theta^*)\,\{\alpha^*\,[\psi\lambda(1+\gamma-\theta)+1-\lambda+\lambda\theta(1-a)]+}{\Delta|_{\beta=0}}$

$$\dfrac{+\psi^*\lambda\,[\alpha(1-\theta)+(\alpha\gamma-\delta)]\}}{\Delta|_{\beta=0}} > 0$$

Hence the fiscal expansion in the foreign economy results in an increase in the foreign output *(17.1)* and an unambiguous fall in the domestic output level *(16.1)*.

A foreign monetary expansion — on the other hand — raises both the foreign *(21.1)* and the domestic output level *(20.1)*. We note that by assuming $\beta = 0$ we obtain exactly the opposite conclusions to the Dornbusch model.

These results can be explained if we investigate the supply side of the domestic model. From equations *(3)* through *(8)* it follows that:

$$\lambda\gamma z = \lambda(1-\theta)p - \lambda\delta R - [1-\lambda+\lambda\theta(1-a)]s + \lambda\gamma\bar{k}$$

Making use of the implications of liberal monetarism that $p = -z$, we obtain:

$$z = -\frac{[1-\lambda+\lambda\theta(1-a)]}{\lambda(1+\gamma-\theta)}s - \frac{\delta}{1+\gamma-\theta}R + \frac{\gamma\bar{k}}{1+\gamma-\theta}$$

A fiscal expansion in the foreign country causes R as well as s to rise which ascertains the negative equilibrium output reaction in the domestic economy. In the case of a monetary expansion in the USA the decline in R is associated with a decline in s in Europe which results in an unambiguous rise in the domestic equilibrium output z.

4. - Real Wage Targetting in Europe

The signs of dz/dg^* and dz/dm^* in equations *(16)* and *(20)* depend not only critically on β but also on θ. By setting $\theta=1$ we obtain results which are qualitatively similar to those of Fitoussi-Phelps. In terms of the two-country model this means that we postulate an alternative hypothesis, namely real wage targetting in the domestic economy. In Europe we assume nominal wages are fully indexed to the cost of living, i.e. $\theta=1$ while the US economy is characterized by $B^* > 0$.

The impact effect of a foreign fiscal expansion on the domestic and foreign output level follows from *(16)* and *(17)* by setting $\theta=1$:

(16.2)
$$\frac{dz}{dg^*} = \frac{[\lambda^*(1+\gamma^*-\theta^*)][\alpha(1-\alpha\lambda)+\psi\lambda\delta]}{\Delta|_{\theta=1}} < 0$$

(17.2)
$$\frac{dz^*}{dg^*} = \frac{-\{[\lambda^*(\beta^*(1-\theta^*)-\delta^*)][\psi\lambda\gamma+1-\lambda a)] +}{\Delta|_{\theta=1}}$$

$$\frac{+1-\lambda^*+\lambda^*\theta^*(1-a^*)][\lambda(\alpha\gamma-\delta)]\}}{\Delta|_{\theta=1}} > 0$$

By setting $\theta = 1$ in equation *(20)* and *(21)* we obtain the impact effect of a foreign monetary expansion on the domestic and foreign output:

(20.2) $$\frac{dz}{dm^*} = \frac{-\lambda^*(1-\theta^*)[\alpha(1-\lambda a)) + \psi\lambda\delta)]}{\Delta|_{\theta=1}} > 0$$

(21.2) $$\frac{dz^*}{dm^*} = \frac{-\lambda^*(1-\theta^*)[\alpha^*(\psi\lambda\gamma + 1 - a\lambda) + \psi^*\lambda(\alpha\gamma - \delta)]}{\Delta|_{\theta=1}} > 0$$

with:

$$\Delta|_{\theta=1} = (-1)\{[\lambda(\alpha\gamma - \delta)][\psi^*\lambda^*(1+\gamma^* - \theta^*) + 1 - \lambda^* + \lambda^*\theta^*(1-a^*)] +$$
$$+ [\alpha^*\lambda^*(1+\gamma^* - \theta^*) + \lambda^*(\beta^*(1-\theta^*) - \delta^*)][\psi\lambda\gamma + 1 - \lambda a]\} < 0$$

A comparison of the results in equations *(16.2)*, *(17.2)* and *(20.2)*, *(21.2)* with the case of liberal monetarism equations *(16.1)*, *(17.1)* and *(20.1)*, *(21.1)* shows that both results are qualitatively similar, i.e. dz/dg^* and dz/dm^* have the same sign in both cases.

These results can again be explained by appealing to the supply side of the domestic model. The supply curve can be rewritten as:

$$z = \frac{1}{\gamma}(p-w) = -\frac{\delta}{\gamma}R - \frac{(1-\lambda)}{\lambda\gamma}s$$

From the assumption of real wage targetting in Europe, i.e. $\theta = 1$, it follows that: $w - p = (1-a)s$.

This rule assures the target of stabilizing real consumer wages. Substituting this expression into the supply curve yields:

$$z = -\frac{(1-a\lambda)}{\lambda\gamma}s - \frac{\delta}{\gamma}R + k$$

Following the reasoning given in the previous section, we know that a foreign fiscal expansion raises R and s. These effects — taken together — explain the unambiguous output contraction in Europe according to the above supply relation. A foreign monetary expansion, on the other hand, causes R and s to fall.

Since both effects work in the same direction the above supply curve ascertains the positive sign of dz / dm^*.

The assumption of real wage targetting in Europe therefore is an alternative hypothesis to explain the results of Fitoussi-Phelps that an expansive foreign fiscal policy is a beggar-thy-neighbor policy while an expansive monetary policy is advantageous for both countries.

I argue that real wage targetting in Europe is a superior explanation since the applied literature indicates an overwhelming case for real wage rigidity in Europe in the first half of 1980's (Bruno-Sachs [2]).

5. - The Dornbusch Model

The Dornbusch [4] is the limiting case of the model in Section 1 if: $\delta = \gamma = \Theta = 0$ and $a = \lambda = 1$.

Intuitively this means that the competitive assumption $p = c$ holds and that $p = q$. The interest rate R disappears from the marginal cost function and nominal wages are assumed to be constant. These assumptions hold correspondingly for the foreign economy.

It is easily seen from equations *(16)* and *(17)* that — with these assumptions — the fiscal impact multiplier for both countries becomes positive, i.e. $dz / dg^* > 0$ and $dz^* / dg^* > 0$; while according to *(20)* and *(21)* the money impact multipliers are: $dz / dm^* < 0$ and $dz^* / dm^* > 0$.

Hence given the above simplifying assumptions and assuming fixed commodity prices in both countries, one obtains the Dornbusch proposition ([4], pp. 199-202).

An increase in government expenditure in the foreign country raises real output in both countries. A foreign monetary expansion increases output in the foreign country but will depress output in the home country.

The key equation to understand the economics of the Dornbusch proposition is the domestic *LM*-curve: $\bar{m} = p + z - \beta i$.

The foreign monetary expansion causes unambiguously a fall in the interest rate i, thereby generating excess demand in the money market. The latter can only be eliminated — provided that domestic money supply and the price level are fixed — by a fall in domestic real output, z.

6. - Conclusions

The Fitoussi-Phelps two-country model provides a convenient framework to examine the transmission of fiscal and monetary policy shocks from the foreign economy to the domestic economy and vice versa. The Fitoussi-Phelps proposition that an expansive fiscal policy is a beggar-thy-neighbour policy while an expansive monetary policy is advantageous for both countries, depends exclusively on their assumption of "liberal monetarism" in the domestic economy. The alternative assumption of Real Wage Targetting in the domestic economy generates results which are qualitatively the same as those of Fitoussi-Phelps.

As such both assumptions are consistent with the model. But the evidence seems to contradict the Fitoussi-Phelps story. This is because during the first half of the 1980's Europe did not experience "liberal monetarism", but rather real wage rigidity.

The generalized two-country-model can be written in matrix notion:

$$
\begin{bmatrix}
1 & 0 & \alpha & -\psi \\
A & 0 & -B & C \\
0 & 1 & \alpha^* & \psi^* \\
0 & A^* & -B^* & -C^*
\end{bmatrix}
\begin{bmatrix}
z \\
z^* \\
R^* \\
s
\end{bmatrix}
=
\begin{bmatrix}
\dot{S}_1 \\
\dot{S}_2 \\
\dot{S}_3 \\
\dot{S}_4
\end{bmatrix}
$$

$$A = \lambda\,(1+\gamma-\theta) \qquad\qquad A^* = \lambda^*\,(1+\gamma^*-\theta^*)$$
$$B = \lambda\,[\beta\,(1-\theta) - \delta] \qquad\quad B^* = \lambda^*\,[\beta^*\,(1-\theta^*) - \delta^*]$$
$$C = [1-\lambda+\lambda\theta\,(1-a)] \qquad C^* = [1-\lambda^*+\lambda^*\theta^*\,(1-a^*)]$$

$$\dot{S}_1 = -\,\alpha\,s^e + g$$
$$\dot{S}_2 = \lambda\,[\beta\,(1-\theta)-\delta]\,s^e + \lambda\,(1-\theta)\,m + \lambda\,(1-\theta)\,\beta\,p^e + \lambda\gamma\,\bar{k}$$
$$\dot{S}_3 = g^*$$
$$\dot{S}_4 = \lambda^*\,(1-\theta^*)\,m^* + \lambda^*\,(1-\theta^*)\,\beta^*\,p^* + \lambda^*\gamma^*k^*$$

The determinant of the coefficient matrix is:

$$\Delta = (-1)\,[(\alpha\,A+B)\,(\psi^*\,A^*+C^*) + (\alpha^*A^*+B^*)\,(\psi\,A+C)] =$$
$$\Delta = (-1)\,\{[\alpha\lambda\,(1+\gamma-\theta)+\lambda) + \lambda\,(\beta\,(1-\theta)-\delta)]\,[\psi^*\lambda^*\,(1+\gamma^*-\theta^*) +$$
$$+\ 1-\lambda^*+\lambda^*\theta^*\,(1-a^*)] + [\alpha^*\lambda^*\,(1+\gamma^*-\theta^*) +$$
$$+\ \lambda^*\,(\beta^*\,(1-\theta^*) - \delta^*)]\,[\psi\lambda\,(1+\gamma-\theta)+1-\lambda+\lambda\theta\,(1-a)]\} < 0$$

Applying Cramers rule we solve the system in terms of the exogenous variables.

$$z = \frac{1}{\Delta}\,\{[\alpha s^e - g]\,[\lambda\,(\beta\,(1-\theta)-\delta)\,(\psi^*\lambda^*\,(1+\gamma^*-\theta^*) +$$
$$+\ 1-\lambda^*+\lambda^*\,\theta^*\,(1-a^*)) + (1-\lambda+\lambda\theta\,(1-a))$$

$(\alpha^* \lambda^* (1+\gamma^*-\theta^*) + \lambda^* [\beta^* (1-\theta^*) - \delta^*])] +$

$- \lambda (\beta (1-\theta) - \delta) \, s^e + \lambda (1-\theta) \, m + \lambda (1-\theta) \beta \, p^e + \lambda\gamma \, \bar{k}]$

$[\alpha (\psi^* \lambda^* (1+\gamma^*-\theta^*) + 1 - \lambda^* + \lambda^*\theta^* (1-a^*)) +$

$+ \psi (\alpha^*\lambda^* (1+\gamma^*-\theta^*) + \lambda^* [\beta^* (1-\theta^*) - \delta^*])] +$

$+ [\lambda^* (1+\gamma^*-\theta^*) \, g^* - \lambda^* (1-\theta^*) \, m^* - \lambda^* (1-\theta^*) \beta^* \, p^* +$

$- \lambda^* \gamma^* \, k^*] [\alpha (1-\lambda+\lambda\theta (1-a)) - \psi\lambda (\beta (1-\theta) - \delta)]\}$

$$z^* = \frac{1}{\Delta} \{[\lambda (1+\gamma-\theta) (\alpha \, s^e - g) + \lambda (\beta (1-\theta) - \delta) \, s^e +$$

$+ \lambda (1-\theta) \, m + \lambda (1-\theta) \beta \, p^e + \lambda\gamma \, \bar{k}] [\psi^*\lambda^* (\beta^* (1-\theta^*) - \delta^*) +$

$- \alpha^* (1-\lambda^* + \lambda^*\theta^* (1-a^*))] - g^* [(\lambda^* [\beta^* (1-\theta^*) - \delta^*])$

$(\psi\lambda (1+\gamma-\theta) + 1-\lambda+\lambda\theta (1-a)) + (1-\lambda^* + \lambda^*\theta^* (1-a^*))$

$(\alpha\lambda (1+\gamma-\theta) + \lambda [\beta (1-\theta) - \delta])] - [\lambda^* (1-\theta^*) \, m^* +$

$+ \lambda^* (1-\theta^*) \beta^* \, p^* + \lambda^*\gamma^* \, k^*] [\alpha^* (\psi\lambda (1+\gamma-\theta) + 1-\lambda +$

$+ \lambda\theta (1-a)) + \psi^* (\alpha\lambda (1+\gamma-\theta) + \lambda [\beta (1-\theta) - \delta])]\}$

$$R^* = \frac{1}{\Delta} \{[\lambda (1+\gamma-\theta) (\alpha \, s^e - g) + \lambda (\beta (1-\theta) - \delta) \, s^e +$$

$+ \lambda (1-\theta) \, m + \lambda (1-\theta) \beta \, p^e + \lambda\gamma \, \bar{k}] [\psi^*\lambda^* ((1+\gamma^*-\theta^*) +$

$+ 1-\lambda^* + \lambda^*\theta^* (1-a^*)] + [-\lambda^* (1+\gamma^*-\theta^*) \, g^* +$

$+ \lambda^* (1-\theta^*) \, m^* + \lambda^* (1-\theta^*) \beta^* \, p^* + \lambda^* \gamma^* \, k^*] [\psi \lambda (1+\gamma-\theta) +$

$+ 1-\lambda+\lambda \theta (1-a)]\}$

$$s = \frac{1}{\Delta} \{[\lambda (1+\gamma-\theta) (-\alpha \, s^e + g) - \lambda (\beta (1-\theta) - \delta) \, s^e +$$

$- \lambda (1-\theta) \, m - \lambda (1-\theta) \beta \, p^e - \lambda\gamma \, \bar{k}] [\alpha^*\lambda^* ((1+\gamma^*-\theta^*) +$

$- \lambda^* (\beta^* (1-\theta^*) - \delta^*)] + [-\lambda^* (1+\gamma^*-\theta^*) \, g^* +$

$+ \lambda^* (1-\theta^*) \, m^* + \lambda^* (1-\theta^*) \beta^* \, p^* + \lambda^*\gamma^* \, k^*] [\alpha \lambda (1+\gamma-\theta) +$

$+ \lambda (\beta (1-\theta) - \delta)]\}$

BIBLIOGRAPHY

[1] BRANSON W. - ROTEMBERG J.: «International Adjustment with Wage Rigidities», *European Economic Review*, vol. 13, n. 3, 1980.

[2] BRUNO M. - SACHS J.: *Economics of Worldwide Stagflation*, Cambridge (Mass.), Harvard University Press.

[3] CURRIE D. - LEVINE P.: «Simple Macroeconomics Rules for the Open Economy», Supplement to the *Economic Journal*, vol. 95, 1984.

[4] DORNBUSCH R.: *Open Economy Macroeconomics*, New York, Basic Books, 1980.

[5] FITOUSSI J-P. - LE CACHEUX J.: «Recession and Recovery in Europe (The EMS and International Transmission Mechanism», Institute d'Etudes Politiques de Paris, Paris, *Observatoire Français des Conjontures Economique*, n. 89-06, 1989.

[6] FITOUSSI J-P. - PHELPS E.: «Causes of 1980's Slump in Europe», *Brookings Papers on Economic Activity*, n. 2, 1986.

[7] — — — —: *The Slump in Europe (Reconstructing Open Economy Theory)*, Oxford, Basil Blackwell, 1988.

[8] SACHS J.: «Comment on Fitoussi and Phelps "Causes of 1980's Slump in Europe"», *Brookings Papers on Economic Activity*, n. 2, 1986.

[9] TAYLOR J.: «What would Nominal GNP Targetting do to the Business Cycle?», *Carnegie-Rochester Conference Series on Public Policy*, n. 22, 1985.

Debts, Deficits and Growth in Interdependent Economies [*]

George Alogoskoufis - **Frederick van der Ploeg**
Athens University,   Univesity of Amsterdam,
Athens (Greece)   Amsterdam (The Netherlands)

Introduction

The 1980s have witnessed a significant average rise in public debt to GDP ratios in the main industrial economies. The average net public debt to GDP ratio in the G-7 rose from about 20% in 1979 to 30% in 1989. This rise has been concentrated in the United States and Europe, as Japan's 1989 public debt to GDP ratio was slightly lower that in 1979. The average growth rate of the G-7 fell from 3.5% in the 1970s to 2.8% in the 1980s. No country escaped this slowdown in economic growth. In addition, world real interest rates in the 1980s have been higher on average than in the previous decade. Finally, Japan's external position improved markedly in the 1980s, in contrast to North America which witnessed a significant deterioration.

This paper investigates the relation between budgetary policies, economic growth current account imbalances, real interest rates and the stock market valuation of capital. We address these issues in the context of a theoretical two-country model of endogenous growth with overlapping generations. The analysis assumes capital mobility

(*) This paper is produced as part of a CEPR research programme on Financial and Monetary Integration in Europe, supported by a grant from the Commission of the European Communities under its SPES Programme (no. E89300105/RES). It also draws on research financed by grants from the Ford and Alfred P Sloan Foundations as part of their support for CEPR's research programme in International Macro-economics.
N.B.: the numbers in square brackets refer to the Bibliography at the end of the paper.

and focuses on international spillovers from capital accumulation. The main differences between countries that we assume lie in the efficiency of production and fiscal policies.

We demonstrate that, in the presence of perfect capital mobility, the endogenous growth rate will be the same in all countries and that relative output levels will not converge. Relative outputs and capital stocks are determined by exogenous differences in productive efficiency. The reason for the equality of the endogenous growth rate is the real interest rate equalization implied by perfect capital mobility. As a result, the marginal product of capital must be the same in both countries. Capital will flow into the country with the more efficient productive technology until the marginal product of capital has been equalized in the two countries. After that, capital stocks need to grow by the same percentage to maintain this equality. Since the rate of growth of the capital stock determines the growth rate in this endogenous growth model, growth rates will then be equal.

With regard to the world economy we demonstrate that savings and growth rates are lower than in a comparable representative-household economy. In the latter type of economy all population growth is within the representative household, and there is no entry of non-interconnected generations. In our overlapping-generations model households are not concerned about the welfare of yet unborn agents, and therefore save less than if they were. Since the savings rate determines the rate of capital accumulation, and the latter determines the growth rate, growth will be slower in an overlapping-generations economy. We also demonstrate that the growth rate falls with increases in both the average public debt to GDP ratio and the average GDP share of public consumption. This is because both reduce global savings and, hence, capital accumulation. Such growth effects do not arise in representative-household economies (Alogoskoufis and van der Ploeg [2], [3]).

With regard to differences between countries, we demonstrate that a relative increase in the public debt to GDP ratio and the GDP share of public consumption produces a relative fall in the ratio of external assets to GDP for the country that experiences it. This is because of the fall in its savings rate (private plus public). On impact, the fall in the national savings rate is higher than in steady state, and the economy enters an adjustment path along which it experiences higher current account deficits and a rising external debt to GDP ratio.

We also examine the case where there are convex adjustment costs for investment. If both countries face the same adjustment costs, then endogenous growth rates are again equalized. The equilibrium global growth rate is lower than in the absence of adjustment costs, while the equilibrium world real interest rate is lower. Higher average public debt to GDP ratios bring about an increase in the world real interest rate and reduce the global growth rate and the stock market valuation of capital. If countries have different investment adjustment costs, then the equilibrium growth rates are no longer equal. The economy in which investment is relatively more costly to adjust ends up growing more slowly. If one assumes that countries have different rates of depreciation of the capital stock, then the country with the higher depreciation rate grows more slowly.

The results suggest that a two-country overlapping generations model of endogenous growth can account for the events of the 1980s in terms of budgetary policies. The fall in the average growth rate and the increase in world real interest rates could be the result of the average rise in public debt to GDP ratios. So could events such as the stock market crash of 1987. The higher current account deficits in countries such as the United States can be seen as a reflection of the relative rise in public deficits and public debt that they experienced. This latter result also obtains in exogenous growth, overlapping generations models, but such models cannot account for the growth effects of budgetary policies (Frenkel and Razin [11], Obstfeld [13], van der Ploeg [14] and Alogoskoufis [1]).

The rest of the paper is as follows: Section 1 presents a model of overlapping generations and endogenous growth. The household sector consists of households with finite horizons and there is entry of new households which are not intergenerationally linked. This creates a consumption externality, as households are not concerned with the welfare of future generations, and save less than otherwise. Alternatively, there is a problem of missing markets, as current generations cannot trade with yet unborn generations. Since savings determine investment in equilibrium, the investment rate is inefficiently low. The product market is competitive, but there are production externalities from the capital stock (or "knowledge") of other firms at home and abroad. Because of these production externalities, the private return of capital falls short of its social return. As a result firms use less capital than is socially desirable, and the equilibrium growth rate is inefficiently low. The government finances public consumption by either lump-sum taxes, or public debt. It is assumed throughout that the government is solvent. Section 2 considers a two-country world in which both countries produce goods that are perfect substitutes in consumption. Their only differences are in fiscal policies and the efficiency of production. There are no barriers to international trade in goods or capital. Section 3 derives the equilibrium, discusses its properties, and considers the effects of alternative budgetary policies on the global growth rate. Section 4 analyses relative budgetary policies, and their effect on external debt. Section 5 discusses an extension of the model to allow for investment adjustment costs. Section 6 contains conclusions.

1. - A Model of Overlapping Generations and Endogenous Growth

Consider a world economy with no barriers to trade, and in which each individual economy produces goods that are perfect substitutes in consumption. As a consequence, the law of one price holds.

Each economy consists of a large number of competitive firms, and a population of households which grows at the rate n. The government spends on public goods, can levy lump-sum taxes and issue debt. Households have no intergenerational bequest motive. New households enter the economy at a rate β, and all households face a constant probability of extinction λ at each instant. Thus, the model, which is based on Alogoskoufis and van der Ploeg [3], incorporates the uncertain lifetimes approach of Yaari [19] and Blanchard [8], with the entry of new households that are not connected to previous generations, as in the model of Weil [18]. Weil [18] and Buiter [9] have shown that the entry of new households, unconnected to previous generations, i.e. a positive birth rate of households, is sufficient for departures from Ricardian debt neutrality (Barro [6]).

1.1 Households and Aggregate Consumption

At time t, a household born at instant v solves the following problem:

(1)
$$\text{Max}_{c(v, s)} \int_t^\infty e^{-(\rho-\lambda)(s-t)} \left(\frac{c(v, s)^{1-\sigma^{-1}}}{1 - \sigma^{-1}} \right) ds$$

subject to the instantaneous flow budget identity:

(2)
$$\frac{da(v, t)}{dt} = [r(t) + \lambda] a(v, t) + \omega(v, t) - \tau(v, t) - c(v, t)$$

where c is consumption, a is non-human wealth, ω is the gross instantaneous non-asset income of the household, and τ is the instantaneous tax it pays to the government. ρ is the pure rate of time preference, σ is the elasticity of intertemporal subsitution, and r is the instantaneous real interest rate. The term λa is an actuarially fair life insurance premium, so that when households are alive they receive an extra return λ on their non-human wealth from insurance companies, and when they die their estate (non-human wealth) accrues to their insurance company. This set-up corresponds to a competitive insurance industry with free entry.

Under the requirement that households are solvent, and that the real interest rate is time invariant, as will be shown to be the case in equilibrium, one obtains the following utility maximizing consumption function for the individual household.

(3)
$$c(v, t) = [\lambda + \sigma\rho + (1 - \sigma) r] [a(v, t) + h(v, t)]$$

where: $h(v, t)$ denotes human wealth. This is defined as:

$$(4) \qquad h(v, t) = \int_t^\infty e^{-(r+\lambda)(s-t)} [\omega(v, s) - \tau(v, s)] \, ds$$

In what follows we shall assume that newly born households do not inherit any non-human wealth, but that non-asset income ω and taxes τ are independent of the age of the household. The fraction of the cohort born at time v which is still alive at time t is $\beta L(v) e^{-\lambda(t-v)} = \beta e^{\beta v} e^{-\lambda t}$, where $L(v) = e^{nv}$ denotes the size of the population at time v. This can be used to define population aggregates, say, $C(t) = \beta e^{-\lambda t} \int_{-\infty}^t c(v, t) e^{\beta v} \, dv$. It is straightforward to show that aggregate consumption and non-human wealth evolve according to:

$$(5) \qquad \dot{C}(t) = [\sigma(r-\rho)+n] \, C(t) - \beta [\lambda+\sigma\rho(1-\sigma)r] \, A(t)$$

$$(6) \qquad \dot{A}(t) = rA(t) + \Omega(t) - T(t) - C(t)$$

Population growth appears in (5) because this refers to aggregate consumption. The probability of death λ does not appear in (6), as the insurance premia received by the surviving households are equal to the non-human wealth of those who die. Therefore, the probability of death does not affect the aggregate return on assets.

The menu of assets held by households consists of physical capital K, government debt D, and external assets F, so that $A = K + D + F$.

1.2 Technology and the Behaviour of Firms

Each economy consists of a large number of identical competitive firms. The objective of these firms is to maximize their net worth.
Technology of firm j is given by:

$$(7) \qquad y(j, t) = \theta \, k(j, t)^{\eta_1} \, K(t)^{\eta_2} \, K^*(t)^{1-\eta_1-\eta_2}$$

$$\theta > 0, \quad 0 < \eta_1 + \eta_2 < 1$$

where θ, η_1 and η_2 are constant technological parameters, $k(j,t)$ denotes the capital stock of firm j at instant t, $K(t)$ denotes the average capital stock in the economy, and $K^*(t)$ denotes the average foreign capital stock. These two latter terms capture the external (or "knowledge") effects of aggregate capital deepening in the economy and the rest of the world. Arrow [5] and Romer [16] have stressed such external effects in the context of a closed economy. Our model is the special case of the Romer model with constant returns to aggregate capital accumulation at the world level (1).

Firm j chooses a path for its capital stock that solves the following problem.

$$(8) \qquad \underset{k(j,v)}{\text{Max}} \int_t^\infty [y(j,v) - \dot{k}(j,v) - \delta\, k(j,v)]\, e^{-\int_t^v r(u)du}\, dv$$

The terms in brackets denote the instantaneous profits of firm j. δ is the rate of depreciation of the capital stock.

The first order condition for a maximum entails:

$$(9) \qquad r(t) = \eta_1 \theta \left(\frac{k(j,t)}{K^*(t)}\right)^{\eta_1 - 1} \left(\frac{K(t)}{K^*(t)}\right)^{\eta_2} - \delta$$

(9) is the condition that the marginal product of capital is equal to the user cost of capital $r + \delta$. Since all domestic firms have the same technology and face the same market and non-market constraints (real interest rate and average domestic and foreign capital stocks), they will all choose the same capital stock. Thus, in domestic equilibrium, $k(j,t) = K(t)$ for all firms. The domestic asset market equilibrium condition then is:

$$(10) \qquad r(t) = \eta_1 \theta \left(\frac{K(t)}{K^*(t)}\right)^{\eta - 1} - \delta$$

where: $\qquad\qquad\qquad \eta = \eta_1 + \eta_2$

---

(1) ROMER [17] surveys the rapidly expanding literature on endogenous growth.

On the other hand, aggregating *(7)* across firms, the domestic aggregate production function is:

(11) $$Y(t) = \theta \, K(t)^{\eta} \, K^*(t)^{1-\eta}$$

1.3 *The Government*

The government finances public consumption G, and interest payments on its debt $r D$, by either lump-sum taxation T, or borrowing D. This gives rise to the flow budget identity of the government:

(12) $$\dot{D}(t) = r \, D(t) + G(t) - T(t)$$

Solvency of the government requires that the sum of the current public debt and the present value of future public consumption does not exceed the present value of future taxes:

(12') $$\int_t^{\infty} e^{-r(s-t)} \, G(s) \, ds + D(t) \le \int_t^{\infty} e^{-r(s-t)} \, T(s) \, ds$$

2. - A Two-Country World

Consider a two-country world. Preferences are the same in both countries, and there are no barriers to goods or capital flows across countries. Since the goods produced in any country are perfect substitutes in consumption, the law of one price will hold. Also, since assets are perfect substitutes internationally, both countries will face the same real interest rate.

We assume that there are two differences across countries. The first is in the efficiency of production, and will be parametrized in terms of differences in θ's. The second difference refers to fiscal policies. Countries are indexed by subscript $i = 1, 2$.

2.1 *Asset Market Equilibrium*

The condition of perfect capital mobility implies that real interest rates will be equal across countries. From *(10)*, and the assumption that the parameter θ differs across countries, we get that the world interest rate and relative capital intensities are determined by the condition that:

$$(13) \quad r(t) = \eta_1 \, \theta_1 \left(\frac{K_1(t)}{K_2(t)} \right)^{\eta-1} - \delta = \eta_1 \, \theta_2 \left(\frac{K_1(t)}{K_2(t)} \right)^{1-\eta} - \delta$$

(13) can be solved for the equilibrium world real interest rate, and the ratio of the equilibrium capital stocks:

$$(14) \qquad\qquad r(t) = \eta_1 \, (\theta_1 \, \theta_2)^{1/2} - \delta$$

$$(15) \qquad\qquad \frac{K_1}{K_2} = \left(\frac{\theta_1}{\theta_2} \right)^{\frac{1}{2(1-\eta)}}$$

From *(14)*, the equilibrium world real interest rate is time invariant as was assumed in Section 1.1 above. It dependes positively on the parameters that increase the marginal productivity of capital stocks,· and negatively on the rate of depreciation of capital.

From *(15)*, the country which, *ceteris paribus*, is more productive in its use of capital, will end up with the higher capital stock. Substituting *(15)* in the aggregate production function *(11)*, we get the following equilibrium aggregate production functions:

$$(16a) \qquad\qquad Y_1 = (\theta_1 \, \theta_2)^{1/2} \, K_1$$

$$(16b) \qquad\qquad Y_2 = (\theta_1 \, \theta_2)^{1/2} \, K_2$$

(16a) and *(16b)* imply that, in equilibrium, the two economies will have the same capital-output ratio, which is constant and determined by the geometric average of θ_1 and θ_2. In both countries, equilibrium output turns out to be proportional to the aggregate capital stock.

If growth in the level of domestic product is defined as $\gamma_i(t) \equiv \dot{Y}_i(t) / Y_i(t)$, then, from the aggregate production functions *(16a)* and *(16b)*, the growth rates of the capital stocks are also equal to $\gamma_i(t)$. Since from *(15)* the equilibrium ratio of capital stocks is constant, it follows that the equilibrium growth rates in the two economies must be equal. Thus, in this model there is no convergence of output levels. "Poor" (low θ) countries have a lower output and capital stock than "rich" (high θ) countries, but a common growth rate. Hence output levels do not converge. The rate of change of labour-augmenting technical progress, or the per-capita growth rate, is defined as $\pi(t) \equiv \gamma(t) - n$. To the extent that both countries have the same rate of population growth, the endogenous growth rate in per-capita output is the same for both countries. However, if the "poor" country had a higher rate of population growth, then its per-capita output growth would be lower than that of the "rich" country.

Combining *(16a)*, *(16b)* and *(14)*, note that:

$$(r + \delta)\, K_i(t) = \eta_1 (\theta_1\, \theta_2)^{1/2}\, K_i(t) \leq Y_i(t).$$

Domestic output exceeds payments to owners of private capital. This is because domestic and international spillovers of knowledge induce additional income for which individual firms do not need to pay. We shall assume that these profits are handed over to the owners of the firms (the household sectors) in a manner that does not depend on their age. This is consistent with our assumption in 1.1 that $\omega(v, t) = \omega(t)$, i.e. independent of the age of the household. Therefore, $\Omega(t) = (1 - \eta_1) Y(t)$.

To summarize, this Section has demonstrated that the equilibrium world real interest rate only depends on exogenous technological parameters. The relative capital stocks and output levels of the two economies only depend on differences in production efficiency, and the capital-output ratio will be the same in both countries. We have also demonstrated that the growth rate of GDP will be the same in both countries, and that there will be no tendency for economic convergence.

2.2 Goods and Labour Market Equilibrium

Equilibrium in product markets requires that the sum of private consumption, public consumption and investment equals national income. National income consists of domestic income Y, plus interest payments on external assets. Thus, in each economy, the product market equilibrium condition is:

$$(17) \quad Y_i(t) + r F_i(t) = C_i(t) + \dot{K}_i(t) + \delta K_i(t) + G_i(t) + \dot{F}_i(t)$$

(17) is based on the familiar accounting identity in an open economy, that national income is equal to absorption plus the current account. The current account is equal to the accumulation of external assets. *(17)* can be re-arranged to give the flow budget identity for the economy as a whole:

$$(17') \quad \dot{K}_i(t) + \dot{F}_i(t) = Y_i(t) + r F_i(t) - C_i(t) - \delta K_i(t) - G_i(t)$$

Labour supply is a constant fraction of the population, and equilibrium in the labour market ensures that all supply is employed.

2.3 Summary

It is convenient to formulate the two-country model in terms of fractions of domestic product. These fractions are denoted by lowercase rather than capital letters, i.e., $c(t) = C(t) / Y(t)$. The model then is as follows:

$$(18) \quad c_i(t) = [\sigma(r-\rho) + n - \gamma(t)] c_i(t) +$$
$$- \beta [\sigma \rho + (1-\sigma) r + \lambda] [k + d_i(t) + f_i(t)]$$

$$(19) \quad \dot{d}_i(t) = [r - \gamma(t)] d_i(t) + g_i - \tau_i, \qquad d_i(0) = d_{i0}$$

$$(20) \quad \dot{f}_i(t) = 1 - [\gamma(t) + \delta] k - c_i(t) - g_i + [r - \gamma_i(t)] f_i$$

$$(21) \quad k = \theta^{-1}; \qquad \theta \equiv (\theta_1 \theta_2)^{1/2}$$

$$(22) \quad \sum_{i=1}^{2} \phi_i f_i(t) \equiv 0$$

(18)-(20) are, respectively, the consumption function, the government flow budget identity and the product market equilibrium condition for each economy. We have used the equilibrium condition that the rates of growth of capital stocks and, therefore, growth rates are the same for both countries. *(21)* is the equilibrium capital-output ratio, which is the same in both countries, and equal to the geometric average of θ_1 and θ_2. Finally, *(22)* is derived from the familiar budget identity that the foreign borrowing of country 1 equals the foreign lending of country 2. ϕ_1 refers to the share of country i's GDP in world GDP. The GDP shares are time independent in this model. It is straightforward to show that $\phi_1 = 1 / [1 + (\theta_1 / \theta_2)^{-1/[2(1-\eta)]}]$. Obviously, $\phi_2 = 1 - \phi_1$.

The simplest way to solve the model is to use the method of Aoki [4], and consider the model of averages and the model of differences.

3. - Budgetary Policies, Savings and Endogenous Growth in the World Economy

We shall first consider the determination of worldwide averages. By using their respective shares in world GDP to take the weighted average of the consumption functions *(18)*, the government flow-budget identities *(19)*, and the product market equilibrium conditions *(20)* for the two countries, after making use of *(21)* and *(22)* we end up with the following average model for the world economy:

$$(23) \qquad \dot{c}_A(t) = [\sigma(r-\rho)+n-\gamma(t)]c_A(t) +$$
$$- \beta[\sigma\rho+(1-\sigma)r+\lambda][\theta^{-1}+d_A(t)]$$

$$(24) \qquad \dot{d}_A(t) = [r-\gamma(t)]d_A(t)+g_A-\tau_A, \qquad d_A(0) = d_{A0}$$

$$(25) \qquad \gamma(t) = -\delta+\theta[1-c_A(t)-g_A]$$

Subscript A denotes that the relevant variables refer to global weighted averages. Note that we have made use of *(21)* to substitute for the average capital-output ratio, and *(22)* which shows that the average external asset to GDP ratio is zero.

3.1 *Budgetary Policies, Private Savings and the World Growth Rate*

We first consider the determination of the average GDP share of world private consumption and the endogenous world growth rate, under the assumption of a constant world public debt to GDP ratio. This assumption will be satisfied if taxes adjust instantaneously to stabilize public debt. Thus, we concentrate on *(23)* and *(25)*, assuming that the average share of taxes is determined by:

(24') $$\tau_A(t) = [r - \gamma(t)] d_A(t) + g_A$$

World equilibrium is depicted in Graph 1. *B-R* (the Blanchard-Romer locus) depicts the steady-state consumption function. It is the locus of consumption-growth combinations that are consistent with the plans of private consumers, and a constant GDP share of private consumption. Assuming a dynamically efficient world economy, in which the real interest rate exceeds the pure rate of time preference, i.e., that $\eta_1 \theta - \delta > \rho$, the *B-R* locus is defined for per-capita growth rates lower than $\sigma (\eta_1 \theta - \delta - \rho)$. The steady state consumption function asymptotically approaches the vertical *R-R* locus, which represents the Ramsey [15], Romer [16] condition that the world per-capita growth rate is equal to the difference between the real interest rate and the pure rate of preference, weighted by the elasticity of intertemporal substitution. This condition, the modified golden-rule, is satisfied at the point $\gamma^* = n + \sigma (\eta_1 \theta - \delta - \rho)$.

The downward-sloping *H-D* line is the product market equilibrium condition *(25)*. It is essentially a modified Harrod-Domar condition for the world economy. *Ceteris paribus*, a lower average share of private consumption in the world economy leaves more room for investment, and the higher investment rate produces more growth. Unlike the model with decreasing returns to aggregate capital, growth never ceases in this model.

World equilibrium is at E_0, the intersection of the *B-R* and *H-D* loci. Since both consumption and the growth rate are jump variables, there are no transient dynamics in the case of a fixed public debt to GDP ratio. Private consumption and the growth rate jump to ensure equilibrium in the global economy.

GRAPH 1

THE EFFECTS OF BUDGETARY POLICIES
ON WORLD CONSUMPTION AND GROWTH RATES

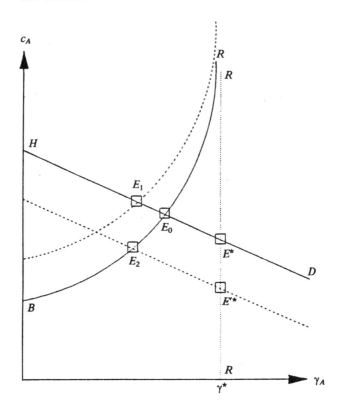

The equilibrium share of consumption is higher, and the equilibrium growth rate lower that in the case of an infinite horizon, representative household global economy. This is because of the entry of new, non-intergenerationally linked households, which cannot trade with current households. This creates a consumption externality and reduces growth. Without this externality, the equilibrium is at E_0^*, the intersection of the *H-R* and *R-R* loci. In the representative household economy, the only growth rate which, is compatible with a constant GDP share of private consumption is the Ramsey-Romer growth rate, $\gamma^* = n + \sigma (\eta_1 \theta - \delta - \rho)$. In that case budgetary policies cannot affect growth rates. Only policies that can affect the marginal product of capital affect growth in such an economy (Barro and Sala-i-Martin [7]).

We turn now to two fiscal policy experiments. The first is a tax financed, steady state rise in the world public debt to GDP ratio, and the second is a global balanced budget increase in government consumption.

A global rise in the public debt/GDP ratio shifts the *B-R* locus to the left. Higher public debt raises consumption at a given growth rate, as part of the lump-sum taxes that will finance the interest payments on the higher public debt are paid by yet unborn generations, for which current generations are not concerned. In equilibrium, the rise in world consumption will reduce the growth rate, as it crowds out capital accumulation. Thus, the new equilibrium at E_1 is associated with higher private consumption and a lower growth rate. Such an effect does not arise in the case of a representative household global economy, as in this case government bonds are not wealth (Barro [6]), and the method of financing government expenditure does not affect private consumption.

A balanced budget global rise in the share of government consumption shifts the *H-D* locus. In the new equilibrium E_2, both private consumption and the growth rate fall relative to the original equilibrium at E_0. The higher taxes used to finance the rise in government consumption crowd out private consumption, but this crowding-out is less than one-for-one, since part of the higher taxes are paid by new, non-intergenerationally linked households. As a result of this, the sum of global private and government consumption rises, total savings and investment get crowded-out, and the growth rate falls. Such an effect does not arise in the representative household economy, in which there is one-for-one crowding out of private consumption. In that case the economy moves from E^* to E'^*.

3.2 *The Dynamic Adjustment of World Savings, Public Debt and Endogenous Growth*

In this Section we concentrate on dynamics. We consider the effects of a transitory tax cut on the dynamic adjustment of the average GDP share of private consumption, public debt and endogenous growth in the world economy. For this purpose we use the average model consisting of equations *(23)* to *(25)*. We supplement the model by a tax rule which is assumed to ensure solvency of the public sector. This tax rule takes the form:

(26) $\tau_A(t) = \tau_0 - \tau_1 d_A(t)$

(26) replaces the tax rule *(24')*. Unlike *(24')* which assumes immediate adjustment to ensure a stable public debt to GDP ratio, *(26)* implies gradual adjustment.

Substituting *(26)* in *(24)*, and the growth rate equation *(25)* in *(23)* and *(24)*, we end up with the following model for the average GDP share of private consumption and the average public debt to GDP ratio.

(27) $\dot{c}_A(t) = [\sigma(r-\rho)+n+\delta-\theta(1-g_A)]\, c_A(t)+\theta\, c_A^2(t)$

$\qquad\qquad - \beta[\sigma\rho+(1-\sigma)r+\lambda][\theta^{-1}+d_A(t)]$

(28) $\dot{d}_A(t) = [r+\delta-\theta(1-g_A)-\tau_1]\, d_A(t)+\theta\, c_A(t)\, d_A(t)+g_A-\tau_0$

The condition for government solvency is that $\tau_1 > r - \gamma_A = r + \delta - \theta(1 - c_A - g_A)$.

The equilibrium and the associated dynamics are depicted in Graph 2.

The locus associated with a constant share of consumption is negatively sloped for low shares of private consumption, since a low share of private consumption leaves more room for investment. This results in a per-capita growth rate that is higher than the difference of the real interest rate and the pure rate of time preference weighted by the elasticity of intertemporal substitution. The slope of the locus turns positive at the point where the share of consumption is high enough to ensure a per-capita growth rate lower than this latter difference. This is at the point: $c_A^* = \frac{1}{2} c_A^*$.

$$c_A^* = 1 - g_A - \theta^{-1}[\sigma(r-\rho) + n + \delta]$$

GRAPH 2

DYNAMICS OF AVERAGE PUBLIC DEBT
AND PRIVATE CONSUMPTION

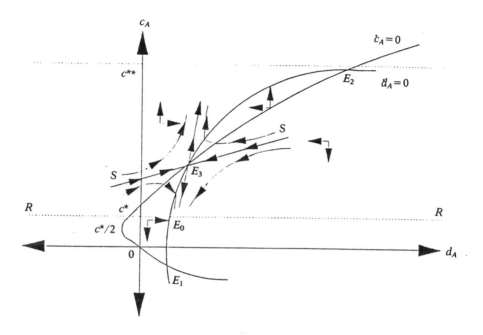

denotes the equilibrium GDP share of consumption associated with the Ramsey-Romer rule, i.e. a representative household economy. $\frac{1}{2} c_A^*$ also denotes the minimum average public debt to GDP ratio, or the highest percentage of GDP that the private sector is prepared to borrow from governments. Note that the Ramsey-Romer share of private consumption is an equilibrium in the model with overlapping generations when governments hold assets equal to the average private capital stock, $d_A = -1 / \theta$.

The locus associated with a constant average public debt to GDP ratio slopes upwards as long as c_A does not exceed:

$$c^{**} = 1 - g_A + \theta^{-1} (\tau_1 - r - \delta).$$

This is the condition for government solvency.

There are three potential equilibria. E_1 can be ruled out because it implies negative average world consumption, whereas E_2 is unstable. Therefore, E_3 is the only meaningful steady state equilibrium, as it is saddlepoint stable which is sensible since d_A is a predetermined variable and c_A a non-predetermined variable. E_0 is the steady state equilibrium in the representative household economy. Comparing E_3 and E_0 one notes that the absence of an intergenerational bequest motive leads to a higher GDP share of private consumption, and a higher public debt to GDP ratio.

Intertemporal shifts in taxation do not affect the GDP share of private consumption in the representative household economy. This is because of Ricardian neutrality. Such shifts only affect the average public debt to GDP ratio (i.e. shifts along the *R-R* curve). In our overlapping generations model, a cut in τ_0 shifts the $\dot{d}_A = 0$ locus to the right, increases the share of private consumption to GDP, reduces the growth rate, and increases the public debt to GDP ratio (Graph 3).

GRAPH 3

DYNAMIC ADJUSTMENT OF AVERAGE CONSUMPTION,
DEBT AND GROWTH AFTER A TEMPORARY TAX CUT

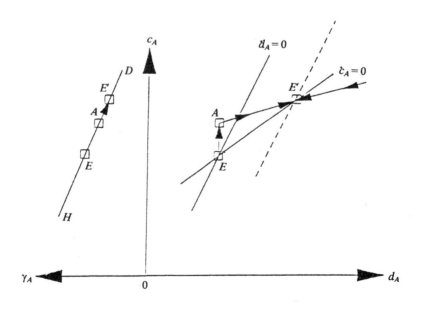

The short-run effects imply an increase in private consumption (shift from E to A), because part of the future taxes will be paid by yet unborn generations. As a result, global savings and the growth rate fall on impact. Over time, there is a rise of the average public debt to GDP ratio which causes further reductions in the savings rate and the growth rate. It also induces increases in the share of taxes (through (26)), which in the end bring us to the new steady state E', with a higher share of consumption and a lower growth rate.

To summarize, in this Section we have investigated the determination of global savings and endogenous growth. We demonstrated that the world savings and growth rates are lower than in a representative-household global economy, and that increases in both public debt and government consumption reduce the world GDP share of total savings and the global growth rate.

We now turn to the effects of differences in fiscal policies between countries.

4. - Relative Budgetary Policies and External Debt

We now turn to the model of differences between countries. This will be used to examine the effects of differences in budgetary policies.

Subtracting the model (18)-(20) of country 2, from the model of country 1, we get the following model of differences:

(29)
$$\dot{c}_R(t) = [\sigma(r-\rho)+n-\gamma]\, c_R(t) +$$
$$-\beta[\sigma\rho+(1-\sigma)r+\lambda]\,[d_R(t)+f_R(t)]$$

(30)
$$\dot{d}_R(t) = [r-\gamma]\, d_R(t)+g_R-r_R, \qquad d_R(0) = d_{R0}$$

(31)
$$\dot{f}_R(t) = [r-\gamma]\, f_R-[c_R(t)+g_R]$$

where subscript R denotes the difference of the relevant ratio between country 1 and country 2.

4.1 *Instantaneous Adjustment of Relative Taxes*

We shall again concentrate first on experiments with constant relative public debt to output ratios. Thus, relative tax rates are assumed to adjust instantaneously to stabilize the relative public debt to GDP ratios. Section 4.2 examines the stability of the relative model when the relative tax rates adjust sluggishly.

With a constant relative public debt to GDP ratio, the model consists of *(29)* and *(31)*. It determines the differences in GDP shares of private consumption, and the differences in net external asset to GDP ratios.

The equilibrium is depicted in Graph 4. The constant relative consumption locus has a positive slope, as in world equilibrium $\gamma < \sigma\,(r-\rho)+n$. If country 1 has a higher public debt to GDP ratio than country 2, this locus will have a positive intercept with the vertical axis. The slope of the locus of constant relative foreign assets could be either positive or negative, depending on whether the real interest rate exceeds or falls short of the common growth rate. The case depicted in Graph 3 is based on the assumption than $r>\gamma$. It is also assumed that the GDP share of public consumption in country 1 is higher than in country 2.

The necessary and sufficient condition for the equilibrium to be saddlepoint stable is that,

(32) $\beta\,[\sigma\,\rho+(1-\sigma)\,r+\lambda] > [\sigma\,(r-\rho)+n-\gamma]\,[r-\gamma]$

This condition will be satisfied if individual households are solvent, and is assumed in Graph 4. It is straightforward to see that if $r\leq\gamma$, *(32)* is satisfied if $\sigma < (r+\lambda)\,/\,(r-\rho)$.

We next consider the implications of a tax financed rise in the relative debt to GDP ratio of country 1, and a tax financed increase in its relative share of government consumption. These two experiments are depicted in Graph 5.

Graph 5*a* depicts the case of a steady state increase in the public debt to GDP ratio of country 1, relative to country 2, leaving the average public debt to GDP ratio unaffected. This shifts the constant relative consumption locus to the left, and the new equilibrium *E'* is associated with higher relative consumption, and a higher external debt for country 1. Initially relative consumption overshoots its steady state increase, as it jumps to put the economies at E_1 on the negatively sloping saddlepath. Subsequently, the relative share of private consumption is falling as country 1 decumulates foreign assets (accumulates foreign debt). Thus the adjustment path is characterized by higher than steady state relative consumption for country 1, and a current account deficit. This pattern could explain the relative position of the USA in the first part of the 1980s.

GRAPH 4

EQUILIBRIUM RELATIVE CONSUMPTION AND FOREIGN ASSETS

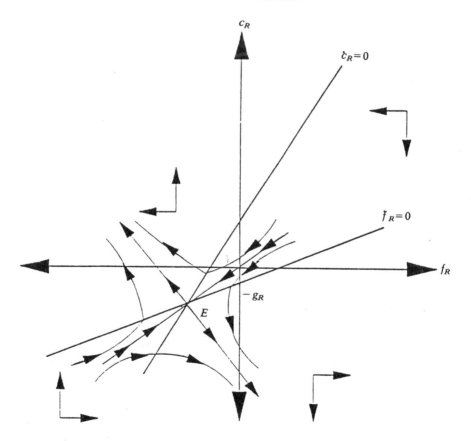

GRAPH 5*a*

A TAX FINANCED STEADY STATE INCREASE
IN RELATIVE PUBLIC DEBT

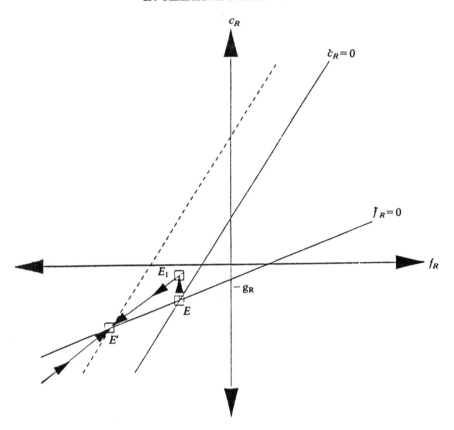

Graph 5*b* depicts the case of a relative increase in the share of government consumption in country 1. This shifts the constant foreign assets locus to the right, and in the new steady state equilibrium country 1 has a lower relative ratio of private consumption to GDP, and a higher external debt. The initial fall in relative consumption undershoots the steady state fall. However, as there is decumulation of foreign assets (accumulation of foreign debt) along the new saddle-path, the relative consumption share gradually approaches its lower equilibrium value at E' .

GRAPH 5*b*

A TAX FINANCED STEADY STATE INCREASE
IN RELATIVE PUBLIC CONSUMPTION

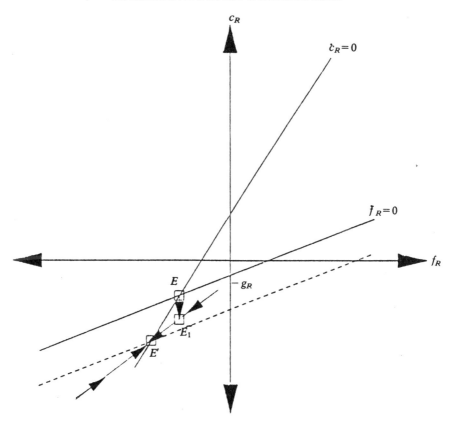

To recapitulate, we have shown that in a world of full capital mobility, an increase in the public debt to GDP ratio in one country will cause a reduction in its relative GDP share of private (and national) savings to GDP, and a rise in its external debt to GDP ratio. On impact, the reduction in private savings is higher than in steady state, and the economy enters an adjustment path along which it experiences higher current account deficits and a rising external debt to GDP ratio. On the other hand, a (relative) rise in the output share of public consumption also reduces national savings, as the reduction in the (relative) GDP share of private consumption is lower than the increase in the share of public consumption. As on impact the reduction in the relative GDP share of private consumption under- shoots the steady state fall, the economy experiences an adjustment path characterized by higher current account deficits, a rising external debt to GDP ratio, and a falling GDP share of private consumption.

4.2 *The Dynamic Adjustment of Relative Savings, External Debt and Public Debt*

In this section we consider the stability of the relative model in *(29)-(31)*, under gradual adjustment of relative tax rates to stabilize differences in the public debt to GDP ratio. Thus, the tax rule takes the form:

(33) $$\tau_R = \tau_0 + \tau_1 \, d_R$$

Substituting *(33)* in *(30)*, the characteristic polynomial of the amended dynamic system *(29)-(31)* is given by:

$$(r - \gamma - \tau_1 - \mu) \{\mu^2 - [(1 + \sigma) \, r - 2 \, \gamma - \sigma \, \rho + n] \, \mu +$$
$$- \beta \, [\sigma \, \rho + (1 - \sigma) \, r + \lambda] + [\sigma \, (r - \rho) + n - \gamma] \, (r - \gamma)\} = 0$$

Since the system consists of one non-predetermined and two predetermined variables, saddlepath stability requires two stable (negative) roots and one unstable (positive) one. It is straightforward to see that in the case where the public sectors are solvent, i.e. $\tau_1 > r - \gamma$, saddlepath stability is satisfied if *(32)* is also satisfied, i.e. if the private sectors are also solvent. If the public sector is solvent, the root associated with public debt is given by $\mu_1 = r - \gamma - \tau_1 < 0$, while if the private sector is solvent, (*(32)* is satisfied), the product of the other two roots will be negative, suggesting that one is negative and the other positive. Hence, the saddlepath condition will be satisfied.

Thus, a relative increase in the share of government consumption in one country will lead to a gradual build-up of public and external debt, and a gradual increase in the relative share of taxes in the country. Thus, while the relative shares of private consumption are not affected initially, there will be a subsequent gradual reduction in the relative share of private consumption for the country that has experienced the relative increase in government consumption. In the new equilibrium, the relative ratios of public and external debt to GDP for the expanding country will have risen, and the relative ratio of private consumption will have fallen. On the other hand, if the initial expansion has been through a relative reduction in the GDP share of taxes, relative private consumption will rise on impact. Subsequently, it will start falling, as the build-up in relative public debt induces a gradual increase in the GDP share of taxes. In the new steady state the relative GDP share of private consumption will be lower for the country that has experienced the initial tax cut, and the relative GDP shares of taxes, public debt and external debt will be higher.

5. - Adjustment Costs for Investment, Real Interest Rates, Stock Markets and Economic Growth

One of the most unsatisfactory aspects of the model used so far is the prediction that the equilibrium world real interest rate only depends on technological parameters, and is independent of demand factors, including the average public debt to GDP ratio. As we have shown elsewhere (Alogoskoufis and van der Ploeg [3]), the interest rate can become endogenous in this type of model if one assumes that investment is subject to adjustment costs. The purpose of this section is to investigate the implications of this extension in our model of interdependent economies.

We assume that firms in both economies face costs of adjusting investment. Instead of (8), firm j chooses a rate of investment that solves the following problem:

$$(34) \quad \max_{I(j,\,v)} \int_t^\infty \left\{ y(j,\,v) - \left[1 + \psi \frac{I(j,\,v)}{k(j,\,v)} \right] I(j,\,v) \right\} e^{-\int_t^v r(u)du} \, dv$$

The maximization is subject to the production function *(7)* and the accumulation equation,

$$(35) \qquad \dot{k}(j,v) = I(j,v) - \delta k(j,v)$$

$I(j,v)$ denotes gross investment of firm j at time v, and the cost of adjustment is proportional to the ratio of its gross investment to its capital stock. Ψ is the factor of proportionality, and measures the intensity of adjustment costs. The first order conditions for a maximum are:

$$(36) \qquad q(j,t) = 1 + 2\psi \frac{I(j,t)}{k(j,t)}$$

$$(37) \qquad \left[r(t) + \delta - \frac{\dot{q}(j,t)}{q(j,t)} \right] q(j,t) = \eta_1 \theta \left(\frac{k(j,t)}{K^*(t)} \right)^{\eta_1 - 1}$$

$$\left(\frac{K(t)}{K^*(t)} \right)^{\eta_2} - \psi \left(\frac{I(j,t)}{k(j,t)} \right)^2$$

q denotes the value of capital to the firm (Tobin's "*Q*"). The interpretation of *(36)* is that the marginal cost of adjusting the capital stock plus the cost of investment goods must equal the value of capital to the firm. The interpretation of *(37)* is that the interest charge, plus the depreciation charge, minus capital gains on equity should equal the marginal productivity of capital, plus the marginal reduction in adjustment costs arising from an additional unit of capital.

Since all domestic firms have the same technology and face the same market and non-market constraints, they will all choose the same investment rate and capital stock. Thus, as before, in domestic asset market equilibrium, $q(j,t) = q(t)$, $k(j,t) = K(t)$, for all firms. Thus, in domestic asset market equilibrium:

$$(38) \qquad q(t) = 1 + 2\psi \frac{I(t)}{K(t)}$$

$$(39) \quad \left[r(t) + \delta - \frac{\dot{q}(t)}{q(t)} \right] q(t) = \eta_1 \, \theta \left(\frac{K(t)}{K^*(t)} \right)^{\eta - 1} - \psi \left(\frac{I(t)}{K(t)} \right)^2$$

where $\eta = \eta_1 + \eta_2$ and *(38)* and *(39)* determine the relation between the real interest rate r and the equilibrium (stock) market valuation of domestic capital q, as functions of technological parameters, the rate of investment, and the world capital stock.

5.1 *Asset Market Equilibrium in a Two-Country World*

We shall assume a two-country world as before. From the assumption of perfect capital mobility, real interest rates and user costs of capital must be equilized. Thus, we shall have that:

$$(40) \quad r_1(t) = r_2(t) = r(t)$$

$$(41) \quad \left[r(t) + \delta - \frac{\dot{q}_1(t)}{q_1(t)} \right] q_1(t) = \left[r(t) + \delta - \frac{\dot{q}_2(t)}{q_2(t)} \right] q_2(t)$$

where *(40)* has been used in *(41)*.
From *(41)*:

$$(42) \quad \dot{q}_1(t) - \dot{q}_2(t) = [r(t) + \delta][q_1(t) - q_2(t)]$$

Since *(42)* is unstable, and the difference in q's is a non-predetermined variable, it will jump to ensure that $q_1(t) = q_2(t)$. Thus, the condition of perfect capital mobility implies that both real interest rates and the stock market values of capital are equalized across countries. If the user cost of capital in country 1 is higher than in country 2, capital will flow into country 2, boosting investment, causing an increase in q and the user cost of capital, until the gross investment ratios and q's are equalized. Thus, in a two-country world in which the only difference between countries is in the value of θ, world asset market equilibrium must satisfy:

(43)
$$q(t) = 1 + 2\,\psi\,\frac{I_1(t)}{K_1(t)} = 1 + 2\,\psi\,\frac{I_2(t)}{K_2(t)}$$

(44)
$$\left[r(t) + \delta - \frac{\dot{q}(t)}{q(t)}\right] q(t) =$$

$$\eta_1\,\theta_1 \left(\frac{K_1(t)}{K_2(t)}\right)^{\eta-1} - \psi \left(\frac{I_1(t)}{K_1(t)}\right)^2 =$$

$$\eta_1\,\theta_2 \left(\frac{K_1(t)}{K_2(t)}\right)^{\eta-1} - \psi \left(\frac{I_2(t)}{K_2(t)}\right)^2$$

From (43), firms in both countries will choose the same rate of gross investment. This will ensure that the marginal cost of adjusting the capital stock and the stock market value of capital q will be the same in both. Using the equilibrium condition (43) in (44), the latter reduces to the requirement that the marginal productivity of capital must be the same in both countries. From this latter requirement, the equilibrium ratio of capital stocks is given as in (15), and the equilibrium world real interest rate is given by:

(45)
$$r(t) = \frac{\dot{q}(t)}{q(t)} - \delta + \frac{\eta_1\,\theta - [(q(t)-1)^2/4\,\psi]}{q(t)}$$

where $\theta = (\theta_1\,\theta_2)^{1/2}$. In equilibrium, as long as the gross investment rate is non-negative, there will be a negative relation between the stock market and real interest rates.

It is straightforward to see that the limit of (45) as Ψ tends to zero is equation (14). It is also straightforward to see that in equilibrium, and for a constant technology, aggregate output is proportional to the aggregate capital stock in each economy, as in (16a) and (16b), with θ

being the factor of proportionality. Thus, the results derived in section 2.1 will hold. In particular, the equilibrium capital-output ratio will be the same in both countries and both countries will be growing at the same rate, as they have the same gross investment rate. The gross investment rate is equal to the rate of depreciation plus the rate of growth of the capital stock. Because of the linearity of the equilibrium output equations in the capital stock, the gross investment rate will be equal to the sum of the growth rate and the depreciation rate. Therefore, $I(t) / K(t) = \gamma(t) + \delta$. Thus, the equilibrium relations between the growth rate, the stock market value of capital and real interest rates are given by:

$$(46) \qquad\qquad q(t) = 1 + 2\psi[\gamma(t) + \delta]$$

$$(47) \qquad r(t) = \frac{\dot{q}(t)}{q(t)} - \delta + \frac{\eta_1 \theta - \psi[\gamma(t) + \delta]^2}{1 + 2\psi[\gamma(t) + \delta]}$$

In equilibrium, and for a constant technology, there will be a positive relation between the global growth rate and the stock market valuation of firms, and a negative relation between the world real interest rate and the growth rate.

5.2 Budgetary Policies, Endogenous Growth and External Debt

We next turn to the question of the determination of the endogenous growth rate and external debt in the world economy. We shall confine ourselves to steady states.

In steady state, the relation between the real interest rate and the growth rate that satisfies global asset market equilibrium is given by setting $\dot{q} = 0$ in *(47)*. Dropping the time index, this gives us the following asset market equilibrium condition.

$$(48) \qquad\qquad r = -\delta + \frac{\eta_1 \theta - \psi[\gamma + \delta]^2}{1 + 2\psi[\gamma + \delta]}$$

For product market equilibrium in the world economy, we use the steady state versions of the average consumption function *(23)* and the Harrod-Domar condition *(25)*. This gives us:

$$(49) \quad \gamma = \sigma\,(r-\rho)+n - \left(\frac{\beta\,[\sigma\,\rho+(1-\sigma)\,r+\lambda]\left[\dfrac{1}{\theta}+d_A\right]}{1-g_A-(\delta+\gamma)/\theta}\right)$$

The product market equilibrium condition *(49)* defines a positive relation between the real interest rate and the growth rate, as long as $(\rho+\lambda)/(\gamma-n) > 1-1/\sigma$. A rise in the real interest rate will, *ceteris paribus*, reduce the world GDP share of private consumption, increase the share of world savings, and cause an increase in capital accumulation and the growth rate.

General equilibrium is depicted in Graph 6. The downward sloping locus is the asset market equilibrium condition *(48)*, and the upward sloping locus is the product market equilibrium condition *(49)*. The presence of adjustment costs for investment results in a lower equilibrium real rate of interest, and a lower growth rate. This result is independent of whether Ricardian debt neutrality holds.

A tax financed steady state rise in the average government debt to GDP ratio, or the GDP share of government consumption will cause a rise in the world real interest rate and a reduction in the endogenous growth rate. From *(46)*, the stock markets will fall.

With regard to relative budgetary policies, the analysis of Section 4 fully applies. A relative rise in the public debt to GDP ratio, or the GDP share of public consumption will cause a fall in relative savings and a rise in external debt for the country that experiences it.

It is also worth noting the model with adjustment costs for investment explains an empirical puzzle found in the literature. If Ricardian debt neutrality holds and preferences are stable, only technological shocks (and distortionary taxes) can cause shifts in the real interest rate. By shifting the asset market equilibrium locus (Graph 6), they induce a positive correlation between real interest rates and growth rates. However, it has not been possible in the literature to document such a positive correlation between real inter-

GRAPH 6

ADJUSTMENT COSTS FOR INVESTMENT
AND THE BURDEN OF DEBT

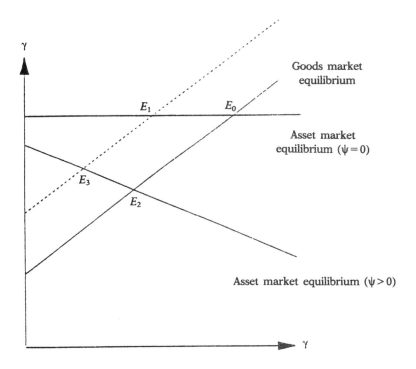

est rates and growth rates. This suggests that one must make allowances for shifts in the goods market equilibrium locus as well. Barro and Sala-i-Martin [7] achieve that in a framework of imperfect competition with technical progress involving new types of consumer products. This is akin to a change in the pure rate of time preference, and they suggest that this factor is at least as significant as technical change involving varieties of capital goods. Our present analysis offers an alternative solution to the above puzzle, that also works in a framework of perfect competition. In our framework, unlike the representative household models, changes in budgetary policies lead to shifts in the goods market equilibrium locus in Graph 6. Such shifts induce a negative correlation between real interest rates and growth rates. If changes in budgetary policies are at least as significant as technological shocks, then one would not expect a significant correlation between real interest rates and growth rates.

5.3 Differences in Growth Rates

Up to now the analysis has been conducted under the assumption that all parameters apart from the θ's are the same in both countries. It would be worth investigating which parameters would make for differences in growth rates. To see that, we need look no further than the asset market equilibrium conditions *(43)* and *(44)*. Assuming that the adjustment cost parameters also differ across countries, the steady state versions of these equilibrium conditions are given by:

(50)
$$q = 1 + 2\,\psi_1\,\frac{I_1}{K_1} = 1 + 2\,\psi_2\,\frac{I_2}{K_2}$$

(51)
$$[r(t) + \delta]\,q(t) =$$

$$\eta_1\,\theta_1\left(\frac{K_1}{K_2}\right)^{\eta-1} - \psi_1\left(\frac{I_1}{K_1}\right)^2 =$$

$$\eta_1\,\theta_2\left(\frac{K_1}{K_2}\right)^{1-\eta} - \psi_2\left(\frac{I_2}{K_2}\right)^2$$

From *(50)* and *(51)*, the equilibrium ratio of the capital stocks in the two countries is given by:

$$\left(\frac{K_1}{K_2}\right)^{\eta-1} = \frac{1}{2}\left(\frac{1}{\eta_1\,\theta_1}\,\frac{(q-1)^2}{4}\,\frac{\psi_2-\psi_1}{\psi_1\,\psi_2} + \right.$$

$$\left. + \left\{\left[\frac{1}{\eta_1\,\theta_1}\,\frac{(q-1)^2}{4}\,\frac{\psi_2-\psi_1}{\psi_1\,\psi_2}\right]^2 + 4\,\frac{\theta_2}{\theta_1}\right\}^{1/2}\right) > 0$$

It is straightforward to show that in equilibrium output will be proportional to the capital stock in both countries, with the factor of proportionality depending on the equilibrium ratio of capital stocks. It is also straightforward to show that if $\theta_1 > \theta_2$, then $K_1 > K_2$. In addition, if $\Psi_1 > \Psi_2$, then $K_1 > K_2$. These implications are straightforward. Capital will be attracted to the country in which it has the higher marginal productivity, and the country with the higher adjustment costs for investment. The reason for the latter result is that the country with the higher adjustment costs for investment will need to have a lower gross investment rate in equilibrium if the q's are equal. If the countries start with the same capital stock, the country with the higher investment adjustment costs will have a higher q, and will therefore attract additional capital, until the ratio of the gross investment rates equals the inverse of the ratio of the adjustment cost parameters in the two countries, a condition that guarantees the equality of q's.

To examine differences in growth rates, we can use the condition that the gross investment rate is equal to the depreciation rate plus the growth rate. Substituting this condition in *(45)*, we get that:

$$(52) \qquad \psi_1 (\gamma_1 + \delta_1) = \psi_2 (\gamma_2 + \delta_2)$$

From *(52)*, the country which, other things equal, faces higher adjustment costs for investment, will end up with a lower endogenous growth rate, as it will need to have a lower gross investment rate in equilibrium. In addition, the country which, other things equal, faces a higher depreciation rate of its capital stock will also end up with a lower endogenous growth rate, as for a given rate of gross investment the net investment rate, and therefore the growth rate are lower.

6. - Conclusions

This paper has examined the implications of budgetary policies for growth, international borrowing and lending, and the relation between economic growth, real interest rates and the stock market valuation of firms. We have used a two-country model of overlapping generations and endogenous growth, in which the only difference between countries is in the efficiency of production. We have demonstrated that in the presence of perfect capital mobility, the marginal productivity of capital and endogenous growth rates are equalized across countries, and that per capita output levels do not converge. Only differences in adjustment costs for investment or the depreciation rate of the capital stock can induce differences in growth rates in this model with international spillovers and perfect capital mobility. Countries whose firms find it more costly to adjust their capital stock, and countries which face higher depreciation rates will end up with lower equilibrium growth rates.

A rise in average public debt to GDP ratios, or the GDP share of public consumption, reduces the global growth rate. The average GDP share of private consumption rises following a rise in average public debt, while it falls following a rise in the GDP share of public consumption. However, in the latter case there is less than full crowding-out, and this is the reason that the global savings rate falls and growth slows down.

A relative rise in the public debt to GDP ratio in one country causes a reduction in its external assets to GDP ratio. Its relative GDP share of private consumption rises, but then gradually falls as the country experiences higher current account deficits, and decumulates foreign assets. In the new steady state, its relative savings rate will be either higher or lower than before the change, depending on whether the real interest rate exceeds the growth rate or vice-versa. A relative rise in the GDP share of public consumption in one country will cause a relative reduction in the GDP share of private consumption. However, as there is less than full crowding-out because of overlapping generations, its relative national savings rate will fall. This will bring about higher current account deficits and a gradual reduction in its external assets to GDP ratio. This reduction will cause a gradual rise in its relative GDP share of private savings, which will eventually stop the external asset decumulation.

In the presence of adjustment costs for investment, the global growth rate is lower than otherwise. There is a positive correlation between the stock market value of firms and the growth rate. An average tax financed rise in the public debt to GDP ratio, or the GDP share of private consumption, reduces growth and the stock market and increases world real interest rates.

This model goes a long way towards accounting for the events of the 1980s in terms of budgetary policies. It does not only explain the wordwide rise in real interest rates and the decumulation of external assets in the United States relative to Western Europe and Japan, but it also explains the generalized slowdown in economic growth.

BIBLIOGRAPHY

[1] ALOGOSKOUFIS G.S.: «On Public Debt Stabilizations in an Interdependent World», London CEPR, *Discussion Paper*, n. 490, 1990.

[2] ALOGOSKOUFIS G.S. - VAN DER PLOEG F.: «On Budgetary Policies and Economic Growth», London, CEPR, *Discussion Paper*, n. 496, 1990.

[3] — — — —: «Endogenous Growth and Overlapping Generations», London, Birkbeck College, University of London, *Discussion Paper*, n. 26/90, 1990.

[4] AOKI M.: *Dynamic Analysis in Open Economies*, New York, Academic Press, 1981.

[5] ARROW K.J.: «The Economic Implications of Learning by Doing», *Review of Economic Studies*, n. 29, 1962, pp. 155-73.

[6] BARRO R.J.: «Are Government Bonds Net Wealth?», *Journal of Political Economy*, n. 82, 1974, pp. 1095-17.

[7] BARRO R.J. - SALA-I-MARTIN X.: «Public Finance in Models of Economic Growth», Cambridge (Mass.), NBER, *Working Paper*, n. 3362, 1990.

[8] BLANCHARD O.J.: «Debts, Deficits and Finite Horizons», *Journal of Political Economy*, n. 93, 1985.

[9] BUITER W.H.: «Death, Birth, Productivity Growth and Debt Neutrality», *Economic Journal*, n. 98, 1988, pp. 279-93.

[10] DOMAR E.D.: *Essays in the Theory of Economic Growth*, Oxford, Oxford University Press, 1957.

[11] FRENKEL J. - RASIN A.: *Fiscal Policies in the World Economy*, Cambridge (Mass.), Mit Press, 1988.

[12] HARROD R.F.: *Towards a Dynamic Economics*, London, Macmillan, 1948.

[13] OBSTFELD M.: «Fiscal Deficits and Relative Prices in a Growing World Economy», *Journal of Monetary Economics*, n. 23, 1989, pp. 461-84.

[14] PLOEG F. VAN DER: «Money and Capital in Interdependent Economies with Overlapping Generation», *Economica*, Forthcoming, 1990.

[15] RAMSEY F.P.: «A Mathematical Theory of Savings», *Economic Journal*, n. 38, 1928, pp. 543-59.

[16] ROMER P.M.: «Increasing Returns and Long-Run Growth», *Journal of Political Economy*, n. 94, 1986, pp. 1002-37.

[17] — —: «Capital Accumulation in the Theory of Long-Run Growth», in BARRO R.J. (ed.): *Modern Business Cycle Theory*, Cambridge (Mass.), Harvard University Press, 1989.

[18] WEIL P.: «Overlapping Families of Infinitely Lived Agents», *Journal of Public Economics*, n. 38, 1989, pp. 183-98.

[19] YAARI M.: «Uncertain Lifetime, Life Insurance and the Theory of the Consumer», *Review of Economic Studies*, n. 32, 1965, pp. 137-50.

A Two-Country Analysis of International Targeting of Nominal GNP (*)

F43

Jeffrey A. Frankel - **Norbert Funke**
University of California,   The Kiel Institute of World Economics,
Berkeley (CA)   Kiel (Germany)

1. - Introduction

The 1980s were the decade when international macroeconomic policy coordination came into its own. To be sure, the subject was not entirely new. In the academic literature, Hamada [26] had applied game theory to one version of the interdependence question. In the policy world, the Bonn Summit of 1978 was an example of coordination in practice.

In the early 1980s, however, Canzoneri and Gray [8], Hamada [27], Oudiz and Sachs [34], and many others began to develop the analysis more thoroughly. It appeared that theory established a powerful case that setting macroeconomic policies cooperatively would yield higher economic welfare for all countries than setting policies independently (1).

Any proposals to put coordination in action were initially rejected out-of-hand by the first Reagan Administration, which believed that each country should be allowed to go its own way. This changed when

---

(*) The authors would like to thank Warwick McKibbin: simulation results reported here draw on joint research with the first author. The second author also thanks Markus Diehl and Monica Mastroberardino for helpful comments and suggestions on an earlier draft.
(1) The area has been surveyed by Cooper [9] and Fischer [12].
N.B.: the numbers in square brackets refer to the Bibliography at the end of the paper.

a new Secretary of the US Treasury took office in 1985, and initiated coordinated intervention in the foreign exchange market at a meeting of finance ministers at the Plaza Hotel in New York in September. At the annual summit meeting of industrialized country leaders in Tokyo the next year, the scope of coordination was broadened from exchange rates to a list of ten economic variables, and the membership of the club was broadened to include all the G-7 countries (2).

In the 1990s, coordination has lost some of the luster it had a short time ago. The academic literature has discovered a variety of limitations to successful coordination. Meanwhile, the G-7 policymaking process seems stalled. It docs not appear to be well-designed to cope with the serious obstacles that any potentially successful coordination faces. The current mechanism of coordination is in particular vulnerable to three sorts of obstacles: compliance, inflation-fighting credibility, and uncertainty. These obstacles are so severe that the institution of international coordination may easily make the world economic worse-off (3).

This paper will analyze a specific proposal for overcoming those obstacles, a cooperative international version of a nominal GNP rule, which may be called *INT*, for International Nominal Targeting. Following the introduction, Section 2 briefly reviews the main obstacles to policy coordination and suggests that *INT* may have good chances of overcoming such obstacles. In Section 3 the proposal of an internationally coordinated version of nominal GNP-targeting is evaluated in a two-country model, in the presence of domestic and foreign shocks to supply, money demand, and goods demand. In this simple framework nominal GNP-targeting comes out fairly promising, although it does not dominate alternative regimes, including coordinated monetary targeting, global price rules or discretionary policy under all circumstances. Furthermore, the results reveal that countries that do not participate in the coordination process may be better or worse-off and thus may possibly have an incentive to join the

---

(2) The story of the management of the dollar in the 1980s is recounted by FUNABASHI [21] and FRANKEL [16]. The history of the G-7 summits is recounted by PUTNAM - BAYNE [35].

(3) For skeptical views on international coordination, see e.g. VAUBEL [39], FELDSTEIN [11] and FRANKEL [13].

agreement. In Section 4 the McKibbin-Sachs global model is used to assess the internationally coordinated version of nominal GNP-targeting under somewhat more realistic assumptions. Simulation results are well in line with the theoretical findings in Section 2. Finally, Section 5 provides some concluding remarks.

2. - Three Obstacles to International Macroeconomic Policy Coordination

The first obstacle to successful and meaningful coordination is the difficulty of ensuring compliance (4). Each country, if it takes the other's policy as given, may have an incentive to renege on earlier agreements and leave the burden of the agreed-upon adjustment to the other country in order to raise its own welfare. Of course, cheating only succeeds as long as the other country does not retaliate. Otherwise, we are back in the non-cooperative equilibrium.

Von Furstenberg and Daniels [40], [41] have conducted a thorough review of 203 specific commitments made in the annual G-7 summit declarations between 1975 and 1989. The average scores assigned to these undertakings were so low that the joint null hypothesis of "no summit ambition" and "no summit effect" could barely be rejected.

If the member countries make commitments to attainable macroeconomic targets that can be monitored — which requires that they be explicit, measurable, and preferably public — then they are less likely to cheat on them. The theory of reputations can be used to show why. The current system seems to violate all of these first basic insights. The presence of so many different indicators on the G-7 list, the vagueness as to whether these variables are in fact forecasts, goals or commitments, and the secrecy surrounding the whole procedure, all imply that substantive enforceable agreements are unlikely to emerge from G-7 meetings. Multiple indicators will nearly always permit to find at least one indicator to justify the course action that a country prefers to take. Pressure can hardly be brought to bear on

---

(4) For a more detailed discussion of the main obstacles see FRANKEL [15], [17].

countries that stray from the agreed-upon targets, if the targets are kept secret.

The second danger that threatens the success of coordination efforts is the risk that cooperative agreements will be biased in favor of expansion, with the result that high inflation rates will re-emerge. Rogoff [36] has demonstrated that the credibility problem of monetary authorities vis-à-vis the private sector may be increased by central bank coordination. Monetary coordination may lead to systematically higher inflation, because it avoids the negative effects associated with undesired exchange-rate depreciations induced by unilateral expansions. Institutional constraints, e.g. in the form of some degree of commitment to a nominal anchor on a longer term basis may help reduce the time-consistent inflation rate and dominate a pure discretionary policy.

The third danger that threatens the success of coordination efforts is uncertainty: *a)* with respect to the initial position of the world economy; *b)* with respect to the effects and transmission effects of a unit change in domestic and foreign macroeconomic policy variables; and *c)* with respect to the correct weights to be put on the various possible target variables. Uncertainty makes it difficult for each country to know what policy changes are in its best interest. This difficulty arises whether the uncertainty centers on the initial position of the economy (the "baseline forecast"), the desired policy targets (e.g., full employment), or the changes in monetary and fiscal policy necessary to produce desired effects (the multipliers). All three kinds of uncertainty make it difficult for each country in the bargaining process to know even what policy changes it could want its partners to make. A number of pessimistic conclusions emerge. Given differing perceptions, the policy-makers may not be able to agree on a coordination package; and even if they do agree, the effects may be different from what they anticipated (5).

To review our conclusions so far, the compliance problem suggests that coordination should involve an explicitly-agreed and publicly-announced target. Furthermore, the target should be robust to

---

(5) For an analysis of coordination under model uncertainty see FRANKEL - ROCKETT [18], FRANKEL - SCOTT - ROCKETT [20]. See also HOLTHAM - HALLET [28], [29].

shocks that occur after the agreement is made. The inflation-fighting credibility problem suggests that the target to which the governments commit should be a nominal variable. The uncertainty problem suggests that governments should commit to a target, where increased knowledge (learning effects) about the true model may be used in future policies. These requirements lead to the suggestion that the nominal target to which the countries should best commit is one that does not even appear on the current G-7 list of indicators at all: nominal GNP.

3. - The Proposal for Simultaneous GNP-Targeting: a Two-Country Analysis

Here it is argued that, whatever the degree of precommitment to a nominal target, nominal GNP makes a more suitable target than the other nominal variables that have been proposed. To consider the problem formally (6), we use a stochastic symmetric two-country rational expectations model in order to compare alternative policy regimes: discretionary policy, a rigid money supply rule, a rigid nominal GNP rule, and rigid price (inflation) rules — with respect to the consumer price index and the producer price index. We distinguish between world-wide and country-specific shocks. Coordination is characterized by the simultaneous decision of both countries to follow the same policy. Monetary policy can have short-run real effects, because nominal wage contracts for period t are set at the end of period $t-1$. The monetary authorities have perfect information on all current shocks and can reach their targets accurately.

As long as shocks are symmetric, coordinated nominal GNP-targeting is the optimal policy in this simple framework, if the authorities assign equal weight to the real income and inflation objective and the

---

(6) Analyses of nominal GNP-targeting in alternative two-country models include ARGY [2], FUNKE [22], [23] and LEDER [30]. Beside alternative rules, Argy considers different wage indexation shemes; FUNKE [23] also critically reviews the chances of *INT* to overcome the main obstacles to policy coordination. These frameworks are extended in particular by the inclusion of price rules, the consumer price index in the authorities' loss-function, as well as discretion from the world perspective.

supply elasticity with respect to unexpected inflation is 1. In the event of money demand disturbances, a coordinated version of GNP-targeting isolates the economy; neither real income nor the price level are affected. This is true for symmetric, asymmetric as well as unilateral shocks. Under all other circumstances, however, fixing nominal GNP still comes out fairly well, although it does not give precisely the right answer.

3.1 *The Two-Country Model*

3.1.1 Aggregate Supply

Aggegate supply is given by a Cobb-Douglas production function (7):

(1) $y_t = c_0 + a \bar{k} + (1 - a) l_t + \mu_t$ $\mu_t \sim N(0, \sigma_\mu^2)$

where y_t is output, k is the fixed capital stock, l_t is labor, c_0 is a constant term, and μ_t is a productivity disturbance (supply shock). Throughout, subscript t denotes time and lower case letters denote natural logarithms. The demand for labor l_t^d is obtained by equating the marginal product of labor to the real producer wage $w_t - p_t$, where w_t is the nominal wage rate and p_t the price of domestic good (producer price).

(2) $l_t^d = \bar{k} + [c_0 + \log(1 - a) + p_t - w_t + \mu_t] / a$

Labor supply expressed in terms of the real consumption wage is:

(3) $l_t^s = \bar{l} + \omega (w_t - p_t^c)$ $\omega > 0$

The consumer price index p_t^c is defined as:

$$p_t^c = g\, p_t + (1 - g)(p_t^* + s_t) = p_t + (1-g)\, z_t$$

(7) See for a similar derivation of aggregate supply CURRIE - LEVINE [10] and for the closed economy case ROGOFF [36].

where $(1 - g)$ is the import content of consumer's consumption, p_t^* the price of the foreign (imported) good, and s_t the nominal spot exchange rate (the price of the foreign currency measured in terms of the domestic currency). Furthermore, z_t is referred to as the real exchange rate $(z_t = p_t^* + s_t - p_t)$. A rise in z_t represents a real depreciation of the home currency. We assume $0.5 < g < 1$, so residents in both countries have a preference for their own good. To simplify algebra without loss of generality, l is set equal to $k + [c_0 + \log (1 - a)] / a$. Nominal wage contracts are set a period in advance before shocks occur with the intention to achieve full employment.

(4)
$$w_k \mid E_{t-1} \, l_t^s = E_{t-1} \, l_t^d$$

Therefore, nominal wage is set at:

(5)
$$w_t = E_{t-1} \, p_t^c - \frac{(1 - g) \, E_{t-1} \, z_t}{\omega \, a + 1}$$

where expectations are formed rationally, so that $E_{t-1} \, p_t^c$ indicates the consumer price index in period t expected in $t - 1$, given the information in $t - 1$.

Hence, *(1)*, *(2)* and *(5)*, together with the analytically convenient normalization that $- c_0 = a \, \bar{k} + (1 - a) \, \bar{l}$ so that $\bar{y} = E_{t-1} \, y_t = 0$, give an open economy Lucas type of supply function.

(6a) $y_t = \beta_1 \, (p_t^c - E_{t-1} \, p_t^c) - \beta_2 \, z_t + \beta_3 \, E_{t-1} \, z_t + (1 + \beta_1) \, \mu_t$

where: $\beta_1 = (1 - a) / a$, $\beta_2 = \beta_1 \, (1 - g)$, and $\beta_3 = \beta_2 / (\omega \, a + 1)$

Therefore, $\beta_3 < \beta_2 < \beta_1$. A similar supply function holds for the foreign country, where the real exchange rate and the expected real exchange rate enter with opposite sign. An asterisk indicates a foreign variable.

(6b) $y_t^* = \beta_1 \, (p_t^{c*} - E_{t-1} \, p_t^{c*}) + \beta_2 \, z_t - \beta_3 \, E_{t-1} \, z_t + (1 + \beta_1) \, \mu_t^*$

3.1.2 Aggregate Demand

The demand side of the home country and the foreign country is described by standard open economy *IS-LM* functions. Domestic functions are denoted by *(a)*, foreign equations by *(b)*.

(7a) $$m_t - p_t^c = -\alpha_1 i_t + \alpha_2 v_t + \varepsilon_t$$

(7b) $$m_t^* - p_t^{c*} = -\alpha_1 i_t^* + \alpha_2 y_t^* + \varepsilon_t^*$$

(8a) $$y_t = -\kappa (i_t - E_t p_{t+1}^c + p_t^c) + \varphi z_t + \delta y_t^* + \eta_t \qquad 0 < \delta < 1$$

(8b) $$y_t^* = -\kappa (i_t^* + E_t p_{t-1}^{c*} + p_t^{c*}) - \varphi z_t + \delta y_t + \eta_t^*$$

(9) $$i_t - i_t^* = E_t s_{t+1} - s_t$$

where m_t represents money supply, i_t the nominal interest rate (not in log). There are two types of demand shocks: a money demand shock (ε_t) and a goods market demand disturbance (η_t). All disturbances are stochastic and uncorrelated (on a national level) with zero mean and constant variances. Positive and negative correlation between ε_t and ε_t^*, η_t and η_t^*, as well as μ_t and μ_t^* is allowed. All elasticities and semi-elasticities α_1, α_2, κ, φ, β are assumed to be larger than zero and identical in both countries.

In the money market nominal money supply is deflated by the consumer price index. This reflects that part of the money demand for transactions is used to buy imports. Demand for the good that firms produce is a function of the real interest rate, the real exchange rate, as well as real income in the other country. Uncovered interest rate parity *(9)* closes the model. To analyze the effects of different monetary policy strategies, alternative policy reaction functions are introduced. We assume that the authorities have an information advantage and can reach their targets accurately:

(10a) $$m_t = -\theta (p_t + y_t)$$

(10a*) $$m_t = -\theta p_t^c$$

(10a**) $m_t = - \theta\, p_t$

(10b) $m_t^* = - \theta\, (p_t^* + y_t^*)$

(10b*) $m_t^* = - \theta\, p_t^{c*}$

(10b**) $m_t^* = - \theta\, p_t^*$

Equations *(10a)*, *(10b)*, *(10a*)*, *(10b*)*, and *(10a**)*, *(10b**)* are the policy-reaction functions for nominal GNP-targeting and price level (inflation rate) rules. We distinguish between inflation rules that try to stabilize the inflation rate as measured by the consumer price index *(10a*)*, *(10b*)* and as measured by the producer price index *(10a**)*, *(10b**)*. If money supply is kept constant in both countries $\theta = 0$, whereas in the case of a perfect nominal income rule $\theta - > \infty$ in *(10a)*, *(10b)*. In the case of a perfect price rule $\theta - > \infty$ in *(10a*)* and *(10b*)* and *(10a**)* and *(10b**)*, respectively (8).

We follow Rogoff [36], who in turn follows Kydland and Prescott, 1977, and Barro and Gordon, 1983, and assume that the market determined level of real income is below the socially optimal level [$\hat{y}$] . Authorities in both countries are tempted to inflate surprisingly in order to raise output beyond the natural rate. The social objective functions in both countries are:

(11a) $L_t = (y_t - \hat{y})^2 + \chi\, p_t^{c2}$

(11b) $L_t^* = (y_t^* - \hat{y})^2 + \chi\, p_t^{c*2}$

where χ is the weight assigned to the inflation objective, since we can normalize the lagged price levels p_{t-1}^c and p_{t-1}^{c*} relative to which p_t^c and p_t^{c*} is measured to zero. We impose $\hat{y} > 0$, which builds in an expansionary bias to discretionary policy-making. The bias is assumed to be identical in both countries.

---

(8) In fact, $\theta - > - \infty$ would also keep nominal income or the price level constant. However, the choice is immaterial, because we do not focus on the transitional mechanism. From an economic pespective it seems more plausible that the authorities increase (decrease) money supply, when nominal income or the price level tend to fall (increase).

It is analytically convenient to decompose the above system into two independent sub-systems, using the method of Aoki [1]. The sum of the single-country models can be called the additive or world model and the difference of the two-country models can be called the difference system. Additive variables or disturbances are denoted by a superscript a, differences by a superscript d:

$$x_t^a = x_t + x_t^* \qquad x_t^d = x_t - x_t^*$$

Thus, after solving the system in x_t^a and x_t^d we can obtain domestic and foreign variables back by:

(12a)
$$x_t = \frac{1}{2}(x_t^a + x_t^d)$$

(12b)
$$x_t^* = \frac{1}{2}(x_t^a - x_t^d)$$

We start by analyzing the additive and difference system separately.

3.2 *The Analysis of the Additive System*

By summing the supply, demand, policy reaction, and loss functions of the two countries, we get the world model *(6'), (7'), (8'), (10'), (11')*. Note, for the description of the supply equation *(6')* and the policy-reaction function *(10'*)*, that in this symmetrical world economy the additive (average) consumer price index is identical to the additive (average) producer price index $(p_t^c + p_t^{c*} = p_t + p_t^*)$ *(9)*.

---

(9) The average real income and price level are $y_t^{av} = y_t^a / 2$ and $p_t^{av} = p_t^a / 2$. As lower case letters denote logarithms, averages refer to the geometric average of the underlying variables (Y_t, P_t), which is approximately identical to arithmetic averages for small changes. In order to be meaningful, the price should always be interpreted as the average price level.

Thus, in the additive system we only have to consider one price rule.

(6')
$$y_t^a = \beta_1 (p_t^a - E_{t-1} p_t^a) + (1+\beta_1) \mu_t^a$$

(7')
$$m_t^a - p_t^a = -\alpha_1 i_t^a + \alpha_2 y_t^a + \varepsilon_t^a$$

(8')
$$y_t^a (1-\delta) = -\kappa (i_t^a - E_t p_{t+1}^a + p_t^a) + \eta_t^a$$

(10')
$$m_t^a = -\theta (p_t^a + y_t^a)$$

(10'*)
$$m_t = -\theta p_t^a$$

(11')
$$L_t^a = (y_t^a - \hat{y}^a)^2 + \chi p_t^{a2}$$

Obviously, the world economy is characterized by a standard closed economy *IS-LM* model along with a closed economy Lucas type of supply function. The average real world output as well as the average world price level are independent of the nominal/real exchange rate in this symmetric two-country world.

Under full discretion, the policy-makers each period choose aggregate demand so as to minimize that period's loss, with aggregate supply including $E_{t-1} p_t^a$ given. From *(11')* and *(6')* we get (10):

(13) $$d L_t^a / d p_t^a = 2 \beta_1 [\beta_1 (p_t^a - E_{t-1} p_t^a) + (1+\beta_1) \mu_t^a - \hat{y}^a] + 2 \chi p_t^a = 0$$

Therefore:

(14)
$$p_t^a (\beta_1^2 + \chi) = \beta_1 \hat{y}^a + \beta_1^2 E_{t-1} p_t^a - \beta_1 (1+\beta_1) \mu_t^a$$

By taking expectations on both side we get under rational expectations:

(15)
$$E_{t-1} p_t^a = \beta_1 \hat{y} / \chi$$

So we can solve *(14)* for the price level under discretion *(DS)*:

(16)
$$p_t^a \mid DS = \beta_1 \hat{y}^a / \chi - \beta_1 (1+\beta_1) \mu_t^a / (\beta_1^2 + \chi)$$

---

(10) The second order conditions for a minimum are met. The minimum is global, because of the quadratic form of L_t^a.

From *(11)* the expected loss under discretion then works out to:

$$(17) \qquad E\,L_t^a \mid DS = (\chi + \beta_1^2)\,\hat{y}^{a2}\,/\,\chi + (1+\beta_1)^2\,\chi\,\sigma_{\mu a}^2\,/\,(\beta_1^2 + \chi)$$

where in the following $\sigma_{\mu a}^2$ is defined as $E\,[(\mu_t^a)^2]$ and so forth.

The first term represents the inflationary bias in the system, while the second represents the effect of the supply disturbance after the authorities have chosen the optimal split between inflation and output. The higher β_1 and the lower the weight on inflation (χ), the greater the inflationary bias.

To compare the outcome of a discretionary policy with the other regimes, we have to solve the above additive system for a money supply rule *(18a)*, *(18b)*, a nominal GNP rule *(19a)*, *(19b)*, and a price level rule *(20a)*, *(20b)* (see appendix).

$$(18a) \qquad y_t^a \mid MS = [-\,\beta_1\,\kappa\,\varepsilon_t^a + \beta_1\,\alpha_1\,\eta_t^a + \kappa\,(1+\alpha_1)\,(1+\beta_1)\,\mu_t^a]\,/\,N_1$$

$$(18b) \qquad p_t^a \mid MS = \{-\,\kappa\,\varepsilon_t^a + \alpha_1\,\eta_t^a - (1+\beta_1)\,[\alpha_1\,(1-\delta) + \kappa\,\alpha_2]\,\mu_t^a\}\,/\,N_1$$

where: $\qquad\qquad N_1 = \alpha_1\,\beta_1\,(1-\delta) + \kappa\,(\alpha_1 + \alpha_2\,\beta_1 + 1)$

$$(19a) \qquad\qquad\qquad y_t^a \mid NI = \mu_t^a$$

$$(19b) \qquad\qquad\qquad p_t^a \mid NI = -\,\mu_t^a$$

$$(20a) \qquad\qquad\qquad y_t^a \mid PL = (1+\beta_1)\,\mu_t^a$$

$$(20b) \qquad\qquad\qquad p_t^a \mid PL = 0$$

where *MS* indicates a money supply rule, *NI* nominal GNP-targeting and *PL* price level (inflation rate) targeting (11).

---

(11) The results for nominal GNP-targeting and price level targeting are straight forward from *(6')*, once it is establisched that $E_{t-1}\,p_t^a = 0$. In the case of GNP-targeting we can substitute $y_t^a = -\,p_t^a$ in *(6')*, and in the case of price level targeting $p_t^a = 0$. Similar considerations hold for the difference system, where the difference of the supply function could also be expressed in terms of the differences in the producer prices.

In the case of a money supply rule, all shocks — money demand, goods market demand disturbances, and supply shocks — influence the world real income and the average world price level. Trivially, if domestic and foreign shocks are perfectly negatively correlated, world real income and the average world price level remain constant ($\varepsilon_t^a = \eta_t^a = \mu_t^a = 0$).

In the case of a nominal-GDP rule or a price level rule, the goods market demand disturbances and money demand disturbances are fully absorbed on the world level (12). This is true for symmetric, asymmetric as well as unilateral shocks. In the event of disturbances to supply, such as the oil price increases of the 1970s, a nominal-GNP rule divides the effect equi-proportionally between an increase in the price level and a fall in output. The short-run output loss associated with a negative supply shock is, however, under nominal GNP-targeting larger than under a money supply rule, if the absolute value of the price elasticity of aggregate demand under a money supply rule is smaller than one. In the world model this is true if:

$$\kappa \, (1 + \alpha_1) / [\alpha_1 \, (1 - \delta) + \alpha_2 \, \kappa] < 1$$

Taylor [38] presents some empirical evidence that aggregate demand is inelastic in the short run. A price level rule has the largest impact on economic activity. To fully compare the alternative regimes, the expected losses are considered:

(21) $\quad E \, L_t^a \mid MS = \hat{y}^{a2} + \{\kappa^2 \, (\beta_1^2 + \chi) \, \sigma^2 \, \varepsilon_a + \alpha_1^2 \, (\beta_1^2 + \chi) \, \sigma_{\eta a}^2 +$

$\quad\quad + (1 + \beta_1)^2 \, [\kappa^2 \, (1 + \alpha_1)^2 + \chi \, [\alpha_1 \, (1 - \delta) + \kappa \, \alpha_2]^2\} \, \sigma_{\mu a}^2\} / N_1^2$

(22) $\quad\quad\quad\quad E \, L_t^a \mid NI = \hat{y}^{a2} + (1 + \chi) \, \sigma_{\mu a}^2$

(23) $\quad\quad\quad\quad E \, L_t^a \mid PL = \hat{y}^{a2} + (1 + \beta_1)^2 \, \sigma_{\mu a}^2$

---

(12) Although a nominal GNP rule may fully absorb demand shocks, it may still increase the volatility of velocity. This observation does, however, not effect the existing pros and cons of alternative rules (FUNKE [24]).

From the world perspective, nominal GNP-targeting and price level targeting dominate the money supply as an anchor for monetary policy in the case of money demand shocks and goods market demand shocks. Compared to a discretionary regime, the credible precommitment to a nominal GNP rule or a price level rule avoids the inflationary bias of a discretionary policy regime (13). Without knowing the parameters of the model it is not possible to determine which rule dominates in the case of supply shocks. However, if the authorities assign equal weights to the real income and inflation target $(\chi = 1)$, nominal GNP-targeting dominates a price rule if $\beta_1 > \sqrt{2} - 1 = 0.414$. Estimates of the slope of the supply relationship vary. Some evidence is reviewed in Frankel-Chinn [19]; most estimates of β_1 are greater than this critical value. If $\chi = 1$ and the elasticity of supply with respect to unexpected inflation $\beta_1 = 1$, nominal GNP-targeting unambiguously dominates discretion. In this case, nominal GNP-targeting is the optimal policy.

As both countries together form a closed economy these results are mostly known (14). It is more interesting to see how the effects of alternative shocks differ between both countries. As we have shown that the main weakness of discretion may refer to its inflationary bias, we focus in the following on the analysis of rigid rules.

3.3 *The Analysis of the Difference System*

Applying definition *(12b)* and making use of:

$$s_t = p_t^{cd} + (2\,g - 1)\,z_t \quad \text{and} \quad p_t^d = p_t^{cd} - 2\,(1 - g)\,z_t$$

we get:

$$(6'') \quad y_t^d = \beta_1\,(p_t^{cd} - E_{t-1}\,p_t^{cd}) - 2\,\beta_2\,z_t + 2\,\beta_3\,E_{t-1}\,z_t + (1 + \beta_t)\,\mu_t^d$$

---

(13) It remains crucial that nominal income targets are consistent with the distorted natural rate (ROGOFF [36]).

(14) Alternative theoretical analyses include: BEAN [5], ROGOFF [36], WEST [42], BRADLEY - JANSEN [6], FRANKEL [15], FUNKE - MASTROBERARDINO [25] and ASAKO - WAGNER [4].

(7") $$m_t^d - p_t^{cd} = -\alpha_1 i_t^d + \alpha_2 y_t^d + \varepsilon_t^d$$

(8") $$y_t^d = -\kappa (i_t^d - E_t p_{t+1}^{cd} + p_t^{cd}) + 2 \varphi z_t - \delta y_t^d + \eta_t^d$$

(9") $$i_t^d = E_t s_{t+1} - s_t = (2 g - 1) E_t z_{t+1} + E_t p_{t+1}^{cd} - (2 g - 1) z_t - p_t^{cd}$$

(10") $$m_t^d = -\theta (y_t^d + p_t^d) = -\theta [y_t^d + p_t^{cd} - 2 (1 - g) z_t]$$

(10"*) $$m_t^d = -\theta p_t^{cd}$$

(10"**) $$m_t^d = -\theta p_t^d = -\theta [p_t^{cd} - 2 (1 - g) z_t]$$

The differences between real income and the consumer and producer price level at home and abroad, are in the case of a money supply rule *(24a), (24b), (24c)* a nominal GNP rule *(25a), (25b), (25c)* and price-level rules with respect to the consumer price index (CPI) *(26a), (26b), (26c)* and with respect to the producer price index (PP) *(27a), (27b), (27c)* (see Appendix):

(24a) $$y_t^d \mid MS = \{ - \beta_1 [\kappa (2 g - 1) + 2 \varphi] \varepsilon_t^d + \beta_1 [\alpha_1 + 2 (1 - g)] \eta_t^d +$$
$$+ (1 + \beta_1) (1 + \alpha_1) [\kappa (2 g - 1) + 2 \varphi] \mu_t^d \} / N_2$$

where:

$$N_2 = (\alpha_1 + \alpha_2 \beta_1 + 1) [\kappa (2 g - 1) + 2 \varphi] + \beta_1 (1 + \delta) [\alpha_1 + 2 (1 - g)]$$

(24b) $$p_t^d \mid MS = \{ - [\kappa (2 g - 1) + 2 \varphi] \varepsilon_t^d + [\alpha_1 + 2 (1 - g)] \eta_t^d +$$
$$- (1 + \beta_1) \{\alpha_2 \mid \kappa (2 g - 1) + 2 \varphi] + (1 + \delta) [2 (1 - g) + \alpha_1] \} \mu_t^d \} / N_2$$

(24c) $$p_t^{cd} \mid MS = \{ - [\kappa (2 g - 1) + 2 \varphi + 2 \beta_2 (1 + \delta)] \varepsilon_t^d +$$
$$- [2 \alpha_2 \beta_2 - \alpha_1 (2 g - 1) \mid \eta_t^d +$$
$$- (1 + \beta_1) \{(2 g - 1) [\alpha_1 (1 + \delta) + \alpha_2 \kappa] + 2 \alpha_2 \varphi \} \mu_t^d \} / N_2$$

(25a) $$y_t^d \mid NI = \mu_t^d$$

(25b) $$p_t^d \mid NI = -\mu_t^d$$

(25c) $p_t^{cd} \mid NI = \{-2(1-g)\,\eta_t^d + [2(1+\delta)(1-g) - \kappa(2g-1) - 2\varphi]\,\mu_t^d\}/N_3$

where: $$N_3 = \kappa\,(2\,g-1) + 2\,\varphi$$

(26a) $y_t^d \mid CPI = \{2\,\beta_2\,\eta_t^d + (1+\beta_1)\,[\kappa\,(2\,g-1) + 2\,\varphi]\,\mu_t^d\} / N_4$

where: $$N_4 = \kappa\,(2\,g-1) + 2\,\varphi + 2\,\beta_2\,(1+\delta)$$

(26b) $p_t^d \mid CPI = \{2\,(1-g)\,\eta_t^d - 2\,(1+\delta)\,[\beta_2 + (1-g)]\,\mu_t^d\} / N_4$

(26c) $$p_t^{cd} \mid CPI = 0$$

(27a) $$y_t^d \mid PP = (1+\beta_1)\,\mu_t^d$$

(27b) $$p_t^d \mid PP = 0$$

(27c) $p_t^{cd} \mid PP = \{-2\,(1-g)\,\eta_t^d + 2\,(1+\delta)\,[\beta_2 + (1-g)]\,\mu_t^d\} / N_3$

The above equations reveal the trivial result that both countries are affected in the same way by symmetric shocks ($\varepsilon_t^d = \eta_t^d = \mu_t^d = 0$), since real income and prices are then identical in both countries ($y_t^d = p_t^{cd} = p_t^d = 0$). Furthermore, the difference in real income and the producer price is independent of goods market demand disturbances and money demand disturbances in the case of nominal GNP-targeting, and a producer price rule. The analysis of the additive and the difference system refer to both the world economy as well as the relative effects on both countries. The effects on both the home country and the foreign country can be derived using these results.

3.4 The Effects of Shocks on the Home Country and the Foreign Country

Using the definition of *(12a)* and *(12b)* we can easily calculate the effects of domestic and foreign shocks on real income and prices at home and abroad. The following example may explain the method. For analyzing the isolated effects of money demand disturbances ($\eta_t = \eta_t^* = \mu_t = \mu_t^* = 0$) under a money supply rule we calculate domestic *(28a)* and foreign *(28b)* real income as follows:

$$(28a) \qquad y_t = \frac{1}{2}\,(y_t^a + y_t^d)$$

$$(28b) \qquad y_t^* = \frac{1}{2}\,(y_t^a - y_t^d)$$

Substituting *(18a)* and *(24a)* in *(28a)* we obtain for the domestic real income:

$$(29a) \quad y_t = \frac{1}{2}\,\{-\beta_1\,\kappa\,\varepsilon_t^a\,/\,N_1 + \beta_1\,[\kappa\,(2\,g-1)+2\varphi]\,\varepsilon_t^d\,/\,N_2\}$$

Based on *(28b)* we obtain for the foreign real income:

$$(29b) \quad y_t^* = \frac{1}{2}\,\{-\beta_1\,\kappa\,\varepsilon_t^a\,/\,N_1 - \beta_1\,[\kappa\,(2\,g-1)+2\varphi]\,\varepsilon_t^d\,/\,N_2\}$$

From this method we can analyze the effects of symmetric, unilateral, perfectly asymmetric shocks or any other combination. In the case of positive symmetric money demand shocks ($\varepsilon_t = \varepsilon_t^* > 0$) we have $\varepsilon_t^d = 0$, but $\varepsilon_t^a > 0$. As $N_1 > 0$ and $N_2 > 0$, we obtain from *(29a)* and *(29b)* that real income drops countries. A unilateral positive domestic money demand shock ($\varepsilon_t > 0$ and $\varepsilon_t^* = 0$) leads to a drop in real income at home. The effect on the foreign country is uncertain without knowing the parameters of the model (19). In the case of a

---

(15) Negative money demand disturbances have identical effects to unanticipated increases in money supply. Thus, the transmission effects of monetary policy are uncertain in this model. An unexpected increase of money supply in the home country may be associated with positive or negative spill-over effects. This results is compatible with simulation results reported by 12 leading econometric models. Most econometric models, however, suggest that fiscal shocks are transmitted positively (BRIANT *et* AL. [7]).

money demand switch ($0 < \varepsilon_t = - \varepsilon_t^*$) real income in the home country falls, whereas real income abroad increases because $\varepsilon_t^a = 0$ and $\varepsilon_t^d > 0$. A similar analysis can be undertaken for all shocks and all regimes. The direction of change of key macroeconomic variables is summrized in Table 1, where a question mark indicates that the direction of change is ambigous without knowing the parameters.

Table 1 reveals that all types of shocks — independent of the country of origin — have an impact on real income and prices in both countries under a money supply rule. In this model, with wage rigidities, flexible exchange rates do not isolate the home country from foreign shocks. Obviously, similar results hold for the forcign country, because of the symmetry. The transmission effects of uni-lateral domestic shocks, however, are mostly uncertain without knowing the parameters of the model.

In contrast, the analysis of coordinated nominal GNP-targeting and coordinated price rules reveal some of the possible advantages of such an agreement. The effects of money demand distrurbances on real income, and the price level are fully absorbed, independent of whether shocks are symmetric, completely asymmetric or unilateral. An x % drop (increase) in money demand is compensated by an x % reduction (increase) of money supply in the respective country. The effects of symmetric goods market demand shocks are also perfectly neutralized. Furthermore, the effects of unilateral goods demand disturbances or *IS*-switches are fully absorbed with respect to real income and the producer price index in the case of nominal GNP-tar-geting or a producer price rule. Price stability measured in terms of the consumer price index is, however, not guaranteed. This occurs, because a change in the nominal exchange rate induces a change of import prices. In general, supply shocks always influence at least one of the macroeconomic target variables. However, domestic (foreign) supply shocks do not have an impact on foreign (domestic) real income and the producer price index in the case of a nominal GNP rule and producer price rule (16).

---

(16) Since in this model all foreign shocks are demand disturbances from the domestic perspective, this implies that a nominal GNP rule and a producer price rule neutralize the effects of all demand disturbances with respect to real income and the producer price level.

TABLE 1

DIRECTION OF CHANGE OF KEY MACROECONOMIC VARIABLE UNDER ALTERNATIVE MONETARY POLICY RULES

Type of shock	World economy		Home country			Foreign country			Real exchange rate
	p_t^{av}	y_t^a	p_t	p_t^c	y_t	p_t^*	p_t^{c*}	y_t^*	z_t
Money supply rules									
Sym. *LM* shock $\varepsilon_t=\varepsilon_t^*>0$	↓	↓	↓	↓	↓	↓	↓	↓	0
Sym. *IS* shock $\eta_t=\eta_t^*>0$	↑	↑	↑	↑	↑	↑	↑	↑	0
Sym. Supply-shock $\mu_t=\mu_t^*>0$	↓	↑	↓	↓	↓	↓	↓	↑	0
LM shock $\varepsilon_t>0$	↓	↓	↓	↓	↓	?	?	?	↓
IS-shock $\eta_t>0$	↑	↑	↑	?	↑	?	↑	?	↓
Supply-shock $\mu_t>0$	↓	↑	↓	↓	↑	?	?	?	↑
LM-switch $0<\varepsilon_t=-\varepsilon_t^*$	0	0	↓	↓	↓	↑	↑	↑	↓
IS-switch $0<\eta_t=-\eta_t^*$	0	0	↑	?	↑	↓	?	↓	↓
Supply-switch $0<\mu_t=-\mu_t^*$	0	0	↓	↓	↑	↑	↑	↓	↑
Nominal-GNP rules									
Sym. *LM* shock $\varepsilon_t=\varepsilon_t^*>0$	0	0	0	0	0	0	0	0	0
Sym. *IS* shock $\eta_t=\eta_t^*>0$	0	0	0	0	0	0	0	0	0
Sym. Supply-shock $\mu_t=\mu_t^*>0$	↓	↑	↓	↓	↑	↓	↓	↑	0
LM shock $\varepsilon_t>0$	0	0	0	0	0	0	0	0	0
IS-shock $\eta_t>0$	0	0	0	↓	0	0	↑	0	↓
Supply-shock $\mu_t>0$	↓	↑	↓	?	↑	0	↓	0	↑
LM-switch $0<\varepsilon_t=-\varepsilon_t^*$	0	0	0	0	0	0	0	0	0
IS-switch $0<\eta_t=-\eta_t^*$	0	0	0	↓	0	0	↑	0	↓
Supply-switch $0<\mu_t=-\mu_t^*$	0	0	↓	?	↑	↑	?	↓	↑
Price (CPI)-rules									
Sym. *LM* shock $\varepsilon_t=\varepsilon_t^*>0$	0	0	0	0	0	0	0	0	0
Sym. *IS* shock $\eta_t=\eta_t^*>0$	0	0	0	0	0	0	0	0	0
Sym. Supply-shock $\mu_t=\mu_t^*>0$	0	↑	0	0	↑	0	0	↑	0
LM shock $\varepsilon_t>0$	0	0	0	0	0	0	0	0	0
IS-shock $\eta_t>0$	0	0	↑	0	↑	↓	0	↓	↓
Supply-shock $\mu_t>0$	0	↑	↓	0	↑	↑	0	↑	↑
LM-switch $0<\varepsilon_t=-\varepsilon_t^*$	0	0	0	0	0	0	0	0	0
IS-switch $0<\eta_t=-\eta_t^*$	0	0	↑	0	↑	↓	0	↓	↓
Supply-switch $0<\mu_t=-\mu_t^*$	0	0	↓	0	↑	↑	0	↓	↑
Producer price rules									
Sym. *LM* shock $\varepsilon_t=\varepsilon_t^*>0$	0	0	0	0	0	0	0	0	0
Sym. *IS* shock $\eta_t=\eta_t^*>0$	0	0	0	0	0	0	0	0	0
Sym. Supply-shock $\mu_t=\mu_t^*>0$	0	↑	0	0	↑	0	0	↑	0
LM shock $\varepsilon_t>0$	0	0	0	0	0	0	0	0	0
IS-shock $\eta_t>0$	0	0	0	↓	0	0	↑	0	↓
Supply-shock $\mu_t>0$	0	↑	0	↑	↑	0	↓	0	↑
LM-switch $0<\varepsilon_t=-\varepsilon_t^*$	0	0	0	0	0	0	0	0	0
IS-switch $0<\eta_t=-\eta_t^*$	0	0	0	↓	0	0	↑	0	↓
Supply-switch $0<\mu_t=-\mu_t^*$	0	0	0	↑	↑	0	↓	↓	↑

Although the analysis of the direction of change of key macro-economic variables hints at the advantages of feed-back rules, the magnitude of the effects is not visible. Furthermore, it should be borne in mind that the political goal of real income ($\hat{y}$) exceeds the natural rate in both countries. A symmetric negative money demand shock that increases real income and the inflation rate under a money supply rule, for example, might coincidentally look better than the same shock under the alternative rules that fully absorb the shock. However, a symmetric positive money demand disturbance would definitively reduce welfare under a money supply rule. Keeping these limitations in mind, Table 1 nonetheless reveals some of the disadvantages of a fixed money supply rule.

To further compare the remaining strategies (17) we can calculate the expected losses. Because of the symmetry it is sufficient to analyze the expected loss of the home country with respect to domestic and foreign shocks. To simplify the algebra, we assume that all shocks are uncorrelated nationally as well as internationally. The expected losses are calculated by substituting y_t and p_t^c in *(11a)*, where y_t and p_t^c are derived from the additive and difference system based on *(12a)*.

$$(30) \qquad EL \mid NI = \hat{y}^2 + \sigma_\mu^2 + \chi \{[\kappa (2\,g-1) +$$
$$+ 2\,\varphi - (1+\delta)(1-g)]^2\,\sigma_\mu^2 +$$
$$+ (1+\delta)^2 (1-g)^2\,\sigma_{\mu*}^2 + (1-g)^2 (\sigma_\eta^2 + \sigma_{\eta*}^2)\} / N_3^2$$

$$(31) \qquad EL \mid CPI = \hat{y}^2 + \{(1+\beta_1)^2 [\kappa (2\,g-1) +$$
$$+ 2\,\varphi + \beta_2 (1+\delta)]^2\,\sigma_\mu^2 + \beta_2^2 (1+\beta_1)^2 (1+\delta)^2\,\sigma_{\mu*}^2 +$$
$$+ \beta_2^2 (\sigma_\eta^2 + \sigma_{\eta*}^2)\} / N_4^2$$

$$(32) \qquad EL \mid PP = \hat{y}^2 + (1+\beta_1)^2\,\sigma_\mu^2 + \chi \{(1+\delta)^2 (\beta_2+1-g)^2$$
$$(\sigma_\mu^2 + \sigma_{\mu*}^2) + (1-g)^2 (\sigma_\eta^2 + \sigma_{\eta*}^2)\} / N_3^2$$

where σ_μ^2 is defined as $E[(\mu_t)^2]$ and $\sigma_{\mu*}^2$ as $E[(\mu_t^*)^2]$ and so forrth.

---

(17) We omit the expected loss of a money supply rule, which results from tedious calculations and remains difficult to interpret.

Obviously, none of these rules is able to avoid the expected losses associated with the political goal of raising real income above the natural rate. Furthermore, it is interesting to note that under all three regimes, the expected loss of goods demand disturbances is independent of the country of origin in this symmetrical world. The expected loss is furthermore identical under a nominal income rule and a producer price rule. In contrast, the expected loss associated with supply shocks is generally higher with respect to domestic supply shocks than with respect to foreign supply shocks. Nominal income targeting remains definitively superior to a producer price rule in the case of domestic supply shocks.

Although the above analysis reveals that the superiority of a rule depends on the structural parameter of the model, the type of shocks, the country of origin as well as the weights in the social objective function, nominal GNP-targeting is never clearly inferior, as e.g. money supply targeting. Thus, nominal GNP-targeting remains a fairly promising candidate for future monetary policy.

3.5 *Asymmetric Rules*

Up to now, we assumed that both countries agreed on following the same rule. In the following Section, it will be analyzed how these results may change, if both countries follow for whatever reason different rules. Starting from a situation where both countries follow a constant money supply rule, we assume that the home country changes its regime (18). We are thus interested in answering the following type of questions. Under which type of shocks does the home country clearly benefit from its regime shift? Is the foreign country better or worse off from the fact that the home country follows a flexible rule?

In the case of a positive money demand shock in the home country, the domestic central bank increases money supply in such a way that the demand disturbance is fully offset under a nominal GNP

---

(18) ARGY [2] presents a similar analysis. His results, however, differ mainly because in his model the government's real income objective is the natural rate and not a higher level $(\hat{y})$.

rule and under both price rules. The home country clearly benefits from the regime shift, as a needless recession is avoided. The foreign country would also be clearly advantaged by the home country's strategy, if the government's objective would be to obtain price stability and to stabilize real income at the natural rate. However, results are less clear-cut if the political goal of real income exceeds the natural rate. Under a constant money supply rule the transmission effects of a unilateral money demand shock is uncertain without knowing the parameters of the model. Thus, if the spill-over effects of a negative unilateral money demand shock were positive with respect to foreign real income, it might coincidentally improve welfare in the foreign country, because the welfare gain of a rising real income may overcompensate for the loss associated with less price stability.

If the money demand disturbance occurs in the foreign country, the impact on the home country's prices or nominal GNP is ambiguous. Therefore, the necessary direction of change of the home country's monetary policy to accommodate the effects of the shock is again uncertain. Since the spill-over effects of monetary policy are ambiguous, the foreign country may be better or worse off.

The analysis of foreign goods demand disturbances or supply shocks leads to similar vague conclusions. In the case of a coordinated money supply rule the spill-over effects of both types of shocks are ambiguous. If nominal income or the corresponding price level tend to increase (decrease) in the home country the authorities will follow a restrictive (expansionary) monetary policy under a nominal income or a price-level rule respectively. The effects of monetary policy are again ambiguous with respect to the foreign policy objectives. The unilateral implementation of a nominal GNP rule or a price level rule may again improve or worsen the situation abroad.

In contrast, the effects of all types of foreign shocks are neutralized with respect to real domestic income and the domestic producer price under a producer price rule or nominal GNP-targeting. The same holds for domestic money demand disturbances and for domestic goods demand disturbances (19). Although it remains diffi-

---

(19) This can be easily seen when the supply functions are expressed in terms of the producer price index.

cult to reach conclusions about the concrete welfare effects, the analysis suggests that a single large country that commits to a nominal GNP rule may still benefit to some extent from the demand-shock-absorbing capacity of this rule.

The above results are derived from a simplified symmetrical two-country model. The gap between the theoretical approach and the real world is still large. Countries are not symmetric, shocks may be permanent and it remains difficult to identify the nature and source of shocks. To further compare the effects of alternative policy regimes, a full model simulation is needed.

4. - Simulation Results of Simultaneous Nominal GNP-Targeting

Warwick McKibbin and Frankel have started to use the McKibbin-Sachs Global (*MSG*) model (20) of the world economy to assess the effects of alternative shocks, including a doubling of the world price of oil, a 5% unilateral US money demand shock as well as a 1% unilateral US real demand shock under alternative policy regimes. The *MSG* model takes into account country specific characteristics and covers altogether seven regions: the USA, Japan, Germany, the rest of the European Monetary System, the rest of the Organization for Economic Cooperation and Development (OECD), non-oil developing countries and the Organization of Petroleum countries. In the simulation analysis it is assumed that the USA, Japan and Germany adopt the same policy regime. The rest·of the OECD countries, which are reported as a unit, are assumed to keep their money supplies fixed. Table 2 reports some of the simulation results.

Table 2 reports the effects of the three types of shocks under four alternative regimes, a constant money supply rule in both countries, nominal GNP-targeting, non-cooperative discretion as well as cooperative discretionary policy. The latter assumes a G-3 central planner who maximizes a world objective function in which the individual objective

---

(20) For a detailed description of the framework see McKibbin - Sachs [31], [32], [33].

TABLE 2

MACROECONOMIC EFFECTS
IN THE McKIBBIN-SACHS GLOBAL MODEL (*)

	Money rule		Nominal income targeting		Non-cooperative discretion		Cooperative discretion	
	1 year	s.e	1 year	s.e	1 year	s.e	1 year	s.e
Oil price shock (100%)								
US economy								
output, % *y*	−1.79	3.05	−2.92	3.81	−2.47	2.79	−2.31	2.62
inflation	3.57	4.52	2.94	3.88	3.09	3.45	3.19	3.58
Japanese economy								
output, % *y*	−1.07	−1.12	−2.14	2.16	−0.61	0.62	−0.52	0.53
inflation	−2.84	3.64	2.16	2.93	3.30	3.31	3.35	3.51
German economy								
output, % *y*	−0.29	3.63	−1.47	2.86	−0.10	0.20	0.00	0.07
inflation	2.46	3.03	1.50	1.95	2.44	3.17	2.52	3.33
Rest of OECD economies								
output, % *y*	−1.35	2.34	−0.98	2.39	−1.15	2.10	−1.20	2.08
inflation	3.38	4.18	4.15	5.14	3.57	4.61	3.48	4.49
US money demand shock (5%)								
US economy								
output, % *y*	−1.21	1.26	0.00	0.01	0.01	0.01	0.01	0.01
inflation	−0.92	1.09	−0.01	0.01	−0.01	0.01	−0.01	0.01
Japanese economy								
output, % *y*	0.12	0.12	0.00	0.00	0.00	0.00	0.00	0.00
inflation	0.18	0.25	0.00	0.00	0.00	0.00	0.00	0.01
German economy								
output, % *y*	0.36	0.49	0.00	0.01	0.00	0.00	0.00	0.00
inflation	0.25	0.33	0.00	0.01	0.00	0.01	0.00	0.01
Rest of OECD economies								
output, % *y*	0.26	0.29	0.03	0.03	0.03	0.03	0.03	0.03
inflation	0.30	0.39	0.03	0.04	0.03	0.04	0.03	0.04
US real demand shock (1%)								
US economy								
output, % *y*	1.33	1.36	0.15	0.33	0.19	0.27	0.19	0.27
inflation	0.52	0.58	−0.24	0.35	−0.22	0.32	−0.22	0.33
Japanese economy								
output, % *y*	0.42	0.43	−0.05	0.06	−0.02	0.03	−0.02	0.03
inflation	0.33	0.39	0.11	0.15	0.13	0.16	0.13	0.27
German economy								
output, % *y*	0.54	0.73	0.02	0.19	0.01	0.01	0.00	0.00
inflation	0.36	0.43	−0.12	0.19	−0.13	0.22	−0.14	0.23
Rest of OECD economies								
output, % *y*	0.51	0.53	0.85	0.92	0.84	0.91	0.84	0.92
inflation	0.40	0.46	0.97	1.21	0.96	1.19	0.96	1.20

(*) Selected results from FRANKEL [17].

functions enter with their shares of GNP. Both discretionary regimes reported here, however, have to be interpreted as being ideal, because they do not yet incorporate any temptation of the government to inflate by surprise. Both regimes would lose some of their advantages in the presence of an "inflationary-bias" (21). The first year effects on output and inflation are reported as percentage deviations from baseline in each first column. The second column of each regime conveys the overall magnitude of effect over 5 years; it is the square root of the sum of the yearly squared effects.

Simulation results are in line with the results of the symmetric two-country analysis. A nominal GNP rule fully neutralizes the effects of money demand shocks and substantially reduces the effects associated to a 1% US real demand shock in the G-3 countries. A doubling of the world price of oil would lead to a greater short-run loss under nominal GNP-targeting than under money supply targeting or the discretionary regimes. Furthermore, Table 2 reveals that the rest of the OECD countries does not necessarily benefit from the introduction of nominal GNP-targeting in the G-3 countries, depending on the weights assigned to the output and inflation objective. Countries that do not participate in the coordination process may possibly have an incentive to join the club or to switch their regimes independently. These results are compatible with those of the two-country model with asymmetric rules, where the foreign country does not necessarily benefit from the domestic regime shift. In the two-country case, both countries may alrealdy be interpreted as a bloc of countries that follows different rules.

5. - Concluding Remarks

A fundamental precondition for any successful international coordination scheme is its ability to overcome three obstacles: compliance, credibility, and certainty.

The incentive to deviate from the international agreement largely depends on the robustness of the coordination scheme with respect to

---

(21) For a detailed description and results see FRANKEL [17].

disturbances that occur after the agreement is made. In a two-country model different monetary policy arrangements were compared, including a simultaneous nominal GNP rule, a simultaneous money supply rule, simultaneous price-level (inflation) rules as well as discretionary policy from the world perspective. As long as shocks are symmetric, nominal income targeting dominates all other regimes, if the authorities assign equal weights to the real income and inflation objective and the supply elasticity with respect to unexpected inflation is 1. The first condition may represent roughly the split that a discretionary policy would favor anyway, while the second condition is close to some empirical estimates. In the event of moncy demand disturbances, a coordinated version of nominal GNP-targeting as well as price rules insulate the economy, neither real income nor the price level are affected. This is true for symmetric, asymmetric as well as unilateral shocks. Under all other circumstances, however, fixing nominal GNP still comes out fairly well, although it does not give precisely the right answer. In particular in the case of supply shocks, an absolute commitment to a nominal GNP rule is unwisely constraining. Simulation results based on the McKibbin-Sachs global model are in line with these findings. All these results, however, are still derived under simplified assumptions and the version of nominal GNP-targeting that is evaluated is a restricted one. It is assumed that both countries eternally fix their rate of nominal growth and are able to hit their targets accurately (22).

Frankel [14] has proposed a cooperative international version of a nominal GNP rule, where the G-7 participants would *a)* loosely commit themselves to broad target ranges for their collective and individual rates of growth of nominal demand (23) for five years into the future, and *b)* commit themselves to somewhat narrower targets for the coming year. A minimum requirement for the credibility of the

---

(22) Asako [3] analyzes nominal GNP-targeting under money supply and multiplier uncertainties.

(23) There is a reason for a choosing nominal demand (defined as GNP minus the trade balance) as the target variable, in place of nominal GNP, even though the latter is a more familiar concept. In the event of a recession, countries need to be discouraged from the temptation to accomplish their expansion of output through net foreign demand — for example, through protectionist measures — as opposed to domestic demand.

authorities' committment vis-à-vis their partners and the private sector is that the agreement should be explicit. The targets would be publicly announced, in the manner that the Chairman of the Federal Reserve Board announced to the US Congress target ranges for $M1$ money supply until recently or the German Bundesbank still does at the end of each year. A significant deviation of the rate of growth of nominal demand from the target value would be noted disapprovingly at the next G-7 meeting. The threat of losing reputation should create the right incentives to stick to the agreement. Nonetheless, for each cooperator the challenge remains to control its own nominal demand target in line with the agreement. Thus, it should best be up to each country how to attain the target, though the tools of monetary policy must presumably take precedence over the tools of fiscal policy for purposes of short-run adjustment.

As long as the coordination process remains stalled, a single country may well start introducing nominal GNP-targeting in a first step, if the preferences of this country are such. The theoretical analysis of asymmetric regimes suggests that this country may still be able to reap at least some of the benefits. If competition about the appropriate monetary strategy leads then to an assimilation of targets, the fundamental basis for *INT* would be created.

1. - Additive System

1.1 *Nominal GNP-Targeting and Money Supply Targeting*

From *(6′), (7′), (8′)* and *(10′)* we get the difference equation of the sum of prices *(A1)* by substituting for i_t^a and m_t^a in equation *(7′)* using *(8′)* and *(10′)* and subsequently substituting y_t^a using equation *(6′)*.

(A1) $\qquad -\alpha_1 \kappa E_t p_{t-1}^a + [\theta \kappa (1+\beta_1)+\kappa (\alpha_1+\alpha_2 \beta_1 + 1) +$

$\qquad + \alpha_1 \beta_1 (1-\delta)] p_t^a - \beta_1 \mid \alpha_1 (1-\delta)+\kappa (\alpha_2+\theta)] E_{t-1} p_t^a = \mu_t^a$

where:

$$u_t^a = -\kappa \varepsilon_t^a + \alpha_1 \eta_t^a - (1+\beta_1) [\alpha_1 (1-\delta)+\kappa (\alpha_2+\theta)] \mu_t^a$$

Forwarding *(A1)* j periods ahead and taking expectations in $t-1$, we obtain:

(A1′) $\qquad -\alpha_1 \kappa E_{t-1} p_{t+i+j}^a + \kappa (\theta+\alpha_1+1) E_{t-1} p_{t+j}^a = 0$

The characteristic root of *(A1′)* is $\lambda = 1 + (1+\theta) / \alpha_1$. Excluding the possibility of an exploding price path for $|\lambda| > 1$, which we get if $\theta < -2 \alpha_1$ or $\theta > -1$, it is conventionally imposed that $E_t p_{t+1}^a = E_{t-1} p_t^a = 0$ in this case. Under these circumstances we obtain *(A2)* for p_t^a:

(A2) $\qquad p_t^a = \dfrac{u_t^a}{\theta \kappa (1+\beta_1)+\kappa (\alpha_1+\alpha_2 \beta_1 + 1)+\alpha_1 \beta_1 (1-\delta)}$

In the case of a money supply rule in both countries $\theta = 0$. *(A3)* is identical to *(18b)* in the text.

(A3) $\qquad p_t^a \mid MS = \{-\kappa \varepsilon_t^a + \alpha_1 \eta_t^a - (1+\beta_1) [\alpha_1 (1-\delta)+\kappa \alpha_2] \mu_t^a\} / N_1$

where:

$$N_1 = \kappa \, (\alpha_1 + \alpha_2 \, \beta_1 + 1) + \alpha_1 \, \beta_1 \, (1 - \delta)$$

In the case of nominal income targeting $\theta \to \infty$

(A4) $$p_t^a \mid NI = \lim_{\theta \to \infty} p_t^a =$$

$$= \lim_{\theta \to \infty} \frac{-\kappa \varepsilon_t^a \, \theta^{-1} + \alpha_1 \, \eta_t^a \, \theta^{-1} - (1 + \beta_1)|\alpha_1 \, (1 - \delta) + \kappa(\alpha_2 + \theta)|\mu_t^a \, \theta^{-1}}{\kappa \, (1 + \beta_1) + \kappa \, (\alpha_1 + \alpha_2 \, \beta_1 + 1) \, \theta^{-1} + \alpha_1 \, \beta_1 \, (1 - \delta) \, \theta^{-1}} = - \mu_t^a$$

Real income is obtained by substituting the above results for the price level in (6') with: $E_{t-1} \, p_t^a = 0$.

1.2 *Price Level Rule*

The results for a price level rule are obtained similarly by solving the difference equation (A5), which is derived from (6'), (7'), (8'), (10'*):

(A5) $$- \alpha_1 \, \kappa \, E_t \, p_{t+1}^a + [\kappa \, (\theta + 1 + \alpha_1) +$$

$$+ \alpha_1 \, \beta_1 \, (1 - \delta) + \alpha_2 \, \beta_1 \, \kappa] \, p_t^a - \beta_1 \, [\alpha_1 \, (1 - \delta) + \alpha_2 \, \kappa] \, E_{t-1} \, p_t^a$$

$$= - \kappa \, \varepsilon_t^a + \alpha_1 \, \eta_t^a - (1 + \beta_1) \, [\alpha_1 \, (1 - \delta) + \alpha_2 \, \kappa] \, \mu_t^a$$

2. - **Difference System**

2.1 *Nominal GNP-Targeting and Money Supply Targeting*

From (6"), (8"), (9") and from (6"), (7"), (9"), (10") we obtain the following pair of (dynamic) equations (A6) and (A7):

(A6) $$\beta_1 \, (1 + \delta) \, p_t^{cd} - \beta_1 \, (1 + \delta) \, E_{t-1} \, p_t^{cd} +$$

$$+ \kappa \, (2 \, g - 1) \, E_t \, z_{t+1} - [\kappa \, (2 \, g - 1) + 2 \, \varphi + 2 \, \beta_2 \, (1 + \delta)] \, z_t +$$

$$+ 2 \, \beta_3 \, (1 + \delta) \, E_{t-1} \, z_t = - (1 + \delta) \, (1 + \beta_1) \, \mu_t^d + \eta_t^d$$

(A7)
$$\alpha_1 E_t p_{t+1}^{cd} - [\theta(1+\beta_1)+\beta_1\alpha_2+1+\alpha_1]\, p_t^{cd} +$$
$$+ \beta_1(\alpha_2+\theta) E_{t-1} p_t^{cd} + \alpha_1(2g-1) E_t z_{t-1} +$$
$$+ [2\theta(1-g+\beta_2)+2\alpha_2\beta_2-\alpha_1(2g-1)]\, z_t - 2\beta_3[\alpha_2+\theta] E_{t-1} z_t =$$
$$= \varepsilon_t^d + (1+\beta_1)(\theta+\alpha_2)\,\theta_t^d$$

After taking expectations in $t-1$ and forwarding j periods ahead the two characteristic roots are:

$$\lambda_1 = 1 + 2\,[\varphi+(1+\delta)(\beta_2-\beta_3)]\,/\,\kappa\,(2g-1) \quad \text{and} \quad \lambda_2 = 1+(1+\theta)\,/\,\alpha_1$$

As all elasticities and semi-elasticities are assumed to be positive and $g>0,5$, and since β_2 is larger than β_3 we always get $\lambda_1>1$. Furthermore, we get $|\lambda_2| > 1$ if $\theta > -2\alpha_1-1$ or $\theta > -1$. To exclude explosive paths, it is conventionally imposed under these conditions that:

$$E_{t-1} z_t = E_{t-1} p_t^{cd} = E_t p_{t+1}{}^{cd} = E_t z_{t+1} = 0.$$

Solving *(A6)* for z_t results then in:

(A8)
$$z_t = \{(1+\delta)(1+\beta_1)\,\mu_t^d - \eta_t^d + \beta_1(1+\delta)\,p_t^{cd}\}$$
$$[\kappa(2g-1)+2\varphi+2\beta_2(1+\delta)]^{-1}$$

Substituting *(A8)* in *(A7)*, and making use of $\beta_2 = \beta_1(1-g)$ in the denominator results in:

(A9)
$$p_t^{cd} \doteq$$

$$= \frac{-[\kappa(2g-1)+2\varphi+2\beta_2(1+\delta)]\,\varepsilon_t^d - [2\theta(1+\beta_2-g)+2\alpha_2\beta_2-\alpha_1(2g-1)]\,\eta_t^d}{[\theta(1+\beta_1)+\alpha_2\beta_1+1+\alpha_1]\,[\kappa(2g-1)+2\varphi]+\beta_1(1+\delta)\,[\alpha_1+2(1-g)]}$$

$$\frac{+(1+\beta_1)\,\{(1+\delta)[2\theta(1-g)-\alpha_1(2g-1)]-(\theta+\alpha_1)[\kappa(2g-1)+2\varphi]\}\,\mu_t^d}{[\theta(1+\beta_1)+\alpha_2\beta_1+1+\alpha_1]\,[\kappa(2g-1)+2\varphi]+\beta_1(1+\delta)\,[\alpha_1+2(1-g)]}$$

In the case of a money supply rule $\theta = 0$ in *(A9)*. Therefore we get *(24c)*. In the case of nominal GNP-targeting $\theta \to \infty$ results in *(25c)*. To calculate p_t^d we use the fact that: $p_t^d = p_t^{cd} - 2(1-g)z_t$ together with *(A8)*. Real income can then easily be calculated by using the supply function:

$$y_t^d = \beta_1 (p_t^d - E_{t-1} p_t^d) - 2(\beta_2 - \beta_3) E_{t-1} z_t + (1+\beta_1) \mu_t^d$$

which is the difference of the supply functions in terms of the difference of the producer prices.

2.2 Prices Level (Inflation-Rate) Targeting: CPI

The calculation follows the same procedure. From *(6")*, *(7")*, *(9")* and *(10"*)* we obtain:

(A10) $\quad \alpha_1 E_t p_{t+1}^{cd} - [\theta + \beta_1 \alpha_2 + 1 + \alpha_1] p_t^{cd} + \alpha_2 \beta_1 E_{t-1} p_t^{cd} +$

$\quad\quad\quad + \alpha_1 (2g-1) E_t z_{t+1} + [2\alpha_2 \beta_1 - \alpha_1 (2g-1)] z_t +$

$\quad\quad\quad - 2\alpha_2 \beta_3 E_{t-1} z_t = \varepsilon_t^d + \alpha_2 (1+\beta_1) \mu_t^d$

Substituting z_t from *(A8)* in *(A10)* along with:

$$E_{t-1} p_t^{cd} = E_{t-1} p_t^{cd} = E_{t-1} z_t = E_t z_{t+1} = 0$$

results in *(A11)*, where we use again $\beta_2 = \beta_1 (1-g)$ in the denominator:

(A11) $\quad\quad\quad\quad\quad\quad p_t^{cd} \mid CPI =$

$$= \frac{-[\kappa (2g-1) + 2\varphi + 2\beta_2 (1+\delta)] \varepsilon_t^d - [2\alpha_2 \beta_2 - \alpha_1 (2g-1)] \eta_t^d}{(\theta + \alpha_2\beta_1 + 1 + \alpha_1)[\kappa(2g-1) + 2\varphi] + \beta_1(1+\delta)[2\theta(1-g) + \alpha_1 + 2(1-g)]}$$

$$\frac{+ (1+\beta_1)\{\alpha_1 (1+\delta)(2g-1) - \alpha_2 [\kappa (2g-1) + 2\varphi]\} \mu_t^d}{(\theta + \alpha_2\beta_1 + 1 + \alpha_1)[\kappa(2g-1) + 2\varphi] + \beta_1(1+\delta)[2\theta(1-g) + \alpha_1 + 2(1-g)]}$$

Taking limit $\theta \to \infty$ in *(A11)* results in *(26c)*. From $p_t^d = p_t^{cd} - 2(1-g)z_t$ we calculate *(26b)*. Substituting the results in the supply equation gives *(26a)*.

2.3 *Price Level (Inflation-Rate) Targeting: Producer Price*

The calculation follows again the same procedure. From *(6″)*, *(7″)*, *(9″)* and *(10″*)* we get:

(A12) $\alpha_1 E_t p_{t+1}^{cd} - [\theta + \beta_1 \alpha_2 + 1 + \alpha_1] p_t^{cd} + \alpha_2 \beta_1 E_{t-1} p_t^{cd} + \alpha_1 (2g-1) E_t z_{t+1} +$

$+ [2\theta(1-g) + 2\alpha_2 \beta_2 - \alpha_1 (2g-1)] z_t - 2\alpha_2 \beta_3 E_{t-1} z_t = \varepsilon_t^d + \alpha_2 (1+\beta_1) \mu_t^d$

Substituting *(A8)* in *(A12)* and using $\beta_2 = \beta_1 (1-g)$ in the denominator along with $E_{t-1} p_t^{cd} = E_{t-1} p_t^{cd} = E_{t-1} z_t = E_t z_{t+1} = 0$ results in:

(A13) $\qquad\qquad\qquad p_t^{cd} =$

$$= \frac{- [\kappa(2g-1) + 2\varphi + 2\beta_2(1+\delta)]\, \varepsilon_t^d - [2\theta(1-g) + 2\alpha_2\,\beta_2 - \alpha_1\,(2g-1)]\,\eta_t^d}{(\theta + \alpha_2\beta_1 + 1 + \alpha_1)\,[\kappa\,(2g-1) + 2\varphi] + \beta_1(1+\delta)\,[\alpha_1 + 2(1-g)]}$$

$$\frac{+ (1+\beta_1)\,\{(1+\delta)[2\theta(1-g) - \alpha_1(2g-1)] - (\alpha_2)[\kappa(2g-1) + 2\varphi]\}\,\mu_t^d}{(\theta + \alpha_2\beta_1 + 1 + \alpha_1)\,[\kappa\,(2g-1) + 2\varphi] + \beta_1(1+\delta)\,[\alpha_1 + 2(1-g)]}$$

Taking limit in *(A13)* results in *(27c)*, where we again make use of $\beta_2 = \beta_1 (1-g)$ in the numerator. *(27a)* and *(27b)* are obtained as above.

BIBLIOGRAPHY

[1] AOKI M.: *Dynamic Analysis of Open Economies*, Academic Press, New York, 1981.

[2] ARGY V.: «Nominal Income Targeting: a Critical Evaluation», Washington (DC), International Monetary Fund, *Working Paper*, n. 91/92, October 1991.

[3] ASAKO K.: «Money Supply versus Nominal Income Targets under Money Supply and Multiplier Uncertainties», *The Economic Studies Quarterly*, vol. 42, n. 2, 1991, pp. 117-23.

[4] ASAKO K. - WAGNER H.: «Nominal Income Targeting Versus Money Supply Targeting», *Scottish Journal of Political Economy*, vol. 39, n. 2, 1992, pp. 167-87.

[5] BEAN C.: «Targeting Nominal Income: an Appraisal», *The Economic Journal*, vol. 93, n. 372, pp. 806-19.

[6] BRADLEY M. - JANSEN D.W.: «The Optimality of Nominal Income Targeting When Wages Are Indexed to Price», *Southern Economic Journal*, vol. 56, n. 1, 1989, pp. 13-23.

[7] BRYANT R. *et AL*: *Empirical Macroeconomics for Interdependent Economies*, Washington (DC), Brooking Institution, 1988.

[8] CANZONERI M. - GRAY J.: «Monetary Policy Games and the Consequences of Non-Cooperative Behavior», *International Economic Review*, vol. 26, n. 3, 1985, pp. 547-64.

[9] COOPER R.: «Economic Interdependence and Coordination of Economic Policies», in JONES R. - KENEN P. (eds.): *Handbook in International Economics*, vol. II, Amsterdam, North Holland, 1985.

[10] CURRIE D. - LEVINE P.: «European Monetary Union or Hard Ems», *European Economic Review*, vol. 36, n. 6, 1992, pp. 1185-204.

[11] FELDSTEIN M.: «Distinguished Lecture on Economics in Government: Thinking about International Economic Coordination», *Journal of Economic Perspectives*, vol. 2, n. 2, 1988, pp. 3-13.

[12] FISCHER S.: «International Macroeconomic Policy Coordination», in FELDSTEIN M. (ed.): *International Policy Coordination*, Chicago, University of Chicago Press, 1988.

[13] FRANKEL J.: «Obstacles to Interantional Macroeconomic Policy Coordination», Washington, International Monetary Fund, *Working Paper*, n. 87/28, Princeton University, *Studies in International Finance*, n. 64, December 1988.

[14] — —: «A Modest Proposal for International Nominal Targetin (Int)», Cambridge (Mass.), National Bureau of Economic Research, *Working Paper*, n. 2856, 1989.

[15] — —: «International Nominal Targeting. A Proposal for Overcoming Obstacles to Policy Coordination», *Rivista di politica economica*, vol. 79, n. 12, 1989, pp. 257-94, and in BALDASSARI M. MCCALLUM J. - MUNDELL R. (eds.): *Global Disequilibrium in the World Economy*, Macmillan Press, Houndmills, 1992.

[16] — —: «The Making of Exchange Rate Policy in the 1980s», Forthcoming, in FELDESTEIN M. (ed.): *American Economic Policy in the 1980s*, Chicago, University of Chicago Press Chicago, Cambridge (Mass), National Bureau of Economic Research, *Working Paper*, n. 3539, University of California, Berkeley Economics, *Working Paper*, n. 91-157, 1990.

[17] — —: «The Obstacles to Macroeconomic Policy Coordination in the 1990s and an Analysis of International Nominal Targeting (INT)», in KOEKKOEK K.A. - MENNESS L.B.M. (eds.): *International Trade and Global Development: Essays in Honour of Jagdish Bhagwati*, London, Routledge House, 1991, pp. 211-36.

[18] FRANKEL J. - ROCKETT K.: «International Macroeconomic Policy Coordination when Policy-Makers Do Not Agree on the True Model», *American Economic Review*, vol. 78, n. 3, 1988, pp. 318-40.

[19] FRANKEL J. - CHINN M.: «The Stabilizing Properties of a Nominal Gnp Rule in an Open Economy, forthcoming in *Journal of Money, Credit and Banking University of California, Berkeley Economics, Working Paper*, n. 91-166, May 1991.

[20] FRANKEL J. - SCOTT E. - ROCKETT K.: «International Macroeconomic Policy Coordination When Policymakers Do Not Agree on the True Model: Reply», *American Economic Review*, vol. 82, n. 4, 1992, pp. 1052-6.

[21] FUNABASHI Y.: *Managing the Dollar: From the Plaza to the Louvre*, Washington (DC), Institute of International Economics, 1988.

[22] FUNKE N.: «International Monetary Policy Coordination: a Classification and Evaluation of Recent Concepts in a Stochastic Two-Country Model. Kiel Advanced Studies», University of California, Kiel Institute of World Economics, *Working Paper*, n. 215, 1991.

[23] — —: *Das Internationale Nominale Sozialprodukt als Geldpolitisches Koordiantionsziel Eine Analyse* (International Nominal Targeting: an Evaluation), Mimeo, 1992.

[24] — —: «Zur Einkommenskreislaufgeschwindigkeit des Geldes Bei Alternativen Geldpolitischen Regeln: Eine Anmerkung» (The Income Velocity of Money under Alternative Monetary Policy Rules: One Remark) *Jahrbücher für Nationalökonomie und Statistik*, forthcoming 1993.

[25] FUNKE M. - MASTROBERARDINO M.: «*Money Supply Targeting versus Nominal Income Targeting: The Small Open Economy Case*»; University of California, Kiel Institute of World Economics, Kiel Advanced Studies, *Working Paper*, n. 201, mar. 1991.

[26] HAMADA K.: «A Strategic Analysis of Monetary Interdependence», *Journal of Political Economy*, vol. 84, n. 4, 1976, pp. 77-9.

[27] — —: *The Political Economy of International Monetary Interdependence*, Cambridge (MA), Mit Press, 1985.

[28] HOLTHAM G. - HALLETT A.H.: «International Policy Coordination and Model Uncertainty», in BRYANT R. - PORTES R. (eds.): *Global Macroeconomics: Policy Conflict and Cooperation*, London, MacMillan, 1987.

[29] — — — —: «International Macroeconomic Policy Coordination When Policymakers Do Not Agree on the True Model: Commenti *The American Economic Review*, vol. 82, n. 4, 1992, pp. 1043-51.

[30] LEDER D.: *The Stabilizing Effects of Pave and of Mixed Monetary Policy Strategies on the World Economy*, Berlin, 1992.

[31] McKIBBIN W. - SACHS J.: «Comparing the Global Performance of Alternative Exchange Rate Arrangements», Cambridge (Mass), National Bureau of Economic Research, *Working Paper*, n. 2000, and *Journal of International Money and Finance*, vol. 7, n. 4, 1986, pp. 387-410.

[32] — — — —: The McKibbin-Sachs Global (MSG2) Model, *Brookings Discussion Papers in International Economics*, n. 78, August 1989.

[33] — — — —: «Implications of Policy Rules for the World Economy: Results from the McKibbin-Sachs Global (*MSG2*) Model», in BRYANT R. - CURRIE D. - FRENKEL J. - MASSON P. - PORTES R. (eds.): *Macroeconomic Policies in an Interdependent World*, Washington (DC), Brookings Institution, 1989.

[34] OUDIZ G. - SACHS J.: «Macroeconomic Policy Coordination Among the Industrialized Economics», *Brookings Papers on Economic Activity*, vol. 1, 1984.

[35] PUTNAM R. - BAYNE N.: *Hanging Together The Seven-Power Summits*, 2ª ed., Cambridge (MA), Harvard University Press, 1987.

[36] ROGOFF K.: «International Macroeconomic Policy Coordination May Be Counterproductive», *Journal of International Economics*, vol. 18, n. 3/4, 1985, pp. 199-217.

[37] ——: «The Optimal Degree of Commitment to an Intermediate Monetary Target», *Quarterly Journal of Economics*, vol. 100, n. 4, 1985, pp. 1169-89.

[38] TAYLOR J.B.: «What Would Nominal GNP Targetting Do to the Business Cycle?» *Carnegie Rochester Conference Series on Public Policy*, n. 22, 1985, pp. 61-84.

[39] VAUBEL R.: «International Collusion or Competition for Macroeconomic Policy Coordination? A Restatement», *Recherches Economiques de Louvain*, vol. 51, n. 3-4, 1985, pp. 223-40.

[40] VON FURSTENBERG G. - DANIELS J.: «Policy Undertakings by the Seven "Summit" Countries: Ascertaining the Degree of Compliance», in MELTZER A. - PLOSSER C. (eds.): *Carnegie-Rochester Conference Series on Public Policy*, vol. 35, Autumn 1991, pp. 267-301.

[41] ————: «Economic Summit Declarations 1975-1989: Examining the Written Record of International Cooperation», *Princeton Studies in International Finance*, n. 72, February 1992.

[42] WEST K.D.: «Targeting Nominal Income: a Note», *The Economic Journal*, vol. 96, n. 384, 1986, pp. 1077-83.

II – REAL AND FINANCIAL INTEGRATION

The Dynamics of Capital Liberalization: a Macroeconometric Analysis

Giancarlo Gandolfo (*) - Pier Carlo Padoan
Università «La Sapienza», Roma

1. - Introduction

This paper examines the dynamics of the liberalization of international capital flows in the Italian economy. The analysis is carried out using the fifth version of the Italian continuous time model (Gandolfo-Padoan [16]).

The use of a continuous time econometric model turns out to be very important for the analysis of the problem at hand. In fact, international capital movements are modelled according to the portfolio adjustment view. Hence they are considered as the flow deriving from the adjustment of the actual to the desired stock of net foreign assets. Thus, one needs in the first place a rigorous estimation of the associated speed of adjustment independently of the sampling interval. This estimation can be obtained only through the continuous time approach to econometric modelling. In this context, capital liberalization takes the form of an increase in the adjustment speed of net foreign assets to their (partial) equilibrium value. The analysis of the consequences of this increase is carried out at two levels. First, stability and sensitivity analysis about the steady state of the model identify a source of instability in the increase in question. Possible stabilizing factors are also considered. In the second place, the

(*) Giancarlo Gandolfo gratefully acknowledges the invitation to CES (Center for Economic Studies of the University of Munich), where he could complete the writing of this paper. The underlying research was carried out thanks to a grant by Consiglio nazionale delle ricerche.

N.B.: the numbers in square brackets refer to the Bibliography at the end of paper.

systemic consequences of capital liberalization are considered by carrying out several simulations with different degrees of capital liberalization (including the case of perfect capital mobility). This paper brings together previous work of ours (Gandolfo-Padoan [17], [18], [19]), and gives new results.

The plan of the paper is as follows. In Section 2 we give an overview of the problem of modelling capital liberalization, and present our solution, which is then followed by a brief description of the relevant parts of our model (Section 3). Section 4 examines the stability of the model around the steady state and gives the results of sensitivity analysis (1). The following sections deal with our simulation exercises. The basic case, i.e. when we simply change the adjustment speed of capital flows, is treated in Section 5. Section 6 shows the importance of exchange rate expectations. Here much attention has been devoted to the role and relative weight of different agents in the foreign exchange market (*chartists* and *fundamentalists*), which is crucial for the onset of possible destabilizing speculative capital flows. The effect of the introduction of a "Tobin tax" (i.e., a tax on all foreign exchange transactions) is examined in Section 7. Section 8 deals with the issue of trade liberalization in relation to capital flow liberalization. Section 9 concludes the paper.

2. - Perfect Capital Mobility: an Overview

The starting point is the Mundellian analysis (Mundell [29]), which — given the assumption of perfect capital mobility — shows the totally different effectiveness of monetary and fiscal policy under fixed and flexible exchange rates. Under fixed exchange rates, perfect capital mobility implies the ineffectiveness of monetary policy and the full effectiveness of fiscal policy. Exactly the opposite is true under flexible exchange rates: monetary policy is fully effective while fiscal policy becomes ineffective. These propositions are 30 years old, but subsequent studies do not seem to have added much to them (refin-

---

(1) By sensitivity analysis we mean the study of the partial derivatives of the characteristic roots of the model with respect to the estimated parameters. For details see GANDOLFO [12].

ements include the distinction between perfect capital mobility and perfect asset substitutability, the reintroduction of some effectiveness of fiscal policy through changes in the real money supply due to exchange-rate changes, etc. (Gandolfo [10], parag. 16.6)).

The recent literature on the relationships between capital controls and crises of the foreign exchange markets points out that, in a regime of fixed but adjustable parities, the removal of capital controls may give rise to speculative attacks capable of exhausting official reserve thus forcing parity realignments. Besides, in the presence of perfect capital mobility, accomodating realignments, i.e. realignments that completely offset the cumulated loss of competitiveness, may give rise to undesirable oscillations in the exchange rate and to vicious circle phenomena (Wyplosz [35], Driffill [6] and Obstfeld [30]). This would increase the frequency of realignments and hence undermine the credibility of the exchange-rate arrangements. The conclusion is that one cannot rely solely on realignments of exchange rates to eliminate external disequilibria. But, again, there is nothing new under the sun: these problems and propositions are, in fact, well known to every student of the Bretton Woods system.

Let us now come to our main point, which is how to model capital controls and liberalization. In some cases (Wyplosz [35]), capital controls are modelled so as to lead to zero capital outflows from residents as only non-residents' capital movements are allowed. While this way of modelling capital controls partly reflects — among others — the Italian past experience of asymmetric capital controls (where only capital inflows were freely allowed) (2) it seems much too extreme especially if the case of developed countries is considered. More accurately, in our view, Khan and Zahler [26], [27] assume that, given an equation for capital movements where flows react to covered interest rate differentials, controls are modelled through the introduction of a coefficient which takes on the value of zero (less than one) in case of total (partial) controls. A more rigorous specification is the one followed by Gros [21] who assumes that capital controls are equivalent to a (positive but not prohibitive) adjustment cost that markets have to bear in order to adjust their financial assets

_____

(2) See, e.g. PAPADIA - VONA [33], PAPADIA - ROSSI [32].

to the desired value whose amount does not depend on controls. Such a specification allows to take into account two features of a world with capital controls: one is that capital controls seldom, if at all, lead to a complete elimination of capital movements; the second is that capital liberalization can be clearly understood as an intrinsically dynamic process. In this respect the view (Palmisani - Rossi [31]) that capital controls, and any other kind of currency restriction, can be thought of as a tax on interest income is not fully convincing. In fact, a tax on interest income changes the desired stock of net foreign assets since it alters the interest differential, but has no effect on the speed at which agents adjust the actual to the desired stock. Thus we believe that the question of the speed of adjustment and the tax on interest income are two aspects that can coexist but should be kept distinct.

This brief review of the literature suggests that the study of the effects of the liberalization of capital movements in an advanced open economy should be carried out according to the following lines: *a)* it should consider the dynamic nature of the process of adjustment towards a liberalized regime. Technically — as recalled above — this means that we should use dynamics and not comparative statics; *b)* it should take account of the role of economic policy and in particular of the behaviour of the monetary authorities as regards international reserves, exchange rates, etc.; *c)* it should consider the effects of the liberalization on the whole economic system. This last point has a twofold nature. On the one hand, it would be insufficient to consider only the effects on the foreign exchange market. On the other, even if one were interested in examining solely the effects on the exchange rate, it should be noted that liberalization influences the foreign exchange market not only directly but also indirectly through the changes in the macroeconomic variables induced by the liberalization. In short, the study should be carried out in the context of economy-wide dynamic macroeconometric models. The existing models are generally not suited to this purpose, at least as regards Italy, partly because they do not contain an adequate modelling of capital movements and lack the technical possibility of embodying perfect capital mobility in a rigorous way.

According to the portfolio view, capital movements are not pure flows but represent the adjustment of the desired to the actual stock of net foreign assets. Now, the parameter representing the adjustment speed depends not only on the behaviour of economic agents but also on the presence of capital controls hence on an institutional arrangement — in the sense that a low adjustment speed is due to the fact that agents are not free to immediately adjust the actual to the desired stock of net foreign assets. To put the same concept in other words, the desired stock of *NFA* (*net foreign assets*) depends on fundamentals, the adjustment speed reflects institutional features such as capital controls.

More precisely, the dynamic version of the portfolio approach to capital movements starts from an equation of the following type:

$$(1) \qquad DNFA = \alpha\,(N\hat{F}A - NFA)$$

where D denotes the differential operator d/dt, α the adjustment speed, and *NFA* the stock of net foreign assets. $N\hat{F}A = \phi\,(...)$ is the *desired* stock, which depends on fundamentals (the arguments of the function ϕ, such as the interest rate differential, etc. These will be specified later on). In equation *(1)*, a low value of α reflects capital controls. In the presence of capital controls, in fact, economic agents are not free to immediately adjust the actual to the desired stock of net foreign assets. While the desired stock of net foreign assets depends on fundamentals, the adjustment speed reflects institutional features such as capital controls.

In this context, the transition to a regime with higher capital mobility is equivalent to an increase in α or, which is the same thing, a decrease in the mean time lag of adjustment. In continuous time, the mean time lag is given by the reciprocal of α, and measures the time required for about 63% of the discrepancy between desired and actual values to be eliminated by the adjustment process.

3. - The Italian Continuous Time Model and Capital Flows

Our model (3) is a medium term disequilibrium model specified and estimated in continuous time as a set of stochastic differential

---

(3) See tables *A* 1 e *A* 2 in the Appendix for a summary view; for a full description see GANDOLFO - PADOAN [10], [16].

equations which stresses real and financial accumulation in an open and highly integrated economy. The Mark V version includes a detailed specification of the financial sector as well as the endogenous determination of the exchange rate.

It considers stock-flow behaviour in an open economy in which both price and quantity adjustments take place. Stocks are introduced with reference to the real sector (where adjustments of fixed capital and inventories to their respective desired levels are present) and to the financial sector which includes the stock of money, the stock of commercial credit, the stock of net foreign assets and the stock of international reserves. The exchange rate is endogenously determined in the exchange market which clears instantaneously. Since we do not privilege any one of the competing theories but believe in an eclectic approach, exchange rate determination is thus related to all the variables present in the model including policy variables. Policy reaction functions cover fiscal variables (government expenditure and taxes) and financial variables such as the interest rate, money supply and international reserves.

Let us take a closer look at the equation which most interests us in the present context, namely the capital movements equation, which is specified as follows:

$$D \log NFA = \alpha_{24} \log \left(\frac{N\hat{F}A}{NFA} \right) +$$

(2)

$$+ \alpha_{25} \log \left(\frac{PMGS_f \cdot E \cdot MGS}{PXGS \cdot XGS} \right), \; \alpha_{25} < 0$$

where:

$$N\hat{F}A = \gamma_{11} \, e^{\beta_{19} \left[i_f + \log \left(\frac{FR}{E} \right) - i_{TIT} \right]} (PY)^{\beta_{20}} (PF_f \cdot E \cdot YF)^{-\beta_{21}}$$

This equation has a twofold nature. First of all, the stock of net foreign assets (*NFA*) adjusts to its desired value *N\hat{F}A*. The latter reflects the portfolio view, in which the scale variables are proxied by the domestic (PY) and foreign ($PF_f \cdot E \cdot YF$) money incomes. Given the scale variables the level of $N\hat{F}A$ is determined by the interest differential term corrected for exchange rate expectations; these are proxied by the ratio of the forward to the spot exchange rate (FR/E).

The second element in the equation refers to capital movements which are not strictly related to portfolio considerations, but rather to trade flows. The ratio of the value of imports to the value of exports is meant to capture the effect of commercial credits on the capital account. A trade deficit — i.e. ($PMGS_f \cdot E \cdot MGS/PXGS \cdot XGS$) > 1; hence log (...) > 0 — is partly financed through commercial credits from abroad, hence an increase in foreign liabilities (D log NFA < 0).

The interest differential term is also included in the interest rate equation. This is consistent with the idea that the domestic interest rate moves to close the discrepancy between its current value and the covered interest parity value. In fact, under perfect mobility and infinite elasticity of arbitrage funds the relation:

$$(3) \qquad\qquad i_{TIT} = i_f + \frac{(FR - E)}{E}$$

should hold. Considerations of imperfect capital mobility can however explain the presence of a gap between the two members. This, in turn, gives rise to a (policy managed) movement of i_{TIT} aimed at the reduction of the gap.

Given the relevance of the topic some further considerations on the modelling of exchange rate expectations seem appropriate. In an open economy with perfect capital mobility, perfect asset substitutability (4) and risk neutral agents, *uncovered interest parity* holds, i.e.:

$$(4) \qquad\qquad i_{TIT} = i_f + \frac{D\tilde{E}}{E}$$

---

(4) Perfect capital mobility is often taken to imply perfect asset substitutability, but the two concepts are best kept apart, see GANDOLFO [10], p. II.398.

where $D\tilde{E} = \tilde{E} - E$ is the expected variation in the exchange rate. If we assume — according to the portfolio approach — imperfect substitutability between domestic and foreign assets, the interest-parity relation becomes:

$$(5) \qquad\qquad i_{TIT} = i_f + \frac{D\tilde{E}}{E} + \omega$$

where ω is a risk premium (5).

However, if we take account of imperfect capital mobility, neither relation *(4)* nor relation *(5)* will hold. A discrepancy between i_{TIT} and the right-hand-side of either eq. *(4)* or eq. *(5)* will not, in fact, cause an instantaneous and huge amount of capital flow. What will take place is a limited amount of capital flows, as described by the first term on the r.h.s. of eq. *(2)*. This flow will also cause a tendency of i_{TIT} to move to close the discrepancy (see eq.*(12)* in table *A*1); the speed of this adjustment depends, inter alia, on the degree of the authorities' control on capital movements. It should be noted that, given the volatility of the risk premium and the difficulty of modelling it precisely, we have not included it explicitly. This does *not* imply the assumption of perfect asset substitutability because we are not considering an equilibrium relation like *(4)* or *(3)*, but a disequilibrium adjustment equation. The observed discrepancy between i_{TIT} and $(i_f + D\tilde{E}/E)$, therefore, reflects both imperfect capital mobility and imperfect asset substitutability. This enables us to keep this discrepancy even under perfect capital mobility.

The problem of exchange rate expectations — as we have mentioned — has been solved by using the forward exchange rate. From the formal point of view, $\log(FR/E) \cong (FR - E)/E$ if we expand in Taylor's series and neglect all higher order terms. From the substantial point of view, in an efficient foreign exchange market with rational expectations, the forward exchange rate is an unbiased predictor of the future spot exchange rate. Hence the expected spot rate can be represented by the forward rate. But what if the foreign

---

(5) See, for example, GANDOLFO [10], p. II.413.

exchange market is not efficient and expectations are not rational, as recent empirical evidence seems to suggest? (6). Let us introduce the concept of "plausible" expectations, i.e. expectations which use easy and plausible information in a simple way, as opposed to rational expectations which use all the existing information efficiently. Now, in the context of plausible expectations the forward exchange rate remains a reasonable candidate for representing the expected spot exchange rate, irrespective of the efficiency of the market. First of all, we observe that in some cases the forward exchange rate outperforms all other forecasts based on econometric analyses (7). Secondly, even admitting that the forward exchange rate is generally not the best unbiased predictor of future spot rates, the problem remains of how agents involved in international transactions form their expectations. The proliferation of exchange-rate forecasting services may suggest that agents rely on these forecasts, but are these better than the forward exchange rate? The findings of Goodman [22], Levich [28], Blake, Beenstock, and Brasse [2], indicate that the forward exchange rate is a predictor of future spot rates which is not worse (and sometimes better) than the predictions of the exchange-rate forecasting services. In addition, the forward exchange rate has no cost. Thus it seems reasonable to assume that a rational agent (not necessarily in the sense of an agent holding rational expectations, but in the general sense of *homo economicus*) uses the forward rate. It should also be noted that the forward exchange rate, which is considered an exogenous variable for estimation purposes, becomes an endogenous variable in the long run (Gandolfo - Padoan [16]).

This as regards the estimated version of the model. When one passes from a situation of capital controls to perfect capital mobility, it is plausible to think that exchange rate expectations undergo a modification as well. Hence it becomes necessary to consider different hypotheses about the formation of these expectations. These will be considered in more detail below.

---

(6) See, for example, Ito [24] and Takagi [34].

(7) Random walk, *ARIMA*, *PPP*, uncovered interest parity, various versions of the monetary model, see Hogan [23].

4. - A First Look at the Consequences of Capital Liberalization. Stability and Sensitivity

The (local) stability of the model has been examined by using the linear approximation about the steady state. The model has two exchange rate regimes (fixed and floating exchange rates), as the sample period covers 1960.4-1984.4. This requires the computation of two steady-states (one for each regime) and, consequently, of two linear approximations. The model is practically stable under both regimes, which show no appreciable difference as regards stability (tables $A3$, $A4$). In fact, all the complex roots have negative real parts and all but one real characteristic root are negative. However, the positive root is not significantly different from zero at the 5% level. We therefore conclude that the hypothesis of stability cannot be rejected.

There is, however, a possible interpretation of this positive root suggested by sensitivity analysis. By sensitivity analysis we here mean the analysis of the effects of changes in the parameters on the characteristic roots of the model. This can be performed in a general way by computing the partial derivatives of these roots with respect to the parameters. If we call A the matrix of the linear approximation of the original non-linear system, we can compute $\partial \mu_i / \partial A$, where μ_i denotes the i-th characteristic root of A. Now, the partial derivative of one real root with respect to α_{24} is positive and very large in relative terms, which implies that the model becomes unstable for sufficiently high capital mobility. This is a worrying result, but sensitivity analysis indicates some possible stabilizing effects. Table $A5$ gives the main results of sensitivity analysis under flexible exchange rates; in this table we present only the results concerning the parameters that crucially affect stability. This table shows a large and positive partial derivative of the possibly positive root with respect to α_{24} (the adjustment speed of net foreign assets). Such a result implies that an increase in α_{24} would cause an increase in this root, hence instability for sufficiently high values of α_{24}. This result holds also under fixed exchange rates. Under flexible exchange rates it is possible to suggest an explanation for this phenomenon. Let us first note that our use of the forward exchange rate as a proxy for the expected spot rate may also be seen as representing rational expectations. Then, if we couple a very high adjustment speed ($\alpha_{24} \rightarrow \infty$) with rational expectations we are in a well-known context. Efficient asset markets with rational expectations imply that the equilibrium state has the saddle-point property, hence at least one positive root. The presence of only one positive root is related to our choice of using also other types of expectations in addition to rational expectations. This is a deliberate choice due to our eclectic approach (8).

There is, however, more to it than that. With $\alpha_{24} \rightarrow \infty$ we have perfect capital mobility which, as shown above, implies instability unless we can rely on rational expectations causing the model to jump on a stable path. Since we do not have generalized rational expectations (see above), full capital liberalization may have destabilizing impact on the model *ceteris paribus*. We wish to stress the *ceteris paribus* clause, because by (directly or indirectly) acting on other parameters one might counteract this destabilizing effect. Sensitivity analysis indicates some possible stabilizing effects. Both an increase in α_5 (the adjustment speed of imports) and an increase in α_8 (the adjustment speed of exports) have a stabilizing effect on the same root. The implication seems to be that the destabilizing impact of an increase in capital mobility can be counteracted by an increase in goods mobility: when one frees capital movements one must also have free trade in goods and services. This interesting result confirms some of the insights of the literature on the order of liberalization mentioned in Section 2. A stabilizing effect is also displayed by an increase in δ_8, a parameter present in the monetary authorities' reaction function. This parameter can be interpreted as the weight that the monetary authorities give to the discrepancy between the desired and the actual stock of international reserves when they decide the intensity of their intervention in the foreign exchange market.

5. - Simulation Exercises: the Basic Case

Further indications on the effects of higher capital mobility may be obtained through simulation analysis. The behaviour of the control

---

(8) Discussed in detail in GANDOLFO - PADOAN [16], and confirmed by the estimates.

solution has been compared with that of versions in which some parameters have been altered to represent capital liberalization. These exercises have been performed by using the original non-linear model. In fact, the parameters being estimated are those of the original non-linear differential model. Hence we can use this non-linear model for simulation rather than the linear approximation. The starting point was the first quarter of 1980 to have, in principle, five years of in-sample behaviour for comparison. The spirit of the exercise is to "rerun history", asking what would have happened had capital movements been liberalized at that point.

In this basic case simulation higher capital mobility has been simulated by imposing and increase in α_{24}, the adjustment speed of net foreign assets to their desired value (9) and eliminating capital controls from the equation of real imports (10). Let us note that an increase in α_{24} would probably be accompanied by an increase in α_{18} and perhaps in α_{17}. These parameters, however, do not affect stability in an appreciable way (they do not, in fact, appear in Table $A5$). Thus we decided not to consider these changes for the sake of brevity.

The value of α_{24} has been set to different values, starting from α_{24} = 0.2 which is the bifurcation value of the parameter derived from sensitivity analysis discussed above. The highest value considered is $\alpha_{24} = 90$, i.e. a mean time lag of one day, an assumption of (almost) perfect capital mobility. The behaviour of the model does not change significantly from a qualitative point of view. By this we mean that the basic features of the reaction mechanism triggered by the increase of α_{24} do not change with the value of the adjustment speed. The only difference lies in the intensity of the movement of the variables. We decided, therefore, to present for each of the first two cases considered (see below) the results obtained with $\alpha_{24} = 90$, i.e. the case of

---

(9) This procedure is similar to that followed (though in a different context) by JONSON - McKIBBIN - TREVOR [25] in their continuous time model of the Australian economy.

(10) The introduction of capital control variables in the equation for real imports reflected an attempt to account for clandestine capital movements. An earlier study (GANDOLFO [8]) found significant empirical evidence for this phenomenon in the Italian economy on the import side. Clandestine outflows are presumably positively related to controls in international capital movements.

full capital liberalization. It should also be stressed, from the purely theoretical point of view, that a very great (let us suppose infinite) speed of adjustment of the net foreign asset position does *not* mean an infinite flow of capital (which, if true, might threaten the non-negativity of the reserves, as pointed out in the discussion). An infinite speed of adjustment, in fact, simply means that economic agents are allowed (and able) to adjust the actual to the desired stock of net foreign assets immediately. The amount of the ensuing capital flow will be equal to the difference between $N\hat{F}A$ and NFA, and this difference is finite because $N\hat{F}A$, according to the portfolio view, is a finite amount as determined by eq. *(12.1)* of the model.

The main result of the simulations is that, after a period of apparently stable behaviour, the dynamic path of some variables, notably the exchange rate, becomes explosive. We may distinguish between an impact effect and an adjustment mechanism (Graph 1). The increase in α_{24} leads to an immediate increase in NFA, which causes an appreciation of the exchange rate E (impact effect). This is a well known effect in portfolio models (Gandolfo [10], Section 18.8.3.3). The change in E, in turn, leads to a decrease in the interest rate (i_{TIT}) and to an increase in the level of international reserves (R). This is the consequence of the "leaning against the wind" components present in both equations. These components cause the interest rate to increase (decrease) and international reserves to decrease (increase) when the change in the exchange rate ($D \log E$) is positive (negative). Finally the improvement of the terms of trade associated with the decrease in E produces an improvement in the current account. From this point onwards a reaction mechanism involving mainly the interest rate and the level of international reserves is set into motion.

The level of R is now higher than the target value which depends on the value of imports (now lower because of the appreciation of the exchange rate). As a consequence, the level of reserves tends to decrease. The level of the interest rate, on the contrary, is pushed upwards by two elements. One is the appreciation of the spot exchange rate relative to the forward rate which increases the target value of i_{TIT}. The other is the monetary squeeze caused by the decrease in international reserves through the money supply equation.

GRAPH 1

THE BASIC CASE
(simulated/base run; simulated-base for *i*)

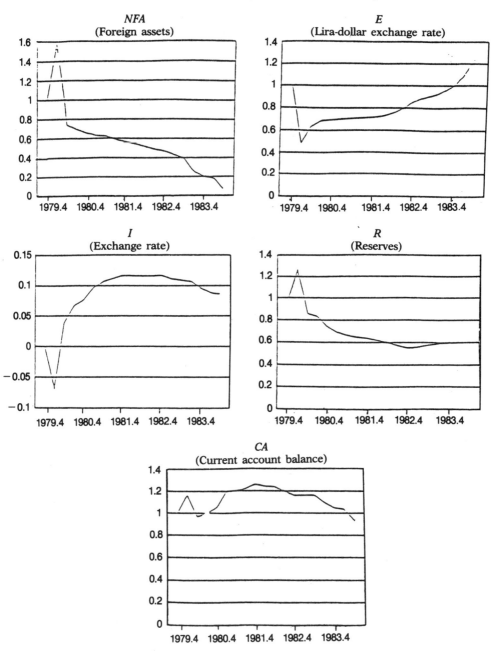

NFA
(Foreign assets)

E
(Lira-dollar exchange rate)

I
(Exchange rate)

R
(Reserves)

CA
(Current account balance)

The increase in i_{TIT} leads to a decrease in the accumulation of net foreign assets.

The decrease in *NFA* pushes towards the depreciation of the exchange rate. This effect is partially offset by the behaviour of the current account (which is improving). At this stage the economy is apparently following a stable path characterized by a lower exchange rate and a higher interest rate. One important real effect is the relatively lower level of fixed investment produced by the tighter monetary and credit conditions. After about three years, however, the pressure for a higher exchange rate overcomes the opposing forces. The exchange rate starts a depreciating movement which soon becomes explosive. The results confirm the widespread view that a decrease in capital controls leads initially to a higher stock of net foreign assets. They also confirm the similarly widespread opinion that the economy can be kept on a relatively stable path with appropriate interest rate and exchange rate policies. This latter opinion, unfortunately, is true only for a few years, and does not hold in the longer run. What this exercise shows, in fact, is that the new regime leads to the build up of market pressures concentrating on the exchange rate which eventually become unsustainable.

6. - Alternative Exchange-Rate Expectations

The role of policy interventions associated with the "leaning against the wind" component was crucial in the basic case. A second group of simulations has been carried out by eliminating this component from the two policy equations (interest rate and international reserves). A second major modification is related to exchange rate expectations which are represented by the ratio of the forward to the spot exchange rate. The forward rate was kept exogenous in the basic case and this fact might have somewhat distorted the result of the exercise.

The role of exchange rate expectations is, in fact, crucial for the onset of possible destabilizing speculative capital flows. Thus we also considered different hypotheses about the formation of exchange rate expectations. The relevant literature is enormous, so we decided to consider, in addition to those included in the estimated version of the model, only the following types of expectations: extrapolative and "normal" or "regressive" as well as a combination of the two. The former simply mean that, if a change has taken place, a further change in the same direction is expected; as regards the latter, they imply that economic agents have an idea of a normal, long-run value of the variable under consideration so that, whenever the current value is different from the normal one, they expect that the current value will sooner or later move towards (or "regress" to) the normal one. It seems plausible to assume the *PPP* value as the long-run normal exchange rate, also because the model possesses a steady state path on which the exchange rate is at its *PPP* value (Gandolfo - Padoan [16]). Hence rational agents, who know the model (and the fact that its steady state is stable) have this normal value in mind.

It is fairly obvious that extrapolative expectations are bound to have a destabilizing effect whereas normal expectations will have a stabilizing effect. The reason for considering these two types of expectations is related to the argument recently put forth by Frankel [7]. From surveys of the forecasts of the agents operating in the foreign exchange market, Frankel concludes that those who forecast at shorter horizons display destabilizing expectations because they tend to extrapolate recent trends, while those who operate with relatively longer horizons tend to have regressive, or stabilizing, expectations. The reasons for this different behaviour are to be seen, according to Frankel, in the fact that short-term traders in the foreign exchange market have to show to their superiors (typically, bank executives) that they are able to make profits over a much shorter time period than that over which the performance of longer-term traders is evaluated. Independently of the reason, we believe that Frankel's distinction is correct, since it corresponds to the distinction between "occasional" and "permanent" speculators introduced long ago by Cutilli and Gandolfo ([3], [4] and [5]).

In the light of this distinction, one should not only consider the two extreme cases (all agents are of the same type, i.e. with either extrapolative or normal expectations), but also the intermediate ones. These are the cases where there are agents of the two types operating simultaneously in the market; the outcome will depend on the relative intensity of action of the two categories (Cutilli and Gandolfo [3], [4], [5]).

6.1 *Extrapolative Expectations*

Expected exchange rate changes were proxied by the rate of change of E, $D \log E$, which replaced $\log (FR/E)$ in both the interest rate and the capital movements equation. In this case too the experiment of capital liberalization leads to an explosive movement of the exchange rate (Graph 2). This movement, however, occurs much earlier (and with a much greater reaction in the variables considered) than in the previous case (Graph 2). The increase in α_{24} produces, as before, an increase in *NFA* and an appreciation of the exchange rate. The absence of leaning-against-the-wind components leaves the interest rate unchanged while international reserves slowly increase. Easier monetary conditions cause the current account to deteriorate. This is due to both higher imports and lower exports (which are inversely related to credit and hence money supply growth). The rather marked deterioration in the current account puts a pressure on the exchange rate which starts a very rapid devaluation course. As a consequence, the economy starts a cumulative process which eventually explodes. The devaluation is generated by the deterioration in the overall balance of payments. This is the result of stock-flow interactions as well as of different adjustment speeds in the balance of payments components. Let us consider, in fact, the relatively low adjustment speeds of real imports and exports. We can then understand that the favourable quantity effect of the devaluation on trade flows will be felt much more slowly than the adverse terms-of-trade effect. This leads to a further devaluation which is accepted by the monetary authorities, since the leaning-against-the-wind components have been suppressed. On the contrary, the central bank accumulates reserves to reach the target value for R. This value, in fact, keeps on increasing due to the increasing value of imports determined by the depreciation of the exchange rate. Higher reserves lead to easier monetary conditions and further current account deterioration.

GRAPH 2

EXTRAPOLATIVE EXPECTATIONS
(simulated/base run; simulated-base for *i*)

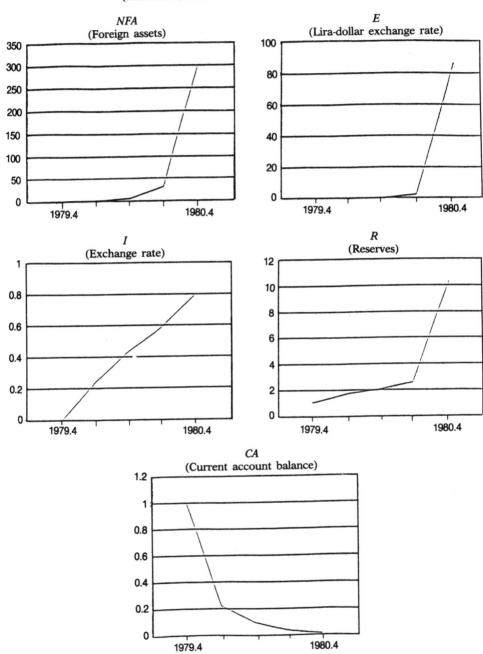

6.2 *Normal Expectations*

In this set of simulations the exchange rate expectations were modelled assuming that traders form an idea of the "normal" or "long run" exchange rate based on the "fundamentals" of the system (relative prices). Accordingly, the expected proportional change in the exchange rate was proxied by the log of the ratio of the "normal" to the spot exchange rate, $\log (\hat{E}/E)$, where $\hat{E} = PXGS/PF_f$ is the ratio of domestic export prices to foreign competitors' export prices in foreign currency, i.e. the exchange rate necessary to maintain price competitiveness. This way of modelling expectations also takes into account the fact that, in the model, monetary authorities adjust international reserves, i.e. intervene in the foreign exchange market, considering price competitiveness in addition to other targets (Gandolfo and Padoan [16]). Normal exchange rate expectations were introduced in the form $\delta_E \log (\hat{E}/E)$, where δ_E was given a set of values ranging from 0.1 to 1.0. However in what follows we will present only the case of $\delta_E = 1.0$ since the dynamic behaviour of this set of simulations does not change in its main characteristics with a change in the value of δ_E. The following cases also include a change in the value of the parameter δ_8, i.e. the parameter associated with the desired value of international reserves in the monetary authorities' reaction function, whose value was set to 1.0 (while its estimated value was 0.282). This change, as recalled above, is suggested by sensitivity analysis (Section 4) which indicates that an increase in δ_8 has a stabilizing effect on the system. The results of the simulation run are summarized in Graph 3.

As in the basic case we can distinguish between an impact effect and an adjustment mechanism. As in the basic case the increase in α_{24} leads to an immediate increase in *NFA* which causes an appreciation of the exchange rate and, consequently, a decrease in i_{TIT}, an increase in the level of international reserves, and an improvement of the trade balance due to better terms of trade. From this moment onwards the adjustment mechanism develops quite differently from the basic case. The level of international reserves adjusts to a lower desired value determined by the lower value of imports which results from the decrease in E. The higher value of δ_8 strengthens this effect thus producing a lower level of R with respect to the basic case. The

GRAPH 3

NORMAL EXPECTATIONS
(simulated/base run; simulated-base for *i*)

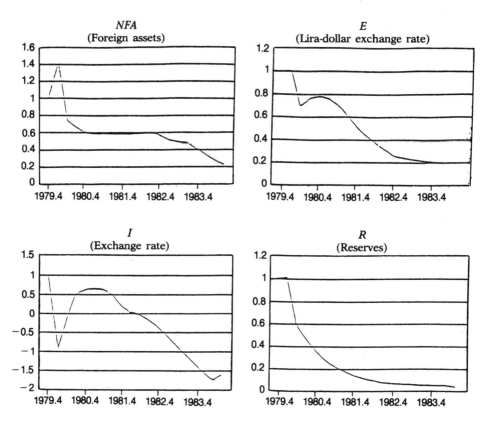

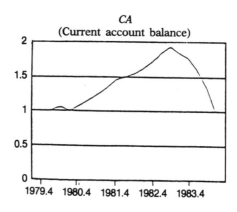

interest rate is initially higher than the control solution but, contrary to the basic case, it begins taking on lower values after nine quarters. This is the consequence of the fact that long term exchange rate expectations indicate an appreciation thanks to the "virtuous" interaction between the decrease in the spot exchange rate and the decline in domestic prices (and hence in export prices); consequently the target value of i_{TIT} decreases. The initial increase in i_{TIT} leads to a decrease in net foreign assets which continues till the end of the simulation, also as a consequence of the behaviour of exchange rate expectations. The current account improves, mainly thanks to the improvement in the terms of trade, for more than twelve quarters.

The forces sustaining this apparently stable path begin to lose strength after three years. While the exchange rate keeps appreciating, a pressure towards depreciation develops both from the decrease in *NFA* and from the change in the behaviour of the current account, which starts to deteriorate. After nineteen quarters the exchange rate inverts its course, and starts a depreciating movement which becomes explosive.

The main lesson from this exercise is that the formation of expectations is crucial in determining the dynamic behaviour of the system. The assumption of "normal" or "long run" expectations has dramatically improved the ability of the system to bear the impact of full capital liberalization with respect to the case of extrapolative expectations. However this was not enough to avoid a final collapse. In this respect what this exercise has shown is that while exchange rate expectations based on "fundamentals" (relative prices) do exert a stabilizing effect, they cannot fully offset the destabilizing effects of financial transactions.

6.3 *Mixed Expectations*

The expected change in the exchange rate is given by:

$$\pi_E \, \delta_E \, D \log E + \pi_N \, \delta_N \log (\hat{E}/E)$$

where $\pi_E + \pi_N = 1$ are the relative weights of the two categories of agents, and the other symbols have the same meaning as before. The combined parameters $(\pi_E \delta_E)$ and $(\pi_N \delta_N)$ where given values ranging from 0.1 to 2.0 in 0.1 increments. This allows for a wide number of possible combinations only a few of which will be discussed here. Given the results of the previous simulation exercises one of the points to be checked was the role of normal expectations in offsetting the destabilizing effect of extrapolative expectations. In order to do this we proceeded as follows. We started with a value of $\pi_E \delta_E = 1.0$ and a value of $\pi_N \delta_N = 0.1$. The main result was that, as in the case where only extrapolative expectations were considered, the behaviour of the exchange rate became explosive. However, the run came to a stop after eight quarters, i.e. a longer time span with respect to the case where normal expectations were not present. Slight increases in the coefficient associated with normal expectations lengthened the period over which the behaviour of the exchange rate, and of the whole model, remained relatively stable. With a value of $\pi_E \delta_E = 1.0$ and $\pi_N \delta_N = 0.5$ the model completed its run over the five year period. We shall refer to this case, which will be discussed in more detail below, as case 1. The experiment was then continued by increasing the value of $\pi_N \delta_N$ while keeping the other coefficient constant at the value of 1.0. One economic interpretation of such an experiment may be the following. Since one of the variables determining the behaviour of monetary authorities in exchange rate intervention (eq. *(16)*) is international competitiveness, an increasing weight of normal expectations in determining market behaviour may reflect the fact that the market considers such a policy commitment as increasingly credible. In other words a variable weight of normal expectations reflects a change in the policy regime (as far as exchange rate intervention is concerned) which is credible. As the simulations show this may prove crucial in affecting capital movements, a fact that has been suggested with respect to the Italian experience in the EMS by Giavazzi and Spaventa [20].

The main result of the increase in the coefficient associated with normal expectations is that the model continues to behave satisfactorily over the five year simulation period and generates different paths of the relevant variables, namely the exchange rate, net foreign assets and the current account. In what follows we will also discuss the case — which we will call case 2 — in which $\pi_N \delta_N$ takes on the value of 2.0 and $\pi_E \delta_E$ the value of 1.0.

6.3.1 Case 1

As in previous cases the first relevant effect is an increase in *NFA* (Graph 4) and, after an initial appreciation, a depreciation of the exchange rate which leads to an increase in the interest rate and a deterioration of the current account because of the adverse terms of trade effect. The deterioration of the two components of the balance of payments further leads to a devaluation which strengthens the effect of a rising interest rate. The devaluation, however, eventually leads to an improvement of the current account, while the stock of net foreign assets keeps on a fairly steady path and then tends to decrease after about ten quarters. The current account keeps on improving although at a rather slow pace. The exchange rate keeps appreciating, thus reinforcing the now positive terms of trade effect. The behaviour of both extrapolative and normal expectations generates a decrease in the level of the interest rate. This, however, is not enough to invert the behaviour of *NFA* which is more strongly affected by favourable expectations. The economy displays both a lower exchange rate and a lower interest rate with respect to the control solution. The difference with respect to e.g. the basic case discussed above, is that now the role of expectations is more important in determining the behaviour of capital movements.

6.3.2 Case 2

As can be seen from Graph 5, the behaviour of the variables is opposite to the previous case.

Net foreign assets increase and the exchange rate devalues. The stronger role of normal expectations is felt in the behaviour of capital movements which flow out of the country as a larger depreciation is now expected. This deteriorates the balance of payments in both of its components, inducing a faster devaluation which deteriorates the current account because of the adverse terms of trade effect. Both of these forces push toward a further devaluation and hence feed negatively on expectations. International reserves must grow to face the higher nominal value of imports generated by the devaluation.

GRAPH 4

MIXED EXPECTATIONS, CASE 1
(simulated/base run; simulated-base for *i*)

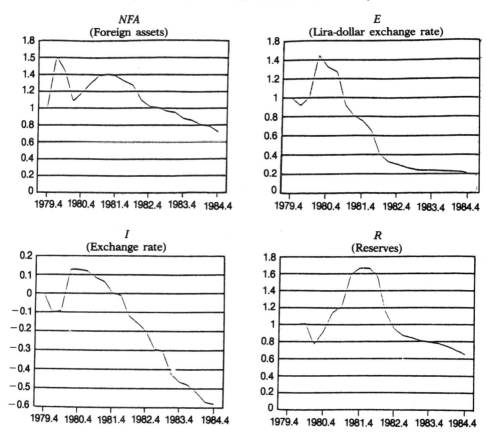

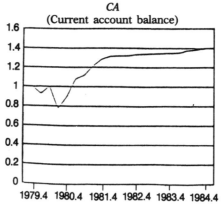

GRAPH 5

MIXED EXPECTATIONS, CASE 2
(simulated/base run; simulated-base for *i*)

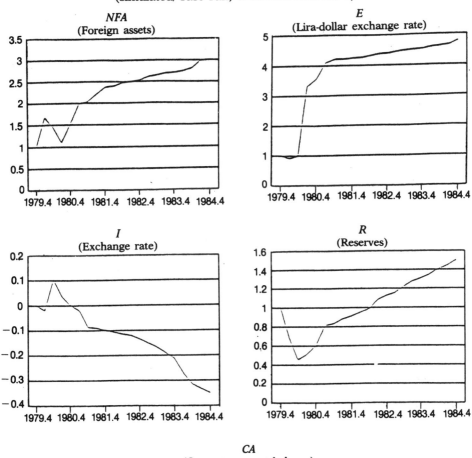

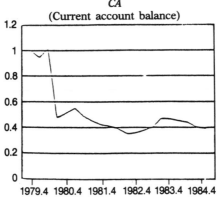

This leads to an expansion in the money supply which feeds both on the current account, through higher demand, and on the interest rate, which decreases as a reaction to a larger money supply, although it assumes a higher level with respect to the previous case because of the different behaviour of exchange rate expectations.

This last case illustrates the influence of policy behaviour on expectations. If the market believes that the authorities will drive the exchange rate to keep up with international competitiveness, it will react by generating a capital account which may eventually become unsustainable. The case just discussed is an extreme one as the weight assigned to normal expectations has proved to be "excessive" with respect to extrapolative ones. In fact, other cases which have not been discussed here, show that, when normal and extrapolative expectations take on approximately equal weights, the behaviour of the model is more satisfactory, i.e. the variables follow paths which are intermediate between those shown in Graphs 4 and 5.

7. - Will a Tobin Tax Help?

In the light of the distinction — recalled above — between "occasional" and "permanent" speculators, the argument in favour of a Tobin tax on all capital flows (so as to avoid the practical enforcement problem of trying to distinguish between foreign exchange purchases for "speculative" purposes versus purchases for the purpose of longer-term investments) seems to receive new support. Such a tax, in fact, would not be much of a deterrent to anyone contemplating the purchase of a foreign security for longer-term investing, but it might discourage the spot trader who is now accustomed to buying foreign exchange with the intention of selling it a few hours later. As Frankel ([7], p. 184), notes there has been little if any attempt to appraise the Tobin proposal in the context of an appropriate macroeconomic model. This is particularly true of Italy, where the Tobin tax has been advocated by various authors (11) without much empirical support.

---

(11) See, for example, BASEVI - CAVAZZUTI [1].

The Tobin tax on capital flows is a tax on the relevant foreign exchange transactions, but it can be translated into an equivalent tax on interest income. It is, in fact, equivalent either to a tax on foreign interest income at a rate which is an increasing function of the Tobin tax rate θ, or to a *negative* tax (i.e., a positive subsidy) on domestic interest income at a rate which is an increasing function of θ. To show this, let us consider the standard method of determining the relative profitability (including the gains due to expected changes in the exchange rate) of placing funds abroad or at home. This amounts to comparing $(1/E)(1 + i_f) \hat{E}$ with $(1 + i_h)$, where the interest rates and $\hat{E}$ (the expected exchange rate) are referred to the same time interval. Let us now introduce a tax at the unit rate θ (to be paid in domestic currency) on both the amount of domestic currency transferred abroad and the amount that will be repatriated (principal plus interest) at the end of the relevant period. The first term of the comparison then becomes $[(1 + \theta)(1 + \theta)^{-1}/E](1 + i_f) \hat{E}$. By simple manipulations (12) one obtains that the relevant interest differential is $[(1 - \theta) i_f - 2\theta](1 + \theta)^{-1} - i_h$ or, equivalently, $i_f - [2\theta + (1 + \theta) i_h][1 - \theta)^{-1}$. It is then easy to simulate the introduction of a Tobin tax in our model, by appropriately modifying the interest differential that appears in the definition of $N\hat{F}A$ (Section 3).

The Tobin tax was tested assuming two different expectation formation mechanisms: extrapolative and normal.

7.1 *Extrapolative Expectations*

The expected proportional change in the exchange rate is given by $\delta_E D \log E$, $\delta_E > 0$. This coefficient was given values ranging from

---

(12) With perfect capital mobility, the relation $[(1 + \theta)(1 + \theta)^{-1}/E]((1 + i_f) \hat{E} = (1 + i_h)$ should hold. If we multiply both members by $(1 + i_f)^{-1} (1 + \theta)/(1 + \theta)$ and subtract 1, we obtain $[(1 + \theta)(1 + i_h) - (1 - \theta)(1 + i_f)]/[(1 - \theta)(1 + i_f)] = (\hat{E} - E)/E$.

By manipulating the left hand side and neglecting, as is usually done, the denominator, we obtain $i_h - [(1 - \theta) i_f - 2\theta](1 + \theta)^{-1} = (\hat{E} - E)/E$ or, equivalently, $[2\theta + (1 + \theta) i_h](1 - \theta)^{-1} - i_f = (\hat{E} - E)/E$. In the absence of the tax, the relation would be $i_h - i_f = (\hat{E} - E)/E$. In both cases, the presence of a risk premium explains why the equality does not hold even with perfect capital mobility.

0.1 to 1.0. In all cases the model produced an explosive (devalu-ationary) behaviour of the exchange rate which developed after very few quarters (no more than four). The other variables followed a behaviour quite similar to that observed in the previous simulation. The introduction of a Tobin tax was modelled by multiplying the foreign interest rate, i_f, by a term $(1 - t)$, with $t = 0.3$. This is equivalent to assuming a Tobin tax rate θ approximately equal to 1.6% (13), a large value if one recalls that θ is applied to the principal and on both the outflow and the inflow. This value was chosen after several runs with alternative values of t had shown that, in order to obtain relevant results, t (and hence θ) had to be large. The introduc-tion of the Tobin tax, however, improved the behaviour of the model only slightly. What happened is that the explosive behaviour of the exchange rate developed from two to three quarters later with respect to the cases without the introduction of the tax.

7.2 *Normal Expectations*

In this exercise the Tobin tax takes on the same value as in the case with extrapolative expectations (about 1.6%, corresponding to a tax of 30% on foreign interest income on a yearly basis).

The results are reported in Graph 6.

The most relevant result is that now the system follows a stable path throughout the simulation period. In this case too we can distinguish between an impact effect and adjustment mechanism. The impact effect is similar to the previous one showing an increase in *NFA* and an appreciation of the exchange rate. The interest rate, however, decreases steadily over the period. This is due to the fact that the Tobin tax lowers the target value for the domestic interest rate. The total effect of the Tobin tax is such that the interest rate differential is, compared to the previous simulations, in favour of the foreign rate. This determines a relatively higher accumulation of net

---

(13) The relationship between θ and t is given by $[(1 - \theta) i_f - 2\theta]/(1 + \theta) = (1 - t) i_f$. With a value of i_f around 12%-13% per annum in the simulation period, this gives a value of θ around 1.6% for $t = 30\%$.

GRAPH 6

NORMAL EXPECTATIONS AND TOBIN TAX
(simulated/base run; simulated-base for *i*)

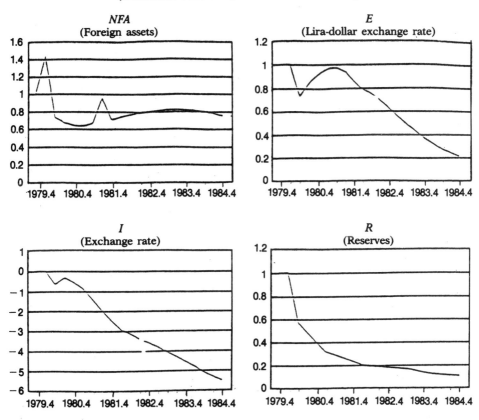

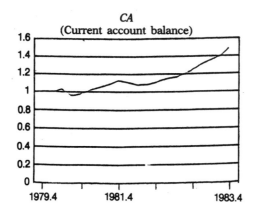

foreign assets (which is, nonetheless, lower with respect to the control solution). The important element, however, is that, contrary to the previous simulations, the level of *NFA* mildly fluctuates around a stable value rather than decreasing steadily. The exchange rate tends to appreciate under the pressure of an improving current account.

The main message from this exercise is that the introduction of a Tobin tax provides a crucial contribution to the stabilization of the system with full capital liberalization and exchange rate expectations geared to relative prices. However there is more to it than that. A Tobin tax allows the system to operate with a lower level of the domestic interest rate as it makes the constraint represented by the foreign rate less stringent. This obviously gives more room for domestic financial policy in terms of e.g. financing of the domestic public debt, an issue which is of paramount importance for the Italian economy. The counter argument for such a tax is that if not all countries adopted it, then the business would simply go to the financial centres where the tax is not present.

8. - Trade and Capital Liberalization

Our final exercise includes the joint liberalization of capital movements and trade flows. The basic model is modified as in case 1 with the addition of an increase in the adjustment speed of both imports and exports of goods and services. Accordingly, both α_5 and α_8 are set equal to 15, i.e. a mean time lag of roughly one week. Lower values of α_5 and α_8, i.e. longer mean time lags, did not alter the results significantly. As sensitivity analysis indicates, an increase in α_5 and α_8 exerts a stabilizing effect on the model. The main result of the simulation (Graph 7) is that the behaviour of the model is more stable. After four years, nevertheless, the unstable movement of the exchange rate emerges as in the previous cases. The behaviour of the system, however, is different. As in case 1 the increase in α_{24} leads to an immediate increase in *NFA*, which causes an appreciation of the exchange rate. This, in turn, leads to a decrease in the interest rate and to an increase in the level of reserves. The current account, on the contrary, heavily deteriorates as the increase in the quantity of

GRAPH 7

TRADE LIBERALIZATION
(simulated/base run; simulated-base for *i*)

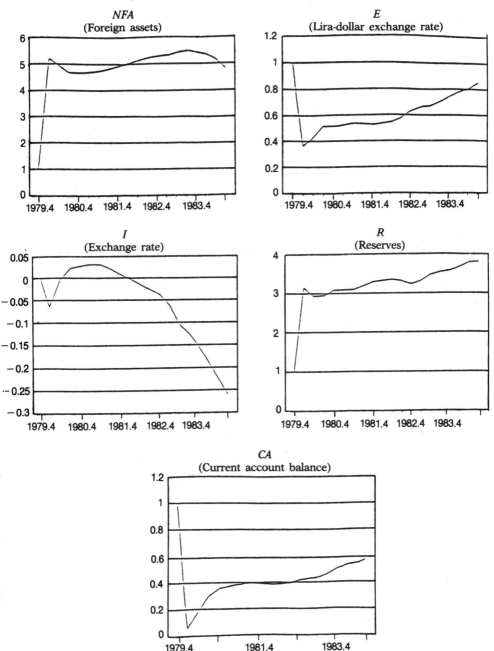

NFA
(Foreign assets)

E
(Lira-dollar exchange rate)

I
(Exchange rate)

R
(Reserves)

CA
(Current account balance)

imports is larger than the increase in the quantity of exports. Following this "impact effect" the model sets itself onto a path characterized by the following properties. The level of reserves stays at the new, higher, level as required by the higher level of imports. This determines a higher money stock which leads to a lower interest rate and hence to lower desired net foreign assets ($N\hat{F}A$).This effect is offset, however, by the lower level (revaluation) of the exchange rate which pushes up NFA. The consequence is a stable behaviour of NFA. Simultaneously, the current account is improving thanks to the catching up of XGS in spite of the negative effect of the lower level of E on exports. If the improvement in the current account had been faster, it could have offset the pressure on the exchange rate. This pressure is due to a level of E which is inconsistent with trade competitiveness. In the end the pressure on the exchange rate leads to instability.

This final experiment confirms that an increase in the adjustment speed of trade flows mitigates the destabilizing effects of financial liberalization. The system, however, still displays instability at the new, more deregulated, regime.

9. - Conclusion

In this paper we have shown that the effects of perfect capital mobility ought to be examined in the context of suitable economy-wide macroeconometric models, where we have suggested a precise way of modelling capital liberalization and related questions (such as exchange rate expectations). The results of simulation exercises carried out by means of our continuous time model of the Italian economy have given interesting insights in this issue, that can be summarized as follows.

First of all, capital liberalization *alone* has a destabilizing effect on the economy in general and on the exchange rate in particular. What should be stressed is that instability is not immediate, but comes about after a period (two or three years) of apparent stability. This result seems to be dramatically confirmed by the events concerning the lira (apparent stability for a couple of years after the liberalization, then huge capital outflows culminating in the devaluation of the lira — realignment on 14 September 1992 and subsequent events). We do not like to play Cassandra, but we have to point out that these delayed destabilizing effects were already stressed in papers of ours well before capital liberalization took place in the Italian economy (Gandolfo and Padoan [14], [15]).

Secondly, exchange rate expectations have a crucial role to play. Their effect, however, varies greatly according to the relative importance of "extrapolative" with respect to "normal" expectations. The former exert a destabilizing effect while the latter have an opposite influence. The current (September 1992) events in the Italian economy undoubtedly reflect the prevalence of agents with destabilizing expectations. If the governement is unable to foster "normal" expectations through appropriate policies, then the inherently destabilizing "one way option" that speculators face in regimes with fixed but adjustable parities and divergent underlying fundamentals will take place. All this is well known to any student of the Bretton Woods system and can be carried over to currency areas and prospective monetary unions (Gandolfo [11]).

Thirdly, a Tobin tax is helpful in stabilizing the system, since it makes purely speculative capital flows (which are typically short term) much less profitable. Finally, trade liberalization is also helpful, but not sufficient. Thus we must conclude that the destabilizing effects of capital liberalization have to be counteracted by a set of measures because a single measure might prove to be ineffective.

TABLE *A* 1

EQUATIONS OF THE MODEL

Private consumption

(1) $D \log C = \alpha_1 \log (\hat{C}/C) + \alpha_2 \log (M/M_d)$

where:

(1.1) $\hat{C} = \gamma_1 \, e^{\,\beta_1 \, D \log Y} (P/PMGS_f \cdot E)^{\,\beta_2} (y - T/P), \; \beta_1 \lessgtr 0 \,; \beta_2 \gtrless 0;$
$$M_d = \gamma_2 \, e^{\,-\beta_3 \, i_{TT}} \, P^{\,\beta_4} \, Y^{\,\beta_5}, \; \beta_3 \gtrless 0$$

Rate of growth in fixed capital stock

(2) $Dk = \alpha_3 \, [\alpha' \log (\hat{K}/K) - k] + \alpha_4 \, Da$

where:

(2.1) $\hat{K} = \gamma_3 \, \tilde{Y} \qquad \gamma_3 = k/u$

Expected output

(3) $D \log \tilde{Y} = \eta \log (\bar{Y}/\tilde{Y})$

Imports

(4) $D \log MGS = \alpha_5 \log (M\hat{G}S/MGS) + \alpha_6 \log (\hat{V}/V) + \alpha_7 \, PCC$

where:

(4.1) $M\hat{G}S = \gamma_4 \, P^{\,\beta_6} (PMGS_f \cdot E)^{\,-\beta_7} \, Y^{\,\beta_8}; \qquad \hat{V} = \gamma_5 \, \tilde{Y}$

Exports

(5) $D \log XGS = \alpha_8 \log (X\hat{G}S/XGS) - \alpha_9 \, Da$

where:

(5.1) $X\hat{G}S = \gamma_6 \, (PXGS/PF_f \cdot E)^{\,-\beta_9} \, YF^{\,\beta_{10}} (\gamma_3 \, Y/K)^{\,-\beta_{11}}$

Output

(6) $D \log Y = \alpha_{10} \log (\tilde{Y}/Y) + \alpha_{11} \log (\hat{V}/V)$

Price of output

(7) $\qquad D \log P = \alpha_{12} \log (\hat{P}/P) + \alpha_{13} Dm + \alpha_{14} \log (M/M_d)$

where:

(7.1) $\qquad \hat{P} = \gamma_7 (PMGS_f \cdot E)^{\beta_{12}} W^{\beta_{13}} PROD^{-\beta_{14}}$

Price of exports

(8) $\qquad D \log PXGS = \alpha_{15} \log (P\hat{X}GS/PXGS)$

where:

(8.1) $\qquad P\hat{X}GS = \gamma_8 P^{\beta_{15}} (PF_f \cdot E)^{\beta_{16}}$

Money wage rate

(9) $\qquad D \log W = \alpha_{16} \log (\hat{W}/W)$

where:

(9.1) $\qquad \hat{W} = \gamma_9 P^{\beta_{17}} e^{\lambda_4 t}$

Interest rate

(10) $\qquad Di_{TIT} = \alpha_{17} \log (M_d/M) + \alpha_{18} [i_f + \log (FR/E) +$
$\qquad\qquad - i_{TIT}] + \alpha_{19} D \log E + \alpha_{20} Dr + \alpha_{21} Dh$

Bank advances

(11) $\qquad D \log A = \alpha_{22} \log (\hat{A}/A) + \alpha_{23} Dk, \qquad \alpha_{23} \gtrless 0$

where:

(11.1) $\qquad \hat{A} = \gamma_{10} e^{\beta_{18} i_{TIT}} M, \quad \beta_{18} \gtrless 0$

Net foreign assets

(12) $\qquad D \log NFA = \alpha_{24} \log (N\hat{F}A/NFA) +$
$\qquad\qquad \alpha_{25} \log (PMGS_f \cdot E \cdot MGS/PXGS \cdot XGS), \quad \alpha_{25} < 0$

where:

(12.1) $\qquad N\hat{F}A = \gamma_{11} e^{\beta_{19} [i_f + \log (FR/E) - i_{TIT}]} (PY)^{\beta_{20}} (PF_f \cdot E \cdot YF)^{\beta_{21}}$

Monetary authorities' reaction function on money supply

(13)
$$Dm = \alpha_{26} (\hat{m} - m) + \delta_3 Dh + \delta_4 Dr$$

where:

(13.1)
$$\hat{m} = m^* + \{\delta_1 [D\log(PY) - (\rho_P + \rho_Y)] + \delta_2 Di_{TIT}\}$$
$$\delta_1 \gtrless 0, \qquad \delta_2 \gtrless 0$$

Taxes

(14)
$$D\log T = \alpha_{27} \log(\hat{T}/T)$$

where:

(14.1)
$$\hat{T} = \gamma_{14} (PY)^{\beta_{22}}$$

Public expenditure

(15)
$$D\log G = \alpha_{28} \log(\gamma_{13} Y/G) + \alpha_{29} D\log Y \qquad \alpha_{29} \gtrless 0$$

Monetary authorities' reaction function on international reserves

(16)
$$D\log R = b\,\delta_5 \log(E_c/E) + (1-b)\,\delta_6 \log(\hat{E}/E) + $$
$$- \delta_7 D\log E + \delta_8 \log(\hat{R}/R)$$

where:

$$\hat{E} = PXGS/\gamma_{14}\,PF_f, \quad \hat{R} = \gamma_{15}\,PMGS_f \cdot E \cdot MGS, \quad b = \begin{cases} 1 & \text{under fixed exchange rates,} \\ 0 & \text{under floating exchange rates,} \end{cases}$$

Inventories

(17)
$$DV = Y + MGS - C - DK - XGS - G$$

Fixed capital stock

(18)
$$D\log K = k$$

Rate of growth in money supply

(19)
$$m = D\log M$$

Public sector borrowing requirement

(20)
$$DH = PG - T$$

Rate of growth in international reserves

(21) $$r = D \log R$$

Rate of growth in bank advances

(22) $$a = D \log A$$

Rate of growth in H

(23) $$h = D \log H$$

Balance of payments

(24) $$PXGS \cdot XGS - PMGS_f \cdot E \cdot MGS +$$
$$+ (UT_a - UT_p) - DNFA - DR = 0$$

VARIABLES OF THE MODEL

Endogenous

A	= nominal stock of bank advances
a	= proportional rate of growth of A
C	= private consumption expenditure in real terms
E	= lira-dollar spot exchange rate
G	= public expenditure in real terms
H	= public sector borrowing requirement
h	= proportional rate of change of H
i_{TIT}	= domestic nominal interest rate
K	= stock of fixed capital in real terms
k	= proportional rate of change of K
M	= nominal stock of money ($M\,2$)
m	= proportional rate of change of M
MGS	= imports of goods and services in real terms
NFA	= nominal stock of net foreign assets
P	= domestic price level
$PXGS$	= export price level
R	= nominal stock of international reserves
r	= proportional rate of change of R
T	= nominal taxes
V	= stock of inventories in real terms
W	= money wage rate
XGS	= exports of goods and services in real terms
Y	= real r net domestic product and income
$\bar{Y}$	= expected real net domestic product and income

Exogenous

E_c	= official lira-dollar parity under fixed exchange rates
FR	= forward exchange rate
i_f	= foreign nominal interest rate
PF_f	= foreign competitors' export price level (in foreign currency)
$PMGS_f$	= import price level (in foreign currency)
$PROD$	= labour productivity
t	= time
$(UT_a - UT_p)$	= net unilateral transfers, in nominal terms
YF	= real world income

CHARACTERISTIC ROOTS OF THE MODEL
UNDER *FIXED* EXCHANGE RATES

Root	Asymptotic Standard error	Damping period (quarters)	Period of cycle (quarters)
0.3114	0.2856		
−0.0009	0.0009	1094.092	
−0.0205	0.0021	48.780	
−0.0745	0.0225	13.428	
−0.0927	0.0200	10.784	
−0.3538	0.1857	2.826	
−0.3921	0.1987	2.550	
−0.4304	0.0753	2.323	
−0.9241	0.1230	1.082	
−4.6670	1.1415	0.214	
−0.0231	0.0073	43.286	247.845
±0.0253*i*	0.0065		
−0.1674	0.0280	5.972	307.220
±0.0204*i*	0.0263		
−0.2596	0.1365	3.852	15.232
±0.4125*i*	0.0571		
−0.5202	0.0927	1.922	44.064
±0.14262*i*	0.0709		
−1.4270	0.1936	0.701	4.474
±1.4043*i*	0.1498		

CHARACTERISTIC ROOTS OF THE MODEL
UNDER *FLEXIBLE* EXCHANGE RATES

Root	Asymptotic standard error	Damping period (quarters)	Period of cycle quarters)
0.3109	0.2841		
−0.0009	0.0009	1091.703	
−0.0205	0.0021	48.773	
−0.0751	0.0237	13.314	
−0.0925	0.0200	10.814	
−0.4134	0.1209	2.419	
−0.9241	0.1230	1.082	
−4.6669	1.1415	0.214	
−0.0232 ±0.0252*i*	0.0072 0.0065	43.193	249.357
−0.1675 ±0.0218*i*	0.0276 0.0259	5.971	287.530
−0.2595 ±0.4111*i*	0.1376 0.0575	3.853	15.283
−0.3737 ±0.0591*i*	0.1040 0.0836	2.676	106.280
−0.5278 ±0.1394*i*	0.0914 0.0573	1.895	45.058
−1.4270 ±1.4043*i*	0.1936 0.1498	0.701	4.474

TABLE A5

SENSITIVITY ANALYSIS WITH RESPECT TO SELECTED PARAMETERS UNDER FLEXIBLE EXCHANGE RATES

Root (μ)	$\partial\mu/\partial\alpha_5$	$\partial\mu/\partial\alpha_8$	$\partial\mu/\partial\alpha_{14}$	$\partial\mu/\partial\alpha_{15}$	$\partial\mu/\partial\alpha_{16}$	$\partial\mu/\partial\alpha_{24}$	$\partial\mu/\partial\beta_6$	$\partial\mu/\partial\beta_7$	$\partial\mu/\partial\delta_8$
0.3109	−0.3153	−1.1513				2.9454			
−0.0009							0.0987	−0.0054	
−0.0751							0.239	−0.076	
−0.1675 ±0.0219i		0.0476	0.3585						
−0.2595 ±0.4111i		−0.5064							
−0.3737 ±0.0591i				0.4899	−0.2342				−0.3068

BIBLIOGRAPHY

[1] BASEVI G. - CAVAZZUTI F.: «Regole del gioco o discrezionalità amministrativa? Il caso della libertà di movimento dei capitali in Italia», *Politica economica*, April 1985.

[2] BLAKE D. - BEENSTOCK M. - BRASSE V.: «The Performance of UK Exchange Rate Forecasters», *Economic Journal*, n. 96, 1986, pp. 986-99.

[3] CUTILLI B. - GANDOLFO G.: «The Role of Commercial Banks in Foreign Exchange Speculation», Banca nazionale del lavoro, *Quarterly Review*, June 1963.

[4] —— · ——: «Wider Band and "Oscillating" Exchange Rates», *Economic Notes*, Jamuary-April 1972.

[5] ——: «Un contributo alla teoria della speculazione in regime di cambi oscillanti», Roma, Ente per gli studi monetari bancari e finanziari Luigi Einaudi, *Quaderno di ricerche*, n. 10, 1973.

[6] DRIFFILL J.: «The Stability and Sustainability of the European Monetary System with Perfect Capital Market», in GIAVAZZI F. - MICOSSI S. - MILLER M. (eds.): *The European Monetary System*, Cambridge, Cambridge University Press, 1988.

[7] FRANKEL J.A.: «International Capital Mobility and Exchange Rate Volatility», in FIELEKE N.S. (eds.): *International Payments Imbalances in the 1980s*, Boston, Federal Reserve Bank of Boston, *Conference Series*, n. 32, 1988, pp. 162-88.

[8] GANDOLFO G.: «Esportazioni clandestine di capitali e sovrafatturazione delle importazioni», *Rassegna economica*, November-Dcember 1977.

[9] ——: *Qualitative Analysis and Econometric Estimation of Continuous Time Dynamic Models*, Amsterdam, North-Holland, 1981.

[10] ——: *International Economics II*, Berlin, Springer-Verlag, 1987.

[11] ——: «Monetary Unions», forthcoming in *The New Palgrave Dictionary of Money and Finance*, London, Macmillan.

[12] ——: «Sensitivity Analysis in Continuous Time Econometric Models», forthcoming in *Computers and Mathematics with Applications*, 1992.

[13] GANDOLFO G. - PADOAN P.C.: «The Mark V Version of the Italian Continuous Time Model», Siena, Università di Siena, *Quaderni dell'istituto di economia*, n. 70, 1987.

[14] ——: «Consequences of Liberalization of Capital Movements in an Advanced Economy: a Systemic Analysis», paper presented at *Conference of the Society for Economic Dynamics and Control*, Tempe, Arizona, 9-11 March 1988.

[15] —— · ——: «Conseguenze della liberalizzazione dei movimenti di capitale: un'analisi sistemica», *Note economiche*, n. 2, 1988, pp. 5-27.

[16] —— · ——: «The Italian Continuous Time Model: Theory and Empirical Results», *Economic Modelling*, April 1990.

[17] —— · ——: «Perfect Capital Mobility and the Italian Economy», in BALTENSPERGER E. - SINN H.W. (eds.): *Exchange - Rate Regimes and Currency Unions*, London, Macmillan, 1992, pp. 36-61.

[18] ——: «Continuous Time Econometric Modelling and the Issue of Capital Liberalization», forthcoming in PHILLIPS P.C.B. - HALL V.B. (eds.): *Models, Methods and Applications of Econometrics*, London, Basil Blackwell, 1992.

[19] ——: «Capital Liberalization and Exchange Rate Expectations: the Italian Case», forthcoming in GANDOLFO G. (ed.): *Continuous Time Econometrics: Theory and Applications*, London, Chapman & Hall, 1992.

[20] GIAVAZZI F. - SPAVENTA L.: «The New EMS, CEPR», *Discussion Paper*, n. 369, 1990.

[21] GROS D.: «The Effectiveness of Capital Controls», IMF, *Staff Papers*, June. 1987.

[22] GOODMAN S.H.: «Foreign Exchange Forecasting Techniques: Implications for Business and Policy», *Journal of Finance*, n. 34, 1979, pp. 415-27.

[23] HOGAN L.I.: «A Comparison of Alternative Exchange Rate Forecasting Models», *Economic Record*, n. 62, 1986, pp. 215-23.

[24] ITO T.: «Foreign Exchange Rate Expectations: Micro Survey Data», *American Economic Review*, n. 80, 1990, pp. 434-49.

[25] JONSON P.D. - MCKIBBIN W.J. - TREVOR R.G.: «Exchange Rates and Capital Flows: a Sensitivity Analysis», *Canadian Journal of Economics*, november 1982.

[26] KHAN M. - ZAHLER R.: «The Macroeconomic Effectis of Changes in Barriers to Trade and Capital Flows: a Simulation Analysis», IMF, *Staff Papers*, june 1983.

[27] —— - ——: «Trade and Financial Liberalization Given External Shocks and Inconsistent Domestic Policies», IMF, *Staff Papers*, May 1985.

[28] LEVICH R.M.: «Analysing the Accuracy of Foreign Exchange Advisory Services: Theory and Evidence», in LEVICH R.M. - WHILBORG C. (eds.): *Exchange Risk Exposure*, Lexington (DC) Heath, (MA), 1980.

[29] MUNDELL R.A.: «Capital Mobility and Stabilization Policy Under Fixed and Flexible Exchange Rates», *Canadian Journal of Economics and Political Science*, November 1963.

[30] OBSTFELD M.: «Competitiveness, Realignments and Speculation: the Role of Financial Markets», in GIAVAZZI F. - MICOSSI S. - MILLER M. (eds.): *The European Monetary System*, Cambridge, Cambridge University Press, 1988.

[31] PALMISANI F. - ROSSI S.: «Aspetti macroeconomici dei controlli valutari. Il caso italiano», *Note economiche*, n. 3, 1988.

[32] PAPADIA F. - ROSSI S.: «Are Asymmetric Exchange Controls Effective?», Roma Banca d'Italia, *Temi di discussione*, n. 131, 1990.

[33] PAPADIA F. - VONA S.: «Exchange Rate Management and Monetary Policy: Issues Raised by the Italian Experience», in BANK OF INTERNATIONAL SETTLEMENTS: *Exchange Market Intervention and Monetary Policy*», Basel, 1988.

[34] TAKAGI S.: «Exchange Rate Expectations: a Survey of Survey Studies», IMF, *Staff Papers*, n. 38, 1991, pp. 156-83.

[35] WYMER C.R. (various dates): «Transfs, Resimul, Continest, Predic, Apredic Computer Programs and Relative Manuals», supplement n. 3 or *Solution of Non-Linear Differential Equation Systems* (mimeos).

[36] WYPLOSZ CHARLES: «Capital Controls and Balance of Payments Crises», *Journal of International Money and Finance*, June 1986.

A Common Monetary Standard or a Common Currency?

EU

F33

Ronald I. McKinnon
Stanford University

Are the major industrial economies ready to reestablish par values for exchange rates on a global basis? To combat burgeoning interbloc protectionism, there is a strong case for severely limiting exchange rate fluctuations in order to preserve free trade in goods and services.

After the breakdown of the Bretton Woods par value system in 1971, the unexpectedly violent fluctuations in untethered relative currency values greatly strengthened the tendency to form regional trading blocs, within which stable exchange rates can be more easily established. For economies closely integrated in foreign trade, a zone of exchange rate stability now seems necessary to preserve free trade in goods and services while reducing investment risk.

The EMS trading bloc in Europe is now paralleled by an emerging North American free trade area, where Canada and Mexico are currently orienting their domestic monetary policies towards keeping their exchanges rates within a narrow range against the US dollar. In the not-too-distant future, a yen-bloc among countries closely linked to the Japanese economy could well emerge. In this limited regional sense, countries now seem more willing to return to a par value system for exchange rates and a common monetary standard.

On the negative side, however, exchange rate swings among the major blocs remain as big as ever. The yen/dollar and mark/dollar exchange rates have moved as much as 25 or 30% both down and up over the past four years. From the mid 1970s onwards, this exchange rate uncertainty has provoked, and is provoking, a resurgence in *interbloc* protectionism. Indeed, when exchange rates are highly volatile and close to being randomly determined, much of the resulting exchange risk cannot be effectively hedged (McKinnon [4] (*)). Consequently, governments tend to offset some of this risk by imposing quantitative restrictions — such as import quotas — on trade between currency areas. Because they insulate the domestic economy from exchange fluctuations with lesser restraint on the volume of trade, quotas are much more efficient than "equivalent" tariffs (McKinnon-Fung [6]). Whence the proliferation of quota protection for agricultural markcts, "voluntary" export restraints in automobiles and steel, market-sharing agreements in textiles and semiconductors, sliding-scale export subsidies, and so on. Largely because of exchange rate instability among trading blocs, in the 1990s the industrial world is lapsing into this rather dangerous mercantilistic rivalry.

But need commitments to the GATT, and to freer global trade based on the most favored nation principle atrophy because of currency instability? After World War II, the great success of the fixed-rate dollar standard in undergirding the GATT suggests not. By the end of the 1960s, quantitative restrictions in trade among the industrial countries had been largely eliminated and tariff protection was moderated.

1. - The Separation of National Fiscal Systems Under a Common Monetary Standard

If everyone agrees on consistent rules of the game (McKinnon [3]), a common monetary standard across geographically diverse economies is feasible. With virtually unchanging par value for exchange rates, both the dollar standard from 1950 to 1970, and the classical gold standard from 1879 to 1914, spanned all the world's major trading economies. By a common monetary standard, I mean a par value regime within which exchange rates still vary within

---

(*) *N.B.:* The numbers in square brackets refer to the Bibliography at the end of the paper.

narrow margins — say 1 to 4% — thus allowing national currencies to circulate separately as a means of payment. By controlling its own note issue and setting reserve requirements for its commercial banks, each national central bank continued to collect seigniorage and act as lender-of-last resort to national banks and to its own government. Nevertheless, under the 19th century gold standard and in the 1950s and 1960s, the major countries followed a common monetary policy: national price levels for tradable goods moved together in the long run (McKinnon [5]).

If national monies remain in circulation, no specific agreements on fiscal policies are required to limit budgetary deficits or national debt to GNP ratios. Each member of an international monetary standard needs only to refrain from using the inflation tax as an *ongoing* instrument of public finance. However, exit from the agreement is possible. If fiscal improvidence forces a government to resort to the inflation tax, an exchange crisis would eventually force the country to devalue and possibly to leave the common monetary standard.

2. - Fiscal Policies Under a Common Currency: Europe Versus the United States

If a common monetary standard succesfully promotes free trade, wouldn't going one step further and squeezing the exchange margins toward zero in the course of adopting a common currency be even better? Certainly tourists would feel less inconvenienced from money changing at airports. Before safely entering a common-currency agreement, however, the fiscal conditions on each member government need to be more stringent than those required of a common monetary standard - indeed, much more stringent than suggested by current debate in Europe.

The European Monetary System (EMS) has successfully evolved into a common monetary standard with 2.25% bilateral bands for exchange rates among member countries. However, the EMS has not imposed direct constraints on member governments' current fiscal deficits or on their outstanding debts. The overhang of national debt in

European economies is now very high, averaging 60% of GDP for EEC members. But fiscal conditions among the member countries are very different, as Table 1 indicates. The ratio of debt/GDP is close to, or over, 100% for Belgium, Ireland, and Italy, while countries like Greece and Portugal only avoid explosions in their debt ratios by resorting to the inflation tax.

Once accumulated, public sector debts of this order of magnitude can only be safely managed if the government in question retains ownership of its central bank. National control over the central bank is necessary both to help manage the debts on a day-to-day basis, but also to reduce the threat of a "run on the government". Each national government can avoid defaulting on the face value of its obligations because everybody knows that, in a crisis, the government can always "print money", i.e., use the inflation tax, to pay interest and principal. This then enables the government to pre-empt the national capital

TABLE 1

FISCAL STRUCTURE
OF THE EUROPEAN ECONOMIC COMMUNITY IN 1991

	Inflation (% per year)		Public finances (% of GDP)		
	deflator of private consumption	nominal unit labour costs	government borrowing requirements	public debt 1991	change from 1990
Belgium	3.2	3.4	6.5	128.1	0.6
Denmark	2.4	1.4	1.3	62.3	−0.1
Germany	3.5	5.4	4.6	45.4	2.4
Greece	18.0	14.2	15.3	86.0	−0.3
Spain	5.9	5.7	2.7	44.5	0.3
France	3.1	3.3	1.6	37.3	0.9
Ireland	3.0	4.9	3.8	97.4	−2.4
Italy..............	6.3	6.9	10.1	103.3	2.6
Luxembourg	3.5	2.8	−1.6	4.7	−1.6
Netherlands	2.8	3.4	4.8	78.8	0.3
Portugal	11.1	14.6	5.5	63.8	−3.5
UK	6.5	8.2	2.2	44.5	1.3
EEC (average)	5.0	5.9	4.6	60.0	1.4

Source: Financial Times, 29, 1991. From forecasts of the EEC commission services.

market to issue Treasury securities at lower interest rates than can high quality private borrowers whose debt is also denominated in the national currency.

Consequently, as long as national currencies circulate separately, at every term to maturity treasury bills through long-term government bonds are widely regarded as being the "safest" of financial instruments denominated in the national currency. In the United States, the highest grade corporate bonds usually pay an interest rate a percentage point or so higher than on long-term US Treasury bonds, and "*B*" grade corporate bonds pay about 2 percentage points higher while unrated "junk" bonds may pay 7 or more percentage points more. The rationale for higher interest rates in the private sector is that companies are subject to commercial risk, i.e. the threat of bankruptcy, which the government is not, and holders of private securities face the same inflation risk as do holders of government securities.

But this traditional low-cost financing of the national debt need not hold if the government loses control over its central bank. For example, with the prospect of moving to a common currency in Europe with some finite probability, the government of Italy is facing the possibility that it will lose control over the Bank of Italy, i.e., over its money issuing authority, to EuroFed. What then are the prospects for the cost of servicing the government debt?

In their empirical analysis, Alesina, Prati, and Tabellini [1] detect an inversion in this traditional relationship between interest rates on private and government debt in Italy. After exchange controls were removed in 1987, they find that the average yield on Treasury Bills was one to three percentage points higher (after adjusting for tax differences) than on "private" bank certificates of deposit of the same maturity. On medium-term maturities, two year Italian government bonds yielded interest a percentage point or so higher than did 18 to 24 month bank certificates of deposit. They also show that three heavily indebted European countries, Belgium, Italy, and the Netherlands, display this interest rate inversion in their domestic capital markets, while other potential members of the European common currency with lower debt ratios do not.

The Italian evidence discriminates between traditional inflation risk on lire denominated debt from the risk of an outright public sector restructuring or default. If investors believe that a move to a common European currency will foreclose the possibility of the Italian government using the inflation tax to solve its debt problems, and if the government debt problem is severe enough, the risk premia incorporated in interest rates on Italian government debt could indeed exceed those on high-grade private debt. In the extreme, moving to a common currency in Europe could provoke a run on the Italian government, much of whose debt is already short-term and turns over every month.

The American monetary union is a useful benchmark for judging the fiscal requirements of moving to a common currency in Europe. The US Federal Government controls the central bank, the Federal Reserve System, which issues the common currency. This control over the national money supply has facilitated the build up of a large Federal Government debt of about 55% of American GNP, which is comparable to the European average in Table 1.

Unlike the fiscal position of the American Federal Government, however, the indebtedness of individual American states is (has been) constrained. If the State of Massachusetts gets into fiscal trouble as it seems to be, then the interest costs of floating new Massachusetts debt (adjusted for federal tax advantages) will rise above the yield on bonds issued by solvent private corporations headquartered in Massachusetts. And if Massachusetts' fiscal problems worsen, its ability to get private credit could dry up altogether *before* a large outstanding *stock* of state debt can accumulate. Not owning their own central banks, American state governments are (have been) effectively disciplined by the "market" in limiting their debt overhangs, unlike European nation states.

Historically, how has this market limitation on state debt been effected? In order to secure better access to the financial markets, the American states (except Vermont) have written some form of balanced budget restriction into their constitutions (Eichengreen [2]). They can borrow only in the short term, or issue special obligation bonds tied to financing particular projects. Otherwise, general purpose spending is limited to projected tax revenues. True, in practice, "prospective" balanced budget projections are often fudged. Nevertheless, compared to the massive indebtedness of the European states shown in Table 1, overhangs of general-obligation bonds of the American states are quite modest.

3. - Against a Common Currency in Europe

Reluctantly, I conclude that national governments in the EEC cannot afford to relinquish control over money issue to EuroFed. Thus a common European currency is not feasible. Debt overhangs are simply too great for any one government (with the minor exception of Luxembourg) to manage its national debt without its own central bank. A future fiscal crisis could well undermine any common-currency regime. How might this happen?

Suppose the circulations of national bank notes in each European country were replaced with ecus, and commercial bank reserves in ecus were held with EuroFed. Instead of national central banks, EuroFed is now the proximate collector of all the seigniorage. Consistency requires that EuroFed be the lender of last resort to domestic banks (and governments?); and from this it would naturally become the regulator guaranteeing the safety of domestic banks.

If one member government got into increasingly severe fiscal difficulties, could EuroFed plausibly stop domestic banks from lending to their own government, e.g. from holding its Treasury Bills? In conducting its own open market operations by buying government bonds to augment the monetary base, could EuroFed deliberately concentrate its purchases of bonds with those countries which had the highest credit rating and exclude others which were in fiscal difficulty? The political obligations of EuroFed as lender of last resort would be ambiguous.

But if a fiscal collapse in one country occurred, exit from the common currency agreement is virtually impossible. Thus the usual way of settling an untenable national debt overhang by devaluation and inflation is blocked.

More specifically, a large country experiencing a fiscal breakdown would, under a common currency, have great leverage on the other member governments. To prevent possible Community-wide bank failures and financial dislocation arising out of that government's threatened default on its ecu debts, the solvent members of the Community might be forced to bail it out, whether through EuroFed or by direct government-to-government lending. Knowing this *exante*, politicians in the errant country might become even less willing to take corrective fiscal action. Moral hazard would be uncomfortably high.

However if the Community was to settle for a common monetary standard with modest exchange margins rather than a common currency, the real possibility of a disruptive Community-wide crisis with fiscal roots would be lessened. One can still have the commitment to fixed exchange rates as within the EMS today — possibly within even narrower margins of, say, one half of one percent. However, any one country's membership in the common monetary standard would last only as long as it was fiscally tenable. Otherwise, the national government in question would likely have to devalue its currency and resign in disgrace — as was true in the 19th century when countries were (temporarily) forced off the gold standard. Consequently, politicians are more likely *exante* to take corrective fiscal action under a common monetary standard than under a common currency.

The general lesson here is clear enough. To curb interbloc protectionism in the world economy, it is both feasible and highly desirable to restore a global monetary standard similar to, but not identical with, that which prevailed in the 1950s and 1960s. Having made the case to return to some kind of par value system for exchange rates, however, going one seemingly natural step further to a common currency can be neither feasible nor desirable, even among nation states as closely integrated as those in the EEC.

BIBLIOGRAPHY

[1] ALESINA A. - PRATI A. - TABELLINI G.: «Public Confidence and Debt Management: A Model and a Case Study of Italy» in DORNBUSCH R. - DRAGHI M. (eds.): *Public Debt Management: Theory and History*, Cambridge, Cambridge University Press, 1990, pp. 94-123.

[2] EICHENGREEN B.: «One Money for Europe? Lessons from the US Currency Union», *Economic Policy*, April 1990, pp. 118-85.

[3] MCKINNON R.: «An International Standard for Monetary Stabilization», Institute for International Economics, *Policy Analysis*, n. 8, March 1984.

[4] — —: «Monetary and Exchange Rate Policies for International Monetary Stability: A Proposal», *Journal of Economic Perspectives*, Winter 1988, pp. 83-103.

[5] — —: «The Rules of the Game: International Money in Historical Perspective», *Journal of Economic Literature*, Forthcoming, 1991.

[6] MCKINNON R.I. - FUNG K.C.: *Floating Exchange Rates and the New Protectionism*, Stanford, Stanford University, November 1991.

Traditional Comparative Advantages vs. Economies of Scale: NAFTA and GATT (*)

Selected Countries F15 F11

Graciela Chichilnisky
Columbia University, New York (NY)

1. - Introduction: Trading Blocs and GATT

Regional free trade zones have been unexpectedly successful in the last decade. Since 1980 the European Community enlarged significantly its membership and its scope. It now includes southern European countries, and market-integrating features allowing goods, people, services and capital to flow freely around an area accounting for about one fourth of world economic output.

In what appears to be a strategic response, the US has been activated to enter into similar agreements with its neighbors. The recent trading and investment agreement with Canada was signed after many decades of doubtful consideration, and the trend is expanding to the rest of the Americas starting with Mexico. The final points needed for the ratification of NAFTA are still undecided (1), even though the US-Canada-Mexico treaty is already signed. This trend is observed also in other regions. The six members of the Association of South East Asian Nations — Singapore, Malaysia,

---

(*) This article was prepared for the United Nations Program of Trade Liberalization in the Americas, ECLAC, Washington (DC).

(1) The US is currently in the process of imposing steel tariffs on a number of countries including Canada, which is seeking exemption.

N.B.: the numbers in square brackets refer to the Bibliography at the end of the paper.

Thailand, Indonesia, the Philippines, and Brunei — have begun this year to build their Asean free trade area Afta as a future counterweight to other international trading blocs, even though at present most of their trade is with Europe, Japan and the US and not with each other. The Japanese have increasingly focused their economic attention in their own region, leading to more investment in and imports from the new East Asian manufacturing exporters. Even the *Andean Pact* seems to be progressing in Latin America after several decades of aimless discussions, with *Mercosur* following suit.

While regional free trade agreements prosper, the negotiation towards the liberalization of global trade are unsuccessful and stalling, with the agricultural markets being a key negotiating problem. Little goodwill has been generated from the GATT discussions, dispelling hopes for a reversal of fortunes in the near future. While the nature of the GATT negotiations is political, it is reasonable to seek explanations for the situation from an economic viewpoint.

The contrast between the lackluster performance of GATT and the success of the regional trade pacts raises disparate reactions. One view is that the emergence of regional trade pacts is a step in the right direction. In this view free trade is not defunct, but rather being organized and approached differently. But another, quite natural, reaction is to fear that "customs unions", as regional free trade pacts are usually called, are inherently opposed to global free trade. Do customs unions increase free trade with insiders at the cost of diverting trade with outsiders? Since the classic works of Meade [17] and Viner [22] classifying the issues into trade creation and trade diversion, there has been little conceptual advance on this issue. But the issue is very alive today, and requires our full attention.

It is the purpose of this paper to re-examine the positive and negative aspects of trading blocs as they relate to gains from free trade. The paper is primarily a discussion of conceptual issues, although it is based on facts and on particular cases which are of interest to the trade liberalization in the Americas.

We take a somewhat different approach to a familiar issue. Rather than asking the standard question of whether regional blocs help or hinder global free trade, we ask a more detailed question: what type of customs union is likely to lead to a trade war between the blocs, and what type of customs union is, instead, likely to lead to expanded global trade. In practical terms: what type of trade policies within the blocs will provide economic incentives for expanding free trade.

We shall compare the impact on the world economy of free trade blocs which are organized around two alternative principles: one is traditional comparative advantages, the other is economies of scale. The aim is to determine how the patterns of trade inside the blocs determine the trade relations among the blocs.

The paper has four parts. Section 2 reviews the existing economics of trading blocs, and uses this to explain the current situation in the EC and NAFTA. Section 3 presents a new conceptual approach to the economics of preferential trade, focusing on the internal organization of the trading blocs and the economic incentives that this generates with respect to the rest of the world. Section 4 is a conclusion which pulls the arguments together for an evaluation of NAFTA and an American free trade zone, and of global free trade. The last Section is an Appendix which provides a formal general equilibrium model of trading blocs with increasing returns to scale and proves the mathematical results which underlie the discussion in the text.

2. - The Economics of Trading Blocs

2.1 *Free Trade and Market Power*

The last ten years have seen new developments in international trade, focusing on the study of economic dynamics and of market imperfections leading to strategic issues in game theory and industrial organization. But the central tenet of the theory remains the Pareto efficiency of the static and competitive world market. In competitive markets, free trade leads to Pareto efficient allocations. There is no way to make a someone better off without making someone else worse off. This is a general proposition which holds for several countries and several markets interacting with each other simultaneously. Called the first theorem of welfare economics, the result that static competitive markets have Pareto efficient equilibria seems to loom the larger, the more special cases of market imperfections are pointed out.

In view of the efficiency of competitive markets, the failure of GATT to bring countries to an agreement about a world of free trade seems, at first sight, irrational. It would appear that countries act as if they could, but prefer not to, achieve a Pareto efficient allocation. Indeed, some believe that the failure of GATT is simply a version of the well-known prisoners' dilemma. The words "prisoners' dilemma" are used to describe a generically inefficient situation, one which, with appropriate coordination, can be altered so as to increase the welfare of each and all players.

Such a view would be incorrect. GATT's problems derive not from irrational behavior, nor from a lack of coordination or "prisoners' dilemma". The reason is that while free trade in competitive markets leads to Pareto optimal solutions, free trade may not lead to Pareto efficient allocations when the countries are large and have market power. For example, large countries may freely choose the quantities they export in order to manipulate to their advantage world market prices, in much the same way that a monopolist freely chooses to supply a quantity that maximizes his profits considering its impact on prices, inducing Pareto inferior allocations. For free trade to be Pareto efficient markets must be competitive, and countries must have no market power. When countries are sufficiently large to have an impact on market prices, then they often have an incentive to impose tariffs on each other.

Furthermore, under classical assumptions, a move from tariffs to free trade will typically make some countries better off but other countries worse off. It is true that if a competitive allocation were reached, it would be Pareto efficient. But in a world with tariffs, as we have today, under traditional assumptions some country will lose if free trade is adopted.

One may ask why large countries have protectionist incentives? The reason is that it is possible for large countries to improve their welfare by improving their terms of trade. This is of course not true in competitive markets where the traders, by definition, have no impact on prices. But the theory of trade proves that under traditional assumptions, a large country does have an economic incentive to impose tariffs on others. This is the standard theorem on the existence of optimal tariffs, which is discussed in more detail in Section 3.5 below. A tariff can improve the terms of trade of a large country, even though it may distort its production and consumption. What the theorem says is that, under traditional assumptions, there is always an optimal tariff, one at which the gains from increasing its terms of trade through tariffs exceeds the losses due to distortions. A textbook analysis of a simple case is found for example in Krugman and Obsfelt [15]. This theorem is widely accepted, understood and applied.

Of course, the argument in favor of optimal tariffs is not true for small countries. It is essential that the country should be large enough to have the ability to have an impact on prices. Furthermore the larger the country, the more market power it has, and the more it can gain from imposing tariffs on others. The implication of this is that if a world of small competitive economies merges into a few trading blocs, then under traditional assumptions, after the blocs are formed, there are more incentives for imposing tariffs than before. In other words, regional free trade associations, under traditional conditions, lead to protectionism.

The optimal tariff which we have just discussed is imposed by one country on others unilaterally. The theorem does not consider the possibility of retaliation by other countries. But what if they retaliate? What if other countries also impose tariffs in response?

We now move to a world of strategic considerations, a world with tariff wars. Each county imposes tariffs on each other, and does so strategically so as to maximize its welfare given the actions of others. The outcome of this tariff game was studied in Kennan and Riezman [12], [13]. If each country chooses as its tariff the best response to the others', a market equilibrium with tariffs is reached. We call this an optimal tariff equilibrium to distinguish it from the free trade equilibrium.

In an optimal tariff equilibrium some countries are better off than they would be at a free trade equilibrium, Kennan and Riezman [12], [13] and Riezman [21]. In other words, not all countries would benefit if the world were to move from the optimal tariff equilibrium into a world with free trade. Furthermore, these works show that the larger the country, the more it can improve its welfare at the optimal tariff equilibrium from the level that it could achieve at a free trade equilibrium.

To a certain extent the current situation in the world economy can be described as an optimal tariff equilibrium. Each country imposes tariffs on others strategically. In this light the difficulties of GATT have a reasonable explanation. The unwillingness of countries to agree to multilateral free trade is neither irrational nor a coordination problem. It is a rational response to economic incentives of countries with market power.

One immediate implication is that, under traditional conditions, regional trade blocs which increase the market power of the market participants will naturally lead to tariff wars. The larger the market power of a trade bloc, the greater is its incentive to impose tariffs on others. Even after retaliatory moves are taken into account the same proposition holds: the larger the market power of the bloc, the greater is its possible gain from a tariff war. Therefore if the formation of regional trade blocs increases the market power of the participants, the creation of regional free trade zones encourages trade wars.

We have remarked that the results on optimal tariffs and on the optimal tariffs equilibria hold under traditional assumptions. Since each of these results predicts that regional free trade zones create incentives against global free trade, it becomes crucial to examine the role of these traditional assumptions closely. For whenever these conditions are satisfied, regional free trade inevitably leads to trade wars. And the larger the free trade zones, the more likely it is that they will lead to trade wars.

We shall examine these conditions in some detail in the next section. This examination will be conceptual, but focused on particular cases of immediate interest. Drawing on the classical results on tariffs of Lerner [16] and of Metzler [19], and on new results on trading blocs with economies of scale Chichilnisky [9] reported also in the Appendix, we shall show that if the blocs are organized internally around the principle of economies of scale, the optimal tariff theorem is defeated. This means that, under increasing returns conditions, it is not true that a country is better off by the unilateral imposition of a positive tariff on its imports. But before we turn to the new results, we shall explore the implications of the optimal tariff theorem on the European Community and on NAFTA.

We shall argue that trade patterns can be based on traditional comparative advantages or on economies of scale. It is to a large extent a matter of policy choice. The trade policies within a trade bloc determine the extent to which the trade bloc will aid or hinder global free trade. The argument for this result, and its implications for trade policy, will occupy the rest of this paper.

2.2 *EC and NAFTA*

We now turn to the possible motivation for the US in forming a free trade zone with its neighbors.

The argument uses simple strategic considerations based on the results discussed in the previous section. NAFTA — and any further extension to a larger free trade zone in the Americas, can be seen as a strategic response by the US to the creation of the European Community trading bloc. The European Community bloc is a free trade zone with a quarter of world output. In seeking to form a trading bloc with its natural trading partners in the Americas, the US appears to respond to the creation of more market power, with an attempt to create more market power. This is a rational response if the US expects a united Europe to impose tariffs on the rest of the world. The emergence of a region with increased market power generally provides an incentive to other regions to seek similar status.

More explanatory power still can be extracted from the results of Kennan and Riezman [12], [13] and Riezman [21] on who wins trade wars. Following the creation of a customs union, the incentives are to create or join another free trade zone, but not at random. The economic incentive is to join another free trade zone with the largest possible market power. This result allows us to predict that the US should not only seek a free trade deal with Canada, but one with as many countries in the Americas as possible. The aim is to reach market power which exceeds that of a unified Europe.

2.3 *Trade Creation and Diversion*

Once a new free trade zone is created, how do we measure the gains and losses from trade?

A naive view is that since free trade in competitive markets is Pareto efficient, any move towards free trade is positive. As we saw, this would not be correct. We argued that regional trade blocs, being larger than their components, will have more market power and therefore an incentive to impose tariffs against outsiders under traditional conditions. Therefore one of the first negative effects of the formation of a trading bloc is that it can hurt the countries outside these areas. We shall argue below that these negative effects can be mitigated if the trading patterns within the blocs are organized around economies of scale.

But are the damages of free trade zones limited to protectionism with the rest of the world? The answer to this question is generally no. There is a second potential damage in the formation of regional trade blocs. Even if the trading blocs are not accompanied by protectionism against the rest of the world, they can still lead to trade diversions. This means that a regional free trade bloc may lead to the wrong specialization within the bloc. The classical argument about trade diversion is found in Viner [22], whose work remains a benchmark of analysis of preferential trade agreements. We shall summarize his argument here in order to show that, if trading within the blocs is organized around economies of scale, then Viner's argument can break down. With economies of scale, the negative effect of trade diversion can be mitigated. The empirical evidence discussed below suggests that this is what has happened in the European Market since 1958.

The essential argument can be captured from the textbook Table 1:

TABLE 1

THE EFFECTS OF TRADING BLOCS
TRADE DIVERSION

Cost of veg. oil	Tariffs		
	0	8	12
Germany	20	20	20
Portugal before EEC	16	24	28
Portugal after EEC	16	16	16
USA......................................	10	18	22

There are three countries, Germany, Portugal and the USA. They trade a commodity, vegetable oil. Initially Germany has a tariff that applies equally to all imported oil. If it imports oil despite the tariff, it will buy initially from the USA, which offers the best price. This appears in the second column, showing a low initial tariff. If the tariff is high enough, however, then Germany will produce its own oil, as in column 3. Now if Germany enters into a free trade agreement with Portugal, what are the welfare implications? If the tariff was initially the higher, the welfare of Germany increases after the regional bloc is created, since it replaces its domestic oil with a less expensive oil and uses its domestic resources in more productive sectors. However, if the tariff was initially as in column 3, after the free trade agreement Germany shifts from American to Portuguese oil, i.e. from a low cost to a higher cost producer. In this case, the free trade zone lowers welfare.

Viner's point is that there are "trade creating" free trade zones, in which the increase in imports by members from one another replaces domestic production. These are desirable. However, free trade blocs could also be "trade diverting" in the case that imports are diverted from a lower cost source outside the bloc to other sources inside the bloc which are less productive, but with more attractive prices after the tariffs were selectively dropped.

The extra trade among the members of the trading bloc is, generally, an improvement of welfare. The trade which is not additional, but a diversion from efficient outside sources to less efficient inside sources lowers welfare. If northern Europe is induced by the entry of southern Europe to buy oil from Portugal rather than an equivalent from the US, and the US source is more efficient but less competitive after the tariffs are dropped in Europe, there has been a welfare loss. Generally speaking Viner's approach evaluates free trade zones by the extent to which more trade is created, rather than existing trade diverted from one source to another.

Viner's original insight remains central to the analysis of preferential free trade zones. But, in practice, it misses an important aspect. The increase size of the market can sometimes lead to more efficiency and competitiveness. Even in the cases where Viner's analysis predicts welfare losses, namely when the trade bloc diverts trade from outside sources to less competitive inside sources, welfare can still increase with economies of scale. This can be explained simply in our numerical example. As Portugal expands its oil production due to its new trade to Germany, it becomes more efficient. This appears in Table 2, column 2. After the tariffs were removed Portugal produces and exports more oil and it becomes more competitive, reaching the US level.

TABLE 2

TRADE IS NOT DIVERTED WITH ECONOMIES OF SCALE

Cost of veg. oil	Tariffs		
	0	8	12
Germany	20	20	20
Portugal before EEC	16	24	28
Portugal after EEC	16	10	10
USA.....................................	10	18	22

Economies of scale can therefore have a major impact on trade policies. We showed that they can check the negative trade diversion effects of a trading bloc. We shall argue in what follows that they can also limit another major negative effect of a trading bloc: the incentives for large blocs with market power to impose tariffs on others.

What does the empirical evidence show? It is widely believed that economies of scale were an important factor in the success of the *Treaty of Rome*. Economies of scale were central to the success of the European Common Market which was formed in 1958. While a strong possibility for trade diversion existed *a priori* in the EC, in reality huge inter-industry trade emerged in manufactures. The increase in market size and the associated rationalization in production led to efficiency gains which took precedence over possible trade diversion. Krugman [14] discusses this issue in some detail, without however offering a conceptual relation between economies of scale and the economics of trading blocs. «Hopes for large benefits from both the US-Canada free trade agreement and Europe 1992 rest largely on an increase in competition and rationalization. In the North American case, the estimate of Harris and Cox, who attempt to take account of competitive/industrial organization effects, suggest a gain for Canada from free trade that is about 4 times larger than those of standard models. In Europe the widely cited and somewhat controversial figure of 7 percent gain due to 1992 presented in the *Cechini Report* Commission of the European Communities 1988 rests primarily on estimates by Alisdair Smith and Anthony Venables of gains from increased competition and rationalization».

In practice, therefore, economies of scale can defeat trade diversion losses, and transform these into gains. I shall also argue below that they can also defeat the incentives for tariff wars between blocs, so that the formation of trading blocs can become a parallel, complementary effort towards the liberalization of world trade.

3. - Trading Blocs with Economies of Scale

3.1 *Trade Inside and Between the Blocs*

Although predictions are inherently dangerous in an area so circumscribed by political action, our conclusion is that regional free trade can have different effects on global markets and it should be to a certain extent the choice of well informed and reasonable economic agents which one will prevail.

Regional trading blocs based on traditional comparative advantages will generally divert trade. They will also typically hinder the prospects of global negotiations. In this case, as the bloc has more market power than its parts, it has the incentive to impose larger tariffs on the rest of the world. Regional blocs then develop incentives for imposing tariffs against each other, and for engaging in trade wars. This type of regional free trade zone works against global free trade.

There is, however, an alternative. If the regional trade zones are oriented to the expansion of trade based not on traditional comparative advantages but rather on increased size and on the productive efficiency and competitiveness that comes with economies of scale, matters could be quite different. In this latter case, the regional free trade zones could unleash an appetite for further expansion of trade. We shall argue that in this case the incentive for blocs to impose tariffs against each other is reduced, and in fact can be defeated by the economic incentives in favor of trade expansion which accompanies economies of scale. The incentives are now for further expansion of trade. The creation of trading blocs which are organized around economies of scale is therefore part of a broader trend towards increasingly open world markets.

3.2 *The Americas: Traditional Comparative Advantages or Economies of Scale*

A central issue in our argument is the pattern of trade inside the blocs. This issue is of particular importance in an American free trade zone. This is because of all the regions, the American area is the one whose trade is currently based on traditional comparative advantages and on the diversity between the traders' economic development rather than on economies of scale.

The matter is not only one of economic reality: it is also one of perceived economic reality. Both the European and the East Asian countries perceive gains from trade as a matter of exploiting economies of scale. The newly industrialized countries in Asia, and the Japanese, have a dynamic vision of comparative advantages. Moving up the ladder of comparative advantages in the production and trade of skilled-labor manufactures, of consumer electronics, and of products based on specialized knowledge and on technological skill, are widespread priorities.

By contrast, within the sphere of influence of the US, the vision of trade based on traditional comparative advantages still prevails. It permeates to a great extent the thinking about international trade at the government level, at the international organization level, at the academic, and even at the journalist level.

The European free trade zone is, to a certain extent, a zone of equals. To encourage this equality, the introduction of free mobility of labor has been one of the first steps in the European market integration of 1992.

The Americas, on the other hand, have the US as a hegemon, a "hub" which concentrates on exporting manufactures and skill-intensive goods to the "spokes" in exchange for their resources. The free mobility of labor between the hub and the spokes is an unspoken issue. It has not even been contemplated in the American negotiations for free trade. It has not been mentioned by any of the governments concerned that labor could move freely between the free trade partners, as it does in the EC region. In some cases, quite to the contrary, the free trade agreement has been mentioned as a way to limit the mobility of labor between the concerned countries, such as Mexico and the US.

To the extent that labor remains a fixed input of production within the countries of the American free trade zone, traditional comparative advantages based on labor will be invoked as a foundation for policy. The concern is that an American free trade zone, if it emerges, may reflect the historical patterns of trade between industrial and developing regions, which is usually called North-South trade.

3.3 *Traditional Comparative Advantages and the Global Environment*

Another reason for concern with respect to traditional comparative advantages arises from the current focus on the environment. Traditional comparative advantages emphasize the South's concentration in the production and export of goods which deplete environmental resources, such as wood pulp and cash crops which overuse rain forests, or minerals whose combustion leads to the emission of greenhouse gases. Recent work in the area of North-South trade with environmental inputs to production (Chichilnisky [7], [8]) shows that ill-defined patterns of property rights on forests, fisheries, and arable land in developing countries may lead to a market-induced over-supply of goods which are intensive in the use of these resources as inputs, and to Pareto inefficient patterns of international trade. What appears as comparative advantages may simply be a reflection of a market failure in the developing countries. Social and private comparative advantages differ and social and private gains from trade may also differ in these circumstances. Traditional tax policies, levying duties on the use of such inputs in the South, may not work, and may indeed lead to more extraction of the resource and more exports of the resource-intensive commodity. Indeed, it is shown in Chichilnisky [7], [8] that differences in property rights on inputs of production are sufficient to explain the patterns of trade between nations. The global environment is therefore another reason for being concerned with traditional comparative advantages as a foundation for trade. Since two thirds of the current exports from Latin America are resources, and the main trade of Ecuador, Venezuela and Mexico with the US is petroleum, this problem is very real. It is also very real with respect to the trading in wood products which lead to the deforestation of the remaining tropical forests, Amelung [1], Barbier *et* Al. [2], Binkley - Vincent [3], Hyde - Neumann [11]. Replacing traditional comparative advantages with economies of scale could be a necessary feature of a program of sustainable development.

3.4 *Skilled Labor and External Economies of Scale*

It seems desirable at this point to distinguish an important difference between two types of economies of scale: internal to the firm, or external to it. The former are simply a reflection that each firm may be more efficient in the use of its inputs to production as the level of its output increases. The firm's per unit costs decrease with the level of output. Such economies of scale are typical of industries which require large fixed costs, such as aerospace, airlines, and communications networks. This type of increasing returns, called internal, can lead to monopolistic competition or other forms of limitations to market entry. As such, there is a loss to the consumer in that the free market outcomes are typically not Pareto efficient.

There is a different type: external economies of scale. These also lead to a decrease in per unit costs as the output expands, but they do so at the level of the industry or of the country as a whole. Each firm's production function faces increasing cost per unit of output, i.e. decreasing returns to scale, which assures competitive behavior. However, as the industry as a whole expands, externalities are created which lead to increased productivity for all the firms. A good example is provided by the electronics industry. Each computer manufacturer faces a rather competitive market. On the other hand, as the overall level of output of the industry expands, knowledge about new technologies develops and this new knowledge, which is easily and rapidly diffused across the industry, leads to lower costs for all. Just about any industry which depends heavily on knowledge has this characteristic. In reality, the factor which leads to increasing returns is the skill of the labor force which embodies knowledge. Knowledge is typically diffused and can be captured and imitated sooner or later, and there are abundant examples in the software and hardware industry to prove this point (2). Knowledge creates skilled labor, and this in turn leads to increasing returns to scale, which usually, although not always, are external to the firm. Because of this skilled labor can simultaneously lead to economies of scale, and to competitive markets. The successful development experience of Korea, of Taiwan, and more recently of the Asian Tigers, showns that export-led policies based on skilled labor intensive goods, for example in consumer electronics, is generally more successful than those intensive in the use of inexpensive and uneducated labor. This point was developed formally in Chichilnisky [4], [6], and more recently in terms of development policies in Dadzie [10].

In this paper we shall concentrate on external economies of scale, which are closely connected with production systems based on skilled labor.

3.5 *Optimal Tariffs: Traditional Theory*

We mentioned above that a large country will typically impose tariffs so as to improve its terms of trade. In doing so it typically

---

(2) Microsoft's Windows excellent imitation of the *Apple* operating systems was tested in the US courts and found without fault.

introduces distortions in its production and consumption. Here we shall show in a simple example how under traditional assumptions there is a tariff that improves welfare, in the sense that the gains from improved terms of trade exceed the losses from distortions. The analysis is completely standard, see e.g. Krugman and Obsfelt [15], but it is included here in order to highlight the differences which arise in economies with increasing returns to scale. This is discussed in the next section.

The analysis in this section relies on one assumption and one simplification. Both are raised in the Appendix, which consider the general case. The assumption here is that the supply and demand curves of the economy are linear and exhibit decreasing returns to scale, and that there are no major income effects. The simplification is to neglect the impact of the tariff revenues on income; this is typically done in textbooks, and will also be done in this section. It is however explicitly analyzed in the Appendix.

We assume that the home country H has a demand curve with equation:

(1) $$D = a - b\tilde{p}$$

where $\tilde{p}$ is the domestic price of the good and a supply curve:

(2) $$Q = e + f\tilde{p}$$

Country H's demand for imports is the difference:

(3) $$D - Q = (a - e) - (b + f)\tilde{p}$$

Foreign export supply is also a straight line:

(4) $$(Q^* - D^*) = g + hp_w$$

where p_w is the world price. The internal price in country H exceeds the world price by the tariff:

(5) $$\tilde{p} = p_w + t$$

In a world equilibrium imports must equal exports:

(6) $$(a - e) - (b + f) \times (p_w + t) = q + hp_w$$

Solving equation (6) for $t = 0$ gives p_f, the world price that would prevail without tariffs. Then a tariff t alters the internal price to:

(7) $$\tilde{p} = p_f + th / (b + f + h)$$

and the world price to:

(8) $$p_w = p_f - t(b + f) / (b + f + h)$$

Note that if the parameters a, e, b, h and f are all positive, then:

(9) $$p_f < \tilde{p} \quad \text{and} \quad p_w > p_f$$

implying that the tariff raises the internal price $\tilde{p}$ and lowers the world price p_w.

It is immediate to show that, under these conditions, it is always possible to find a tariff t that increases the country's welfare. Let q_1 and d_1 be the free trade levels of consumption and production. Since the internal price is higher after the tariff, domestic supply rises from q_1 to q_2 and demand falls from d_1 to d_2:

(10) $$q_2 = q_1 + tfh / (b + f + h)$$

and:

(11) $$d_2 = d_1 - tbh / (b + f + h)$$

The gain in welfare from a lower world price is the area of the rectangle in Graph 1, the fall in the price multiplied by the level of imports after the tariff:

(12) $$\text{gain in welfare} = (d_2 - q_2) \times t(b+f) / (b+f+h) =$$
$$t \times (d_1 - q_1) \times (b+f) / (b+f+h) - (t)^2 \times h(b+f)^2 / (b+f+h)^2$$

GRAPH 1

GAINS AND LOSSES FROM TARIFFS:
TRADITIONAL CASE

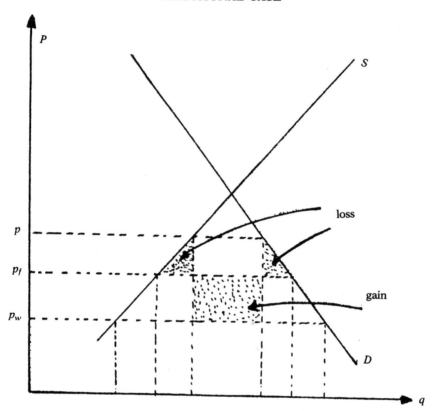

The loss from distorted consumption is the sum of the areas of the two triangles in Graph 3:

$$(13) \qquad \text{loss in welfare} = (1/2) \times (q_2 - q_1) \times (\tilde{p} - p_f) +$$

$$+ (1/2) \times (d_1 - d_2) \times (\tilde{p} - p_f) = (t)^2 \times (b+f) \times h^2/2\,(b+f+h)^2$$

The net effect on welfare is therefore:

$$(14) \qquad\qquad \text{gain - loss} = t \times U - (t)^2 \times V$$

where U and V are constants. The net effect is the sum of a positive number times the tariff rate and a negative number times the square of the tariff rate. It follows that when the tariff is sufficiently small the net effect must be positive, since t^2 is smaller than t, for t near zero. This establishes that, when supply and demand, income effects of the tariff income are neglected and are linear and tariffs are small, there exists a positive tariff which increases the welfare of the country beyond that which can be obtained under free trade.

The size of the country matters. If the importing country is small, then foreign supply is highly elastic i.e. h is very large, so from *(8)* we verify that the tariff has little or no effect on world prices p_w while raising domestic prices $\tilde{p}$ almost one-to-one.

3.6 *Optimal Tariffs with Economies of Scale*

The argument in the previous section shows that a large country is better off by imposing tariffs than it is under free trade. This proposition holds under traditional conditions, one of which is that the supply of goods should increase with prices across market equilibria. In our example, this is formalized by the parameters in the supply function in equation *(2)*, which is upward sloping. However, this assumption ceases to be valid when the economy has economies of scale. In such economies the larger the output the lower the costs, and therefore, in principle, the lower the prices. Then $f < 0$ in equation *(8)*, which in turn can lead to a negative welfare gain from the tariff from equation *(12)*.

A good example of this phenomenon is provided by the electronics industry, for example computer hardware. The last fifteen years have seen a dramatic decrease in prices together with a dramatic expansion of output of computer hardware. This occurs because the expansion in output leads to rationalization and the corresponding increased efficiency in production. In the hardware industry this takes the form of technological change which improves productive efficiency and lowers the costs of the industry as a whole. Even though a technological breakthrough may in principle be patented, and therefore could be captured by one firm with the corresponding increase in its market power and deviation from competitive behavior, in practice the computer industry is very competitive. This is because the knowledge which drives the technological innovation in this industry is easily diffused.

A standard textbook analysis of such economies of scale is for example Nicholson [20], pages 252-5, who documents that most studies of long-run cost curves have found that average costs are decreasing up to a point and then constant. Examples provided are agriculture, electricity generation, railroads, and commercial banking, all activities which are broadly associated with economic development. The same textbook analysis explains how competitive markets can lead to a negative association of quantities and prices across equilibria. This was the content of the famous debate in the 1920's between J.H. Clapham, A.C. Pigou and D.H. Roberston, which was resolved positively, and which appeared in the Economic Journal between 1922 and 1924 (3). Chichilnisky and Heal [5] have discussed in some detail the policy implications of international trade in economies with increasing returns to scale in a report on trade policies in the 1980's to the Secretary General of UNCTAD, and they reach similar conclusions.

We shall now show how the analysis of optimal tariffs in the last section breaks down when there are increasing returns to scale. In such economies there may be no gains from imposing tariffs, even if the country is large and has substantial market power. The optimal tariff theorem no longer holds. We shall now explain how this happens in a concrete case.

It is useful to remind ourselves how tariffs increase welfare in the economy of the previous section. Tariffs increase welfare by lowering the world prices p_w: this was seen in equation *(7)*. The country's terms of trade thus improve after the tariff. It imports fewer lower cost goods from the rest of the world. The welfare gains were computed in equation *(12)*: these depend crucially on the fact that, after the tariff, the consumers pay lower prices for the goods they import.

However, this argument no longer holds with economies of scale. With economies of scale the world price may increase rather than

---

(3) See NICHOLSON [20], p. 332.

decrease after the tariff. The welfare gains from tariffs are the drop in world prices times the quantity imported. But if the world price increases, the gains are transformed into losses.

The possibility that after a tariff the terms of trade deteriorate for the country was studied in Lerner [16] and Metzler [19]. They argue mostly in terms of income effects. A similar phenomenon occurs in our economy, but due to different causes. In contrast with the economy of the previous section, the parameter *f* in equation *(8)* is now negative rather than positive; this means that across equilibria the prices drop as quantities increase, or otherwise said, prices increase when quantities drop. If the tariff decreases the quantity produced and traded, this will lower the productive efficiency of the economy. Costs increase and therefore prices increase too. The tariff defeats the gains from rationalization in production produced by the larger market size. This is represented in Graph 2. It shows a negative correlation between market clearing prices and the quantity of goods sold at an equilibrium, and how this leads to an increase in the world prices after the tariff, corresponding to a decrease in output.

We saw that after the tariff, the world price p_w can be higher rather than lower as it is in the traditional case with decreasing returns to scale. The terms of trade for the country are therefore worse after the tariff. Consumers in the country are worse off: the price of their imports have increased. All of this is formally reflected in the systems of equations presented above. In equation *(7)* the parameter *f* describing the relation between supply and prices, which was previously positive, is now negative. In practical terms the following conditions are sufficient for the world price to increase rather than decrease after the tariff:

(15)
$$b < |f| < h$$
$$f < 0, \; b, h > 0$$

Conditions *(15)* are satisfied under a variety of circumstances. For example *(15)* holds when foreign export supply increases with, and is highly responsive to, prices ($h > 0$ and large), a resonable assumption for the world, when the country has increasing returns to scale ($f < 0$)

GRAPH 2

LOSSES FROM TARIFFS WITH ECONOMIES OF SCALE

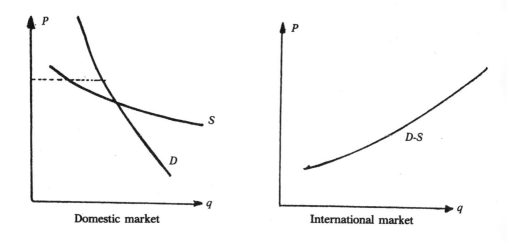

Domestic market   International market

AFTER THE TARIFF, THE WORLD PRICE p_w INCREASES
DUE TO ECONOMIES OF SCALE

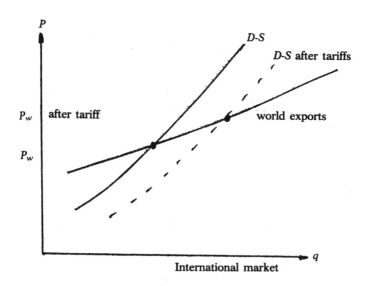

International market

and the quantity produced is more responsive to price than is the demand ($b > 0$, $b < |f|$).

The main condition is the existence of economies of scale in the economy ($f < 0$). Under these conditions, the optimal tariff theorem is no longer true, as the countries may have no economic incentive to impose tariffs on others: they lose by restricting trade.

Consumer electronics, semiconductors, software production, banking and financial services, and just about any sector whose productivity depends mostly on knowledge and information have these characteristics. Software production is today actively developed in India as an export business. It is a sector which is simultaneously labor intensive and subject to informational economies of scale. As already discussed, the remarkable economic development of the *Asian Tigers* over the last fifteen years profited from the expansion of their international trade of skilled-labor intensive products such as consumer electronics. This sector is simultaneously labor intensive and subject to informational economies of scale.

All the arguments just presented hold equally for countries or for trading blocs. To the extent that sectors with economies of scale expand within the free trade zone, the zone itself loses its economic incentives to use its market power to restrict trade and wage tariff wars against others.

4. - Conclusions

We have argued that the formation of trading blocs typically harms the global liberalization of markets when the blocs are themselves organized under the principle of traditional comparative advantages. Under these conditions, the larger the market power of the bloc the greater its incentives to impose tariffs on others. Protectionism emerges from the increased market power of the traders.

Relation can lead to a tariff war between the blocs. Furthermore under traditional assumptions, the larger country wins the tariff ware. Therefore the larger the trading bloc, the more likely it is to impose tariffs and to win a trade war.

Trading blocs of this nature have no economic incentive to favor the GATT negotiations. They are better off with tariffs than with free trade. Indeed, the economic incentives of such trading blocs are contrary to the GATT's intentions. We argued that, to a certain extent, this explains the floundering of the GATT negotiations.

We discussed the example of the EC bloc in contrast with NAFTA or with an eventual American free trade zone. The empirical evidence suggests that the EC trading bloc benefited from increasing returns to scale.

NAFTA, and any eventual America free trading bloc, emerged as a strategic response to the increased market power of the European trading bloc. By contrast with the EC trading bloc, the emerging NAFTA appears to be organizing under the traditional theory of comparative advantage.

The lack of any provision for the mobility of labor between the countries of the region reinforces this trend. NAFTA does not contemplate the mobility of labor between Mexico and the US. The lack of labor mobility tends to lock-in the traditional comparative advantages between the countries within the area. Their trading on the basis of comparative advantages within bloc will create incentives for trade wars between the blocs.

A different scenario contemplates a NAFTA organized around economies of scale. Example for such scenarios include the Indian software trade, and the *Asian Tigers'* specialization in consumer electronics. Typically, electronic-based industries have increasing returns derived from the creation and diffusion of knowledge as output expands. This leads to rationalization in production and to increased efficiency and thus lower costs. The expansion of output is accompanied by lower rather than higher prices. From the point of view of the exporter, these markets are less likely to be protected because the importer, having increasing returns to scale in this industry, has less incentives to rely on tariffs than it does in other industries with decreasing returns. With increasing returns, tariffs decrease trade and can increase world prices, thus decreasing the welfare of the importing country. Economies of scale produce incentives to expand trade.

We formalized this issue by showing that economies of scale can defeat the standard result of optimal tariffs. While under traditional conditions, a trading bloc is always better off with tariffs than it is with free trade, we showed that with increasing returns to scale this is no longer true. Tariffs decrease the size of the market, and therefore decrease productive efficiency in economies with increasing returns. This decrease in efficiency leads lo increased rather than lower world prices, and the main purpose of the tariff, which is to improve the countries' terms of trade, is defeated. Under these conditions trading blocs are better off with free trade, and with the corresponding expanded markets, than they are with tariffs. To the extent that NAFTA organizes itself around economies of scale in the international trade within the region, the incentives for a trade war between NAFTA and the EC are mitigated.

It seems useful to remind ourselves that the choice of products and of technology are to a large extent the subject of policy. They need in no way interfere with market efficiency. The first welfare theorem about the efficiency of competitive markets applies to a market with given technologies and with given products. The theorem does not explain how different technologies or products arise: it proves that once technologies and products are given, competitive markets lead to Pareto efficiency. Once the product mix and the technologies are chosen the market can operate efficiently. This implies that the organizing principles within the blocs — traditional comparative advantages or economies of scale — are, to a great extent, a matter of policy choice. Choosing different trade policies, for example, choosing technologies and the product mix, can be achieved without market distortions or loss of market efficiency. This point was already made by Meade [18] several years ago.

The emergence of an American trading bloc which reinforces the current tendency towards the exploitation of traditional comparative advantages is a source of concern. It has been argued Chichilnisky [4], [5], [6] that export-led policies based on (unskilled) labor intensive products can defeat the goals of development and trade by depressing the country's terms of trade and overall consumption. Trade between the countries of the Americas is organized today around traditional comparative advantages: labor and resource intensive exports from the South and capital and skill-intensive exports from the North. If the emergence of an America free trade zone is based on similar principles, then not only may this continue a depressing growth trend in Latin America, but in addition it could create or reinforce incentives against the global liberalization of free trade.

We have argued that another reason to avoid trade policies between the countries of the Americas based on traditional comparative advantages is that they tend to deplete environmental assets such as forests, fisheries or fertile land, and overuse minerals which are exported by the developing countries to the North. Some of these minerals are the source of potentially dangerous CO_2 emissions. Petroleum exported from Mexico, Ecuador and Venezuela to the USA fits this description. Indeed, any concept of sustainable development requires a rethinking of trade policies away from those based on comparative advantages. This general premise is particularly well suited to the NAFTA, and to the Americas as a whole, since two thirds of Latin American exports today are resources.

The main point of this paper is that the characteristics of trading policies within the trading blocs can determine the extent to which the blocs will favor or harm the global negotiations towards free trade. Trading policies based on comparative advantages are generally negative towards GATT. We argued that trading policies based on economies of scale could have the positive effect towards global free trade: they could mitigate the economic incentive of tariffs and trade restriction in favor of an expansion of world trade. The emergence of such blocs could advance in tandem with the global liberalization of world trade.

1. - Trading Blocs with Increasing Returns to Scale

This appendix develops an international trade model and proves formally the propositions on customs unions stated in the body of the paper.

The model presented here extends the North-South model introduced in Chichilnisky [4], [5], [6], to the case of economies which trade goods produced under conditions of increasing returns to scale, and proves formally the proposition that with increasing returns to scale, large countries can achieve higher welfare levels with free trade than with tariffs. This model consider Cobb-Douglas production functions, and it assumes that there exist economies of scale in production which are external to the firm, such as in the example of the electronic industry discussed in the text.

The model describes two countries, 1 and 2, producing and trading two goods B (basic goods) and I (industrial goods) with each other; these goods are produced using two inputs, labor L and capital, K. The economies of the two countries are competitive, so that in each country prices are taken as given by consumers and producers. Producers maximize profits, and consumers maximize utility subject ot their budget constraints. Walras' law is satisfied, so that the value of the excess demand is equal to zero. At an equilibrium all markets, for goods and for factors, clear.

The increasing returns to scale considered here are "external" to the firm as in the example of parts of the electronics industry discussed in the text. This means that in the production functions, formalized below, there exists a parameter denoted γ which increases with the level of output of the economy. As the outputs of the economy expand, the production function varies, formalizing the notion that factors are more productive at higher levels of aggregate output. However, the firm takes this parameter γ as given — this is the assumption that the increasing returns are external to the firm.

For each given value of the parameter γ the firm has constant returns to scale. The firms are therefore competitive, and in particular zero profits are achieved at an equilibrium.

Consider the model of one country first. The production functions are:

$$(16) \qquad\qquad B^S = \gamma\, L_1^\alpha\, K_1^{1-\alpha}$$
$$I^S = \gamma\, L_2^\beta\, K_2^{1-\beta}$$

where α, β, $\in (0,1)$, γ is a positive parameter, L_1 and K_1 are the inputs of labor and capital in the B sector, and L_2 and K_2 the inputs of labor and capital in the I sector. The total amount of labor and capital in the economy are L^S and K^S respectively. Prices are p_B and p_I; we assume that I is the numeraire so that:

$$(17) \qquad\qquad\qquad p_I = 1$$

Factor prices are denoted as usual: w for wages and r for rental on capital. We shall assume for simplicity that the demand for basic goods at an equilibrium is known:

$$(18) \qquad\qquad\qquad B^d = \bar{B}^d$$

so that by Walras' law the demand for industrial goods in equilibrium is given by:

$$(19) \qquad\qquad I^d = (wL^S + r K^S - p_B\, \bar{B}^d)$$

because of zero profits. More general demand functions than those postulated in *(18)* can be given without a major effect on the results, see for example the various forms of demand functions utilized in Chichilnisky [6]. Indicating the equilibrium level of exports by X_B^{S*}

and the equilibrium level of imports by X_I^{d*}, the model of the world economy is formalized by the following equilibrium conditions:

(20)
$$p_B^* \, B^{S*} + I^* = w^* \, L^* + rK^*$$
(zero profits)

$$K^* = K^S = K_1 + K_2$$
(capital market clears)

$$L^* = L^S = L_1 + L_2$$
(labor market clears)

$$B^{S*} = B^{d*} + X_B^{S*}$$
(B market clears)

$$I^{d*} = I^{S*} + X_I^{d*}$$
(I market clears)

2. - Solving the Model

The model for the world economy consists of two countries, indicated with the indices 1 and 2, each specified as above. To solve the model, there are therefore five prices to be determined: the "terms of trade" p_B, and two factor prices in each country: w and r. The quantities to be determined in an equilibrium are: the use of factors in each sector of each country: K_1, K_2, L_1, L_2, the outputs of the two goods B^S and I^S, and the corresponding parameter γ determining the external economies of scale, the exports and imports of each of the two goods in each of the two countries, X_B^{S*} and X_I^{d*}, and the demand for each good in each country: B^{d*} I^{d*}. There is a total of twenty seven variables to be determined endogenously, including all prices and quantities in all markets and both countries.

In the following proposition 1 we shall prove that all of these variables can be determined once the variable giving the terms of trade in equilibrium p_B is known. Furthermore we shall prove that there exists one "resolving equation" which determines the equilibrium value of the terms of trade as a function of all the exogenous parameters of the model, of which there are six in each country: α, β, σ, B^{d*}, L^S and K^S, and a total of twelve in the world economy.

3. - The Effects of a Tariff on the Terms of Trade

Proposition 1: if the importing country 1 has external economies of scale;

$$\gamma = \gamma(B) = B^\sigma, \ \sigma > 1$$

and the foreign supply is highly elastic $(\partial X_B^{S2}/\partial p_B) > 0$ and very large then no tariff can increase the welfare of the country relative to that which the country can achieve under free trade.

Proof: consider a world economy with two countries defined as in equations *(16) (17) (18) (19) (20)*. We shall now solve the model by finding an explicit expression for the equilibrium terms of trade p_B^* in the world economy. This consists of writing the market clearing conditions in the B market, exports equal imports, and expressing it as a function of one variable: p_B. From the terms of trade in equilibrium, we show that all other endogenous variables can be found. We shall use the indices 1 and 2 to distinguish the parameters of the two countries. Note first that we have given no specification of demand or supply behavior outside of an equilibrium; in particular, there is no information for carrying out stability analysis. Since the model has constant returns to scale, profit maximising supply functions are, as is standard, undefined. As is standard in models with constant returns to scale, we derive the equilibrium relations between supplies and prices from the condition of full employment of factors together with an equilibrium condition which incorporates the external economies of scale.

Denote:

$$l_1 = L_1 / K_1$$
$$l_2 = L_2 / K_2$$

Since by assumption each firm takes the parameter γ as given, from the production functions *(16)*, marginal conditions and zero profits imply:

(21)
$$w = \gamma\alpha\,(L_1 / K_1)^{\alpha-1}\, p_B = \gamma\alpha l_1^{\alpha-1}\, p_B$$

$$r = \gamma\,(1 - \alpha)\, l_1^{\alpha}\, p_B$$

$$w = \gamma\,\beta l_2^{\beta-1}$$

$$r = \gamma\,(1 - \beta)\, l_2^{\beta}$$

so that:

(22)
$$\frac{r}{w} = \left[\frac{(1 - \alpha)}{\alpha}\right] l_1 \quad\text{and}\quad \frac{r}{w} = \left[\frac{(1 - \beta)}{\beta}\right] l_2$$

and in particular:

(23)
$$l_1 = \frac{[(1 - \beta)\,\alpha]}{[\beta(1 - \alpha)]}\, l_2$$

Our next step is to define an equation (called the "resolving equation" and denoted $F = 0$) which yield the equilibrium value of the terms of trade p_B as a function of all the exogenous parameters of the model of which there are 12 as listed above, and from which all other endogenous variables at equilibrium are explicitly computed.

Indicating logarithms with the symbol "~" the four equations in *(21)* can be rewritten as:

(24)
$$\tilde{w} = (\alpha - 1)\,\tilde{l}_1 + \tilde{\alpha} + \tilde{p}_B + \tilde{\gamma}$$

$$\tilde{r} = \alpha\tilde{l}_1 + (1 \simeq \alpha) + \tilde{p}_B + \tilde{\gamma}$$

$$\tilde{w} = (\beta - 1)\,\tilde{l}_2 + \tilde{\beta} + \tilde{\gamma}$$

$$\tilde{r} = \beta\tilde{l}_2 + (1 - \beta) + \tilde{\gamma}$$

so that:

(25)
$$(\alpha - 1)\,\tilde{l}_1 + \tilde{\alpha} + \tilde{p}_B = (\beta - 1)\,\tilde{l}_2 + \tilde{\beta}$$

$$\alpha\tilde{l}_1 + (1 \simeq \alpha) + \tilde{p}_B = \beta\tilde{l}_2 + (1 \simeq \beta)$$

or equivalently:

(26)
$$(\alpha - 1)\,\tilde{l}_1 + (1 \simeq \beta)\,\tilde{l}_2 = \tilde{\beta} - \tilde{p}_B - \tilde{\alpha}$$
$$\tilde{\alpha}\,\tilde{l}_1 - \beta\tilde{l}_2 = (1 \simeq \beta) - \tilde{p}_B - (1 \simeq \alpha)$$

Solving for $\tilde{l}_1$, $\tilde{l}_2$ we obtain:

(27)
$$\tilde{l}_1 = \frac{[(\tilde{\beta} - \tilde{p}_B - \tilde{\alpha})(-\beta) - (1 - \beta)[(1 \simeq \beta) - \tilde{p}_B - (1 \simeq \alpha)]}{[\beta - \alpha]} -$$

and:

(28)
$$\tilde{l}_2 = \frac{[(\alpha - 1)[(1 \simeq \beta) - \tilde{p}_B - (1 \simeq \alpha)] - [(\tilde{\beta} - \tilde{p}_B - \tilde{\alpha})\alpha]]}{[\beta - \alpha]}$$

From (27) and (28) we obtain:

(29)
$$\tilde{l}_1 = \frac{\tilde{p}_B}{(\beta - \alpha)} + A$$

and:

$$\tilde{l}_2 = \frac{\tilde{p}_B}{(\beta - \alpha)} + B$$

where:

$$A = \frac{[(\tilde{\beta} - \tilde{\alpha})(-\beta) - (1 - \beta)[(1 \simeq \beta) - (1 \simeq \alpha)]]}{(\beta - \alpha)}$$

and:

$$B = \frac{[\alpha - 1][(1 \simeq \beta) - (1 \simeq \alpha)] - \alpha\,(\tilde{\beta} - \tilde{\alpha})}{(\beta - \alpha)}$$

$$A > 0 \quad \text{and} \quad B < 0 \quad \text{if} \quad \beta < \alpha$$

Therefore:

$$(30) \qquad l_1 = e^A \, p_B^{1/(\beta - \alpha)}$$

and:

$$l_2 = e^B \, p_B^{1/(\beta - \alpha)}$$

Now:

$$(31) \qquad l_2 = \frac{(L^S - L_1)}{K^S - K_1} \Rightarrow L^S - L_1 = l_2 \, (K^S - K_1)$$

or:

$$L_1 = L^S - l_2 \, (K^S - K_1)$$

and:

$$(32) \qquad l_1 = L_1/K_1 \Rightarrow L_1 \, l_1 \, K_1$$

so that:

$$L^S - l_2 \, (K^S - K_1) = l_1 \, K_1$$

or:

$$(33) \qquad K_1 \, (l_1 - l_2) = L^S - l_2 \, K^S \Rightarrow K_1 = (L^S - l_2 \, K^S) / (l_1 - l_2)$$

From *(31) (32) (33)* we obtain:

$$(34) \qquad K_1 = \frac{(L^S - l_2 \, K^S)}{(l_1 - l_2)}$$

and:

$$(35) \qquad L_1 = \frac{(l_1)}{(l_1 - l_2)} \, (L^S - l_2 \, K^S)$$

from which together with *(30)* we obtain the levels of supply of labor and capital used in each sector, at an equilibrium as a function of the equilibrium level of the relative price of *B*:

$$(36) \qquad L_1 = \frac{e^A L^S}{(e^A - e^B)} - \frac{e^A e^B}{(e^A - e^B)} K^S p_B^{1/(\beta - \alpha)}$$

and:

$$(37) \qquad K_1 = \frac{L^S}{e^A - e^B} p_B^{1/\alpha - \beta} - e^B (e^A - e^B) K^S$$

From *(16) (36)* we obtain the quantity of *B* and *I* produced at each level of relative prices, p_B. Now taking $\gamma = 1$, we denote these as ϕ (p_B) and ψ (p_B) respectively. Therefore from *(16)* we obtain the equilibrium level of outputs as a function of equilibrium prices:

$$(38) \qquad\qquad B^S = \gamma \phi (p_B)$$

and:

$$I^S = \gamma \psi (p_B)$$

Note that this does not fully express output as an explicit function of equilibrium prices because $\gamma = \gamma (B)$. In order to obtain outputs as explicit functions of equilibrium prices we must also find out the equilibrium value of $\gamma = \gamma^* (B)$, which is "fixed point" problem, since γ depends on *B* and *B* depends on γ. We solve this as follows.

The economy has increasing returns which are external to the firm, and the parameter γ increases with the level of output of *B* and *I*:

$$(39) \qquad\qquad \gamma = B^\sigma$$

At an equilibrium equations *(38)* and *(39)* must be satisfied simultaneously, i.e.:

$$(40)$$

$$\gamma = [\gamma \cdot \phi (p_B)]^\sigma$$
$$= \gamma^\sigma \phi (p_B)^\sigma \quad \text{or} \quad \gamma^{1-\sigma} = \phi (p_B)^\sigma$$

so that:

$$\gamma = \phi\,(p_B)^{\sigma/(1-\sigma)}$$

Therefore at an equilibrium from *(38)* we obtain a relation between the outputs of B and I, and p_B:

(41)

$$B^S = \phi\,(p_B)^{\sigma + 1/(1-\sigma)}$$
$$I^S = \psi\,(p_B)^{\sigma + 1/(1-\sigma)}$$

Note that:

$$\text{when } \sigma > 1, \; \theta = \sigma + 1/1 - \sigma < 0$$

so that when $B^S = \phi\,(p_B)^{\sigma + 1/(1-\sigma)}$ decreases with p_B across equilibria, since $\phi\,(p_B)$ is an increasing function of p_B for each fixed γ, see Graph 3.

If $\sigma \to 1$, $\theta \to -\infty$.

To solve the model we now consider the market clearing condition in B. At a world equilibrium, the B market must clear so that:

(42) $\quad B^{d,1}\,(p_B + t) - B^{s,1}\,(p_B + t) = B^{s,2}\,(p_B) - B^{d,2}\,(p_B)$

or:

$$F(p_B,\, t) = B^{d,1}\,(p_B + t) - B^{s,1}\,(p_B + t) - B^{s,2}\,(p_B) + B^{d,2}\,(p_B) = 0$$

From *(18) (19) (21) (30)* and *(41)*, equation *(42)* is a function of the variable p_B alone, which we call a reduced form "resolving" equation for this model. Solving this equation gives the equilibrium values of p_B from where all other variables can be computed as shown above. The model is thus solved.

We may now study the changes in the terms of trade as a function of the tariff t. By the implicit function theorem:

(43)
$$\partial p_B / \partial t = \frac{-\,\partial F / \partial t}{\partial F / \partial p_B}$$

$$= \frac{-\,(\partial (B^{d,1} - B^{s,1} / \partial\,(p_B + t))}{B^{d,1}/\partial\,(p_B + t) + \partial B^{d,2}/\partial p_B - \partial B^{s,1}/\partial\,(p_B + t) - \partial B^{s,2}/\partial P_B}$$

GRAPH 3

EACH FIRM FACES AN UPWARD COST CURVE.
THE COUNTRY AS A WHOLE FACES A DOWNWARD COST CURVE
DUE TO EXTERNAL ECONOMIES OF SCALE

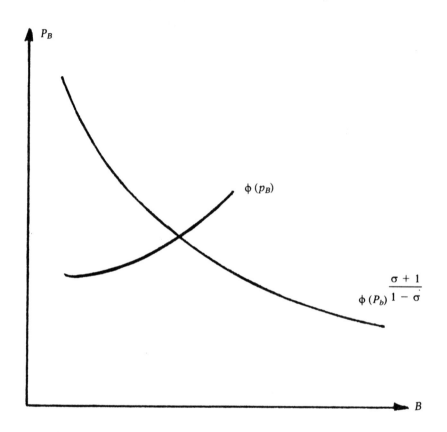

By the assumptions on demand for B, if $\sigma_1 > 1$, then $\partial B^{s,1}/\partial (p_B + t) < 0$ and therefore the numerator of *(43)* is negative. The denominator is also negative, so that $\partial p_B/\partial t > 0$. As the tariff t increases, p_B also increases. The terms of trade of the country decrease, since it imports B and must now pay more for it, as we wished to prove.

BIBLIOGRAPHY

[1] AMELUNG T.: «Tropical Deforestation as an International Economic Problem», Linz (Austria), Egon Sohmen Foundation, Paper presented at the Conference on *Economic Evolution and Environmental Concerns*, August 30-31, 1991.

[2] BARBIER E.B. - BURGER J.C. - MARKANDYA A.: «The Economics of Tropical Deforestation», *Ambio*, vol. 20, n. 2, 1991, pp. 55-8.

[3] BINKLEY C.S. - VINCENT J.R.: «Forest Based Industrialization: a Dynamic Perspective», Washington (D.C.), World Bank, *Forest Policy Issues Paper*, 1990.

[4] CHICHILNISKY G.: «Terms of Trade and Domestic Distribution: Export Led Growth with Abundant Labor», *Journal of Development Economics*, n. 8, 1981, pp. 163-92.

[5] CHICHILNISKY G. - HEAL G.: *The Evolving International Economy*, Cambridge, Cambridge University Press, 1987.

[6] CHICHILNISKY G.: «A General Equilibrium Theory of North-South Trade», Part 1: *Equilibrium Analysis, Essays in Honor of Kenneth Arrow*, Cambridge, Cambridge University Press, 1986, pp. 3-56.

[7] ——: «Global Environment and North-South Trade», Stanford, Stanford Institute for Theoretical Economics, Stanford University, *Technical Report*, n. 31, 1991.

[8] ——: «North-South Trade and the Dynamics of Renewable Resources», Columbia University, *Working Paper*, 1992.

[9] ——: «Customs Unions with Economies of Scale», Columbia University, *Working Paper*, 1992.

[10] DADZIE K.: «Accelerating the Development Process: Challenges for National and International Policies in the 1990's», Report by the Secretary General of UNCTAD to UNCTAD VIII, New York, United Nations Conference on *Trade and Development*, 1991.

[11] HYDE W.F. - NEUMANN D.H.: «Forest Economics in Brief-with Summary Observations for Policy Analysis», Washington (DC), World Bank, First Report on *Agricoltural and Rural Development*, 1991.

[12] KENNAN J. - RIEZMAN R.: «Do Big Countries Win Tariff Wars», *International Economic Review*, vol. 29, n. 1, 1988, pp. 81-5.

[13] —— - ——: «Optimal Tariff Equilibria with Customs Union», *Canadian Journal of Economics*, vol. XXIII, n. 1, 1990, pp. 70-83.

[14] KRUGMAN P.: «The Move to Free Trade Zones», Department of Economics, MIT, *Working Paper*, 1991.

[15] KRUGMAN P. - OBSTFELT M.: *International Economics*, Illinois, Boston, London, Scott, Foresman and Company, 1988.

[16] LERNER A.: «The Symmetry Between Import and Export Taxes», *Economica*, n. 3, 1936, pp. 306-13.

[17] MEADE J.: *The Theory of Customs Unions*, Amsterdam, North-Holland, 1955.

[18] ——: *The Theory of Indicative Planning*, London, Allen Unwin, 1971.

[19] METZLER L.: «Tariffs the Terms of Trade and Distribution of National Income», *Journal of Political Economy*, n. 57, 1949, pp. 1-29.

[20] NICHOLSON W.: *Microeconomic Theory*, Hinsdale (Ill.), The Dryden Press, 1978.

[21] RIEZMAN R.: «Customs Unions and the Core», *Journal of International Economics*, n. 19, 1985, pp. 355-65.

[22] VINER J.: *The Customs Union Issue*, New York, Carnegie Endowment for International Peace.

III - THE COMPLEX CONNECTIONS BETWEEN NORTH AND SOUTH

f1 4

Trade in Primary Products:
Price Instability, Causes and Remedies

David M. Newbery (*)
Cambridge University

1. - Introduction

Table 1 reproduces information from the World Bank's *World Development Report, 1991* on the importance of primary products in the exports of the poorer developing countries in 1965 and in 1989 (the most recent year for which data are available). Although most Asian countries have been able to dramatically decrease their dependence on primary products, Sub-Sahara Africa is still critically dependent on primary products, and so, to a surprising extent is Latin America. The most striking change over this period is the shift in dependence towards "fuels, minerals and metals" and away from "other primary products", reflecting, in part, the dramatic change in the relative price and quantity of petroleum relative to tropical products.

Clearly, many countries are still heavily dependent on primary products, and for them, and possibly for the rest of the world, price instabilities that give rise to income fluctuations have potentially important effects. Nor are poor countries the only ones affected. The value of oil in Norway was estimated at 71% of total wealth for 1980,

(*) Reserarch support under the ESRC grant *The Economics of Missing Markets. Learning and Games* is gratefully acknowledged.

TABLE 1

STRUCTURE OF MERCHANDISE EXPORTS
(percentages weighted averages)

	1965	1989
Low-income economies (*)		
Fuels, minerals, metals	16	25
Other primary commodities	60	23
All primary commodities	76	48
Low-income economies excl. India and Cina		
Fuels, minerals, metals	22	43
Other primary commodities	65	30
All primary commodities	87	73
Sub-Saharian Africa		
Fuels, minerals, metals	24	53
Other primary commodities	68	36
All primary commodities	92	88
Latin America and Caribbean		
Fuels, minerals, metals	43	33
Other primary commodities	50	33
All primary commodities	93	66
Severely indebted countries		
Fuels, minerals, metals	33	29
Other primary commodities	45	29
All primary commodities	78	58

(*) Definitions of country groupings defined in WORLD BANK, 1991.
Source: WORLD BANK, 1991, Table 16.

at a price of oil of $ 16.4 ($ 1980) per barrel (1). At various times since 1980 the forecast price of oil has been twice and half this level in real terms, as Graph 6 below shows, Given that Norwegian oil is costly to extract, the effect of doubling or halving the long run expected price

(1) See ASLAKSEN - BJERKHOLT [1], Table 5. The assumed price of oil was roughly the real price of the period 1975-1980.

of oil would be to more than double or halve the value of oil reserves, indicating that the price of oil has a profound effect on the estimated value of Norway's assets, and hence on her estimated, sustainable consumption level.

Table 2 lists developing countries in the order of dependence on a

TABLE 2

COMMODITY SHARE OF COUNTRY EXPORTS (*)
(average 1982-1984)

Country	Main commodity	Share	Country	Main commodity	Share
Angola........	petroleum	93.0	Fiji	sugar	44.3
Uganda	coffee	93.0	Burma (**) ..	rice	42.4
Congo, P.R. ..	petroleum	88.3	Trin. & Tob...	petroleum	41.8
Burundi	coffee	87.3	Mali	cotton	41.7
Iraq	petroleum	86.9	Sudan	cotton	39.0
Zambia	copper	79.1	Guyana (**) ..	bauxite	38.9
Mexico	petroleum	76.9	Belize........	sugar	38.7
Cuba	sugar	76.2	Madagascar ..	coffee	37.0
Gabon	petroleum	74.4	Swaziland	sugar	36.1
Venezuela	petroleum	72.7	Sri Lanka	tea	36.0
Chad	cotton	69.4	Tanzania	coffee	35.2
Rwanda	coffee	67.8	Paraguay	cotton	33.9
Liberia........	iron ore	63.4	Dom. Rep. ..	sugar	33.5
Egypt,			Central Afr.		
Arab Rep. ..	petroleum	60.8	Rep.	coffee	32.4
El Salvador....	coffee	59.1	Honduras	bananas	31.3
Syrian Arab Rep.	petroleum	56.7	Guatemala....	coffee	31.3
Zaire	copper	54.1	Gambia	groundnuts	30.3
Ecuador	petroleum	53.7	Solomon Is. ..	timber	30.2
Malawi	tobacco	53.2	Haiti	coffee	27.4
Burkina	cotton	51.3	Nicaragua	coffee	26.8
Colombia......	coffee	50.1	Bolivia	tin	26.6
Mauritania	iron ore	49.6	Costa Rica (**)	coffee	26.3
Vanuatu	cocoa	49.1	Ivory Coast ..	cocoa	26.2
Togo	phosphate rock	48.5	Kenya	coffee	26.0
Chile	copper	46.1	Morocco	phosphate rock	25.8
Indonesia	petroleum	45.1	Namibia	copper	25.1
Tunisia	petroleum	44.9			

(*) Countries with single commodity shares above 25%.
(**) Countries whose second largest export commodity also accounts for more than 25%
Source: WORLD BANK, 1988, Table 9.

single primary commodity (down to a level of 25% share of total exports), though as noted in the table, three also have a share of more than 25% on a second commodity. Thus Burma earns 75.5% of its export revenue from two primary commodities, Guyana earns 74.3%, and Costa Rica 52.8%. Coffee, petroleum, copper and sugar are the typical products of such heavily dependent economies. Given the substantial instability in all primary commodity markets, such countries are likely to experience sharp fluctuations in export earnings and their underlying wealth. To the extent that these fluctuations are transmitted to domestic consumption they will be costly, and we would expect the countries to seek ways of managing these risks and reducing their costs.

International commodity prices are notoriously volatile, and there is no evidence that volatility has decreased in the recent past — if anything it has probably increased. Newbery and Stiglitz [16] estimated the price variability of six agricultural primary commodities of importance to LDCs over the period 1951-1975. They estimated the coefficient of variation (*CV*) of prices in a number of different ways. Three measures are of particular relevance. The first is the *CV* of price changes from one year to the next, or, to be precise, the standard deviation of $2 (p_t - p_{t-1})/(p_t + p_{t-1})$. This is a crude measure of the year to year variability. A rather better measure of the unpredictability of commodity price movements is the *CV* of the price forecast errors. Newbery and Stiglitz used a simple first order autoregressive formula to predict prices, but in principle more sophisticated time series methods could be used. One natural choice would be the error in the one-year ahead futures price compared to the eventual spot price. Finally, they gave the *CV* of deviations fron 5-year centred moving averages, which measures the potential reduction in price instability that might be achieved with some time-averaging of prices, and gives a better measure of the deviations fron the underlying time path of prices to which the economy would have to adjust.

They found that the 5-year moving average gave the lowest measures of instability, slightly lower than the forecast errors, that in

---

(*) *N.B.:* The numbers in square brackets refer to the Bibliography at the end of the paper.

TABLE 3

COMMODITY PRICE INSTABILITY, 1950-1986
(coefficient of variation, percentages)

Commodity	1950-1969		1970-1986	
	5-yr MA (*)	price change (**)	5-yr MA	price change
Cocoa	21	25	22	28
Coffee	12	16	24	35
Tea	7	11	19	23
Sugar	35	39	38	47
Cotton......................	6	13	13	19
Jute	20	22	12	18
Rubber	16	24	18	23

(*) 5-year *MA* is the *CV* of deviations from 5-year centred average price.
(**) *Price change* is the standard deviation of $2 (p_t - p_{t-1}) / (p_t + p_{t-1})$.
Source: NEWBERY [15], Table 5.1.

turn were slightly lower than the *CV* of price changes, though the differences were slight. Newbery [15] recently updated estimates of the variability of 7 "soft" commodities, and two measures of price instability are given in Table 3.

Graph 1 gives a typical time series of the real price of coffee between 1900 and 1987 (2).

Graphs of quarterly commodity prices show similar volatility, and most commodity time series exhibit the characteristic spikes with much flatter troughs. Graph 2 shows quarterly sugar prices (deflated by an index of manufacturing unit value) for a recent 30-year period. In both figures, the dotted graph is the plot of the logarithm of prices, so that equal proportional changes are represented by equal vertical displacements, while the continuous line is the plot of actual prices (with the scale shown on the other vertical axis). It shows that the characteristic spikes also appear over shorter time periods, and that

(2) The time series comes from the data of GRILLI - YANG [7], deflated by the US CPI. The aim of the deflator is to make the fluctuations relative to levels reasonably clear, and the reader is cautioned not to draw conclusions about long-run trends which are very sensitive to the choice of deflator.

GRAPH 1

REAL COFFEE PRICES
1900-1989

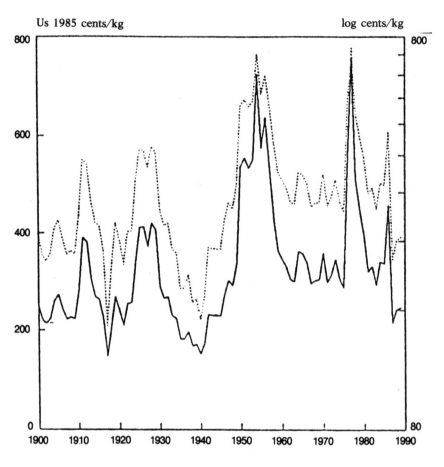

Us 1985 cents/kg   log cents/kg

——— coffee   .... coffee (log price)

Source: WORLD BANK, COMMODITIES DIVISION.

GRAPH 2

SUGAR PRICES 1960-1989
Deflated by MUV

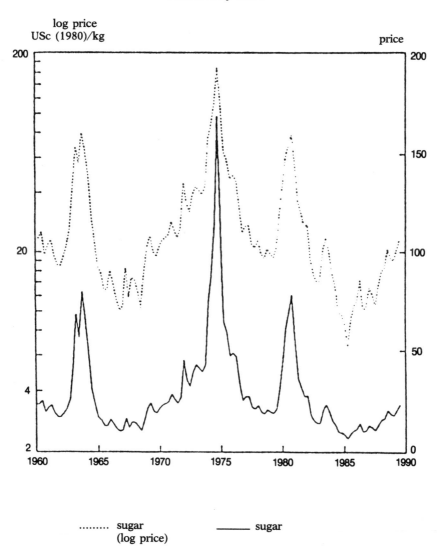

log price
USc (1980)/kg

price

.... sugar
(log price)

———— sugar

Source: WORLD BANK, COMMODITIES DIVISION.

the difference between the spikes and troughs are more pronounced when graphing price levels than the log of price — percentage changes may be more symmetrically distributed than absolute changes from the mean. Note that sugar has more pronounced spikes than coffee, and is also more volatile. This can be seen dramatically in Graphs 3 and 4, where equal vertical displacements indicate equal proportional changes. Both Graphs 3 and 4 give logarithmic plots of real commodity prices for three tropical foodstuffs, and for three non-food stuffs. Notice the wide range of price movements — the y-axis covers a range of 100:1, and the most volatile commodity, sugar, has a peak to trough ratio of almost 40:1. Graph 5 repeats the time series for cocoa, giving both logarithmic (left scale) and arithmetic plots (right scale), with a 10:1 scale rather than the 200:1 scale of Graph 3.

Describing the stochastic properties of these price series is clearly a first step in understanding the nature of volatility and the possibility of measures to offset the harmful effects it might have. If successive annual prices were independently and identically distributed (i.i.d.) about a constant mean, then relatively simple smoothing systems, in particular by lending and borrowing, would be remarkably effective in stabilising revenue streams. At the other extreme, if commodity prices evolved according to a random walk, then any stabilisation would be extremely difficult, for reasons that will be discussed more fully below.

What is the evidence? Cuddington and Urzua [3] have attempted to identify the extent to which price changes of primary commodities persist, using Grilli and Yang's [7] annual data on 24 commodity prices for the period 1900-1987, deflated by an index of manufacturing unit values. They regress the change in the log of the real commodity price on a constant plus error, $e(t)$, which is in turn expressed as $A(L)u(t)$, where $u(t)$ is white noise. Their measure of persistence is then Σa_i, where a_i are the coefficients of $A(L)$, and is a measure of the extent to which the price change will persist. Table 4, reproduced from Cuddington and Urzua [3], gives the persistence measures of three groups of commodities, each group ranked in increasing order of persistence. (It also gives the highest order significant lag for the more parsimonious lag specification). Thus if one looks at cocoa, 65% of a price change is expected to persist, and

GRAPH 3

COMMODITY PRICES 1960-1989
Deflated by MUV

US cents (1980)/kg

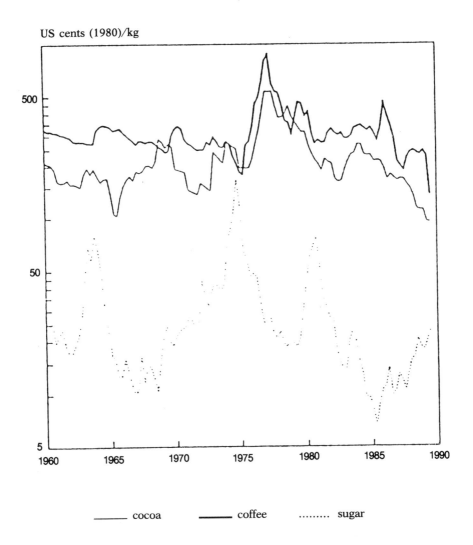

_____ cocoa   _____ coffee   .... sugar

Fonte: WORLD BANK, COMMODITIES DIVISION.

GRAPH 4

COMMODITY PRICES 1960-1989
Deflated by MUV

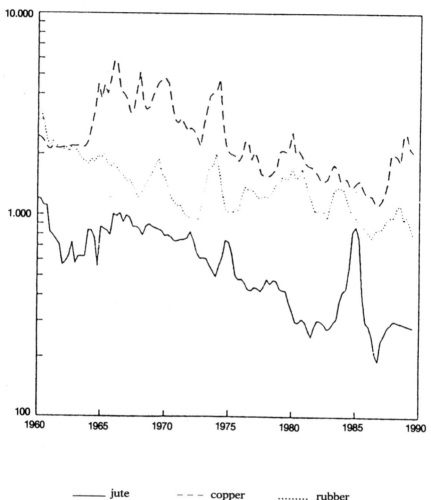

US $ (1980)/Mt

——— jute   – – – copper   .... rubber

Source: WORLD BANK, COMMODITIES DIVISION.

GRAPH 5

COCOA PRICES 1960-1989
Deflated by MUV

US 1985 cents/kg

log cents/kg

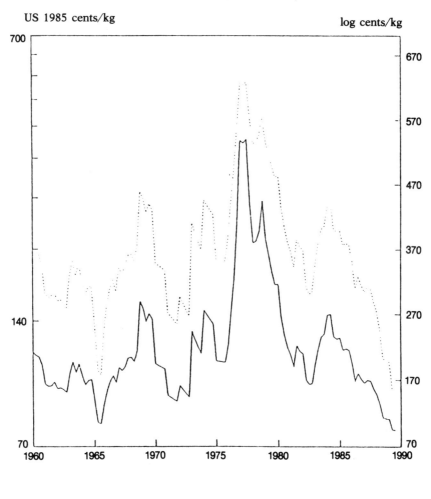

_____ cocoa   .... cocoa (log price)

Source: WORLD BANK, COMMODITIES DIVISION.

TABLE 4

PERSISTENCE OF PRICE SHOCKS, 1900-1987 (*)

Commodity	Persistence		Longest
	autocorr. measure	Deaton PER20	lag years
Rice	0.11	0.18	9
Palm oil	0.13	0.13	5
Coffee	0.38	0.17	11
Bananas	0.45	0.59	10
Wheat	0.46	0.24	10
Sugar	0.52	0.11	6
Cocoa	0.65	0.29	2
Tea	0.72	0.37	2
Beef	1.00	—	—
Maize	1.10	0.19	10
Lamb	1.30	—	4
average	**0.61**	—	**6.28**
Timber	0.10	—	8
Wool	0.35	—	2
Jute	0.40	0.19	5
Hides	0.43	—	2
Cotton	0.67	0.39	3
Tobacco	0.73	—	4
Rubber	1.00	—	—
average	**0.51**	—	**3.43**
Petroleum	0.51	—	11
Silver	0.65	—	8
Tin	0.65	0.43	5
Lead	0.73	—	3
Aluminium	0.93	—	5
Zinc	1.00	0.31	—
Copper	1.00	—	—
Coal	1.00	—	—
average	**0.81**	—	**4.00**

(*) Annual data. The first measure is the sum of the statistically significant autocorrelation coefficient, as calculated by Cuddington and Urzua and explained in the text. Deaton and Laroque's measure of persistence is *PER* 20, given in Table 5, and explained therein. The longest lag is the highest order statistically significant lag.

Sources: CUDDINGTON - URZUA [3], DEATON - LAROQUE [5], Table 2, DEATON - LAROQUE [6], Table 1.

the remaining 35% can be accounted by short term fluctuations, with a maximum (statistically significant) lag of two years.

In each group the average persistence is over 50%, and for many commodities prices seem to follow a random walk with persistence of 100%. It was impossible to reject the null hypothesis that all commodity price series followed a random walk using the (rather weak) statistical tests available. One must interpret this rather careful-ly, for even if it is hard to reject the hypothesis that commodity price follow random walks, there are no plausible theories which suggest that these prices should follow random walks, and rather good arguments why eventually they should return to an equilibrium determined by demand and supply.

Deaton and Laroque [6] have also studied this problem, using more sophisticated methods, but the same commodity price data. Their measures of persistence are the sum of all autocorrelation coefficients (whether significant or not), with the sums being linearly declining weighted averages over the window widths of 20 or 40 years. Their results are reported in Table 5.

Where the same commodity appears in both studies the measures of persistence from both studies are given in Table 4. In some cases the agreement is close — thus either 45 or 59% of the price shock in bananas is persistent, similarly for rice and palm oil. For others the differences are considerable, with Deaton and Laroque's (more reli-able) measures tending to be lower than those of Cuddington and Urzua, which Deaton and Laroque argue are likely on statistical grounds to be biassed upwards. If one takes the Cuddington and Urzua evidence then perhaps one-half of price shocks are persistent for many of the important export crops of developed countries. If one takes Deaton and Laroque's estimates then about one-quarter of price shocks are permanent. Even in this case, though Table 4 shows the high first-order autocorrelations, so three-quarters or more of the price shocks will persist for at least a year, and even after two years typically 60% of the price shock will persist. The evidence suggests, therefore, that serial correlation is prevalent for the world prices of summary commodities, and this fact should be taken into account in designing methods for consumption smoothing.

How can the characteristic features of commodity price fluctu-

TABLE 5

VARIABILITY AND PERSISTENCE
OF ANNUAL COMMODITY PRICES, 1900-1987 (*)

Commodity	CV	AR1	AR2	PER20	PER40
Bananas	0.17	0.91	0.82	0.59	0.52
Cocoa	0.54	0.83	0.66	0.29	0.24
Coffee	0.45	0.80	0.62	0.17	0.11
Copper	0.38	0.84	0.64	0.31	0.22
Cotton........................	0.35	0.88	0.68	0.39	0.13
Jute	0.33	0.71	0.45	0.19	0.09
Maize	0.38	0.76	0.53	0.19	0.10
Palm oil	0.48	0.73	0.48	0.13	0.05
Rice..........................	0.36	0.83	0.61	0.18	0.08
Sugar	0.60	0.62	0.39	0.11	0.06
Tea	0.26	0.78	0.59	0.37	0.28
Tin	0.42	0.90	0.76	0.43	0.18
Wheat........................	0.38	0.86	0.68	0.24	0.11

(*) *CV* is the coefficient of variation. *AR1* and *AR2* are the first and second order autocorrelation coefficients of the deflated series of prices. *PER20* and *PER40* are the Campbel-Mankiw-Cochrane measures of persistence with window widths of 20 and 40 years. Deaton and Laroque [6] give only *PER40*, together with measures of skewness and kurtosis.

Source: Deaton - Laroque [5], Table 2, Deaton - Laroque [6], Table 1.

ations be explained? Most commodities can be stored, and have active futures markets that allow the risks of storage to be shifted onto speculators. Price variability provides a motive for buying when cheap, storing in the expectation of selling at a higher future price. When the price falls, the incentive is to remove some supply from the market for a speculative storage and to arbitrage prices. On the other hand, if stocks are depleted when demand is strong, then the physical fact that storage cannot be negative prevents the price being damped by sales from storage. Storage therefore provides a simple explanation for the spikes in the price series, which correspond to stock-outs, and the rounded valleys, which correspond to periods in which excess supply is accumulated as inventories.

If demand is deterministic and static, and the supply process stochastic, then an optimal storage rule can be numerically calculated, following the path-breaking work by Gustafson [9]. Newbery and

Stiglitz [16] [17] developed analytical techniques for special cases, and numerical approximation techniques for other cases. Williams and Wright [25] give the mots comprehensive treatment of modelling storage using Monte Carlo simulation and curve fitting techniques, while Deaton and Laroque [6] develop a different computer-based solution algorithm for the same problem. Both Williams and Wright ([25], p. 159), and Deaton and Laroque [6] then calculate the effect on uncorrelated production disturbances of storage and show that plausible auto-correlations can be induced by optimal storage. Thus Williams and Wright [25] show that with a linear demand schedule of elasticity -0.2 at the pre-storage mean price, and with inelastic supply with a coefficient of variations of output of 10%, zero storage costs and 5% interest rate, the best estimate of the first order auto-correlation in prices induced by optimal storage is 0.467, comparable to that for sugar. Deaton and Laroque [6] Table 2, report similar results, though it is worth pointing out that to achieve high auto-correlations, very inelastic demands are required which in turn imply high price variability in the absence of storage (50% in this case). In this case storage reduces the *CV* of price from 50% to 27% (Williams and Wright [25], Table 4.1, p. 110). As a very rough rule, optimal storage appears to halve the unstabilised coefficient of variation, and hence reduce the costs of instability by three-quarters (3).

Deaton and Laroque use their storage model to interpret time series price data and estimate the parameters of the storage rule. As they point out, most of the identification arises from the very infrequent periods of stock-out when prices rise in a spike, and efficient estimation requires very long time series of the order of hundreds of years. Given the relatively short run price series data available, the precision of estimates is quite low, but they claim reasonable support for the explanatory power of their model of storage in explaining the resulting variability of prices. The main weakness of their model is that it suggest implausibly low discount rates (the rate of interest plus the storage costs amount to typically less than 2% per annum) and

---

(3) If demand is stationary and deterministic, and mean output unchanged, then the average price is well-defined (though it may be affected by storage), and the *CV* is measured relative to this mean price. Deaton and Laroque's measures of the *CV* are similarly relative to the average real price for the entire time series.

rather lower implied serial correlation than that observed. Williams and Wright show that if weather is auto-correlated, then storage will typically be lower, and price auto-correlations higher, and would go some way to accounting for the very high observed price auto-correlations. An unexplored, but potentially quite important additional explanatory factor must be the serial correlation in income shifting demand, especially for the pro-cyclical fuels, minerals and metals.

At this point one should also ask whether producer cartel behaviour influences the stochastic properties of the price time series. Graph 6 shows two natural candidates for significant cartel behaviour — for oil, where OPEC became a key player in 1973, and for phosphate rock, where Morocco and Florida together have a dominant market position. Again, both price levels and log prices are graphed, the former to note the distinctive time series properties, and the latter to show the proportional price changes more clearly. What is striking is that the oil price exhibits three step changes (up in 1974 and 1980, down in 1986) with plateaus in between (and gradual real price declines as the $ deflator rises), whereas phosphate rock a price spike like the other more competitively supplied commodities, though perhaps with a more sluggish price fall after the spike. One possible interpretation is that for cartelized commodities there may be an attempt to resist price declines, either by greater storage or by production controls. Newbery [18] shows that cartels may be prepared to undertake greater price stabilisation via storage than would occur on competitive markets, though they will be equally helpless in preventing the price associated with stock-outs. Another possible explanation is that the ability of a cartel to operate effectively depends on the tightness of market conditions, and is facilitated by an increase in demand relative to supply. Once established, collusion might persist until weakening market conditions precipitate cheating, which might in turn precipitate a trigger response to competitive behaviour (Green and Porter [10]).

To summarize, the observed complexity and time series properties of the prices of competitively supplied primary commodities con in considerable part be explained by two crucial features of primary commodity markets — that the commodity can be stored by forward-looking agents, and that aggregate storage cannot be negative. To-

GRAPH 6

OIL AND PHOSPHATE ROCK
Deflated by MUV

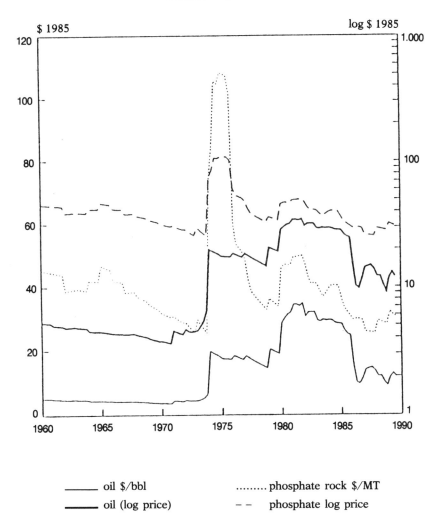

—— oil $/bbl	········ phosphate rock $/MT
—— oil (log price)	– – phosphate log price

Source: WORLD BANK, COMMODITIES DIVISION.

gether these features enable price falls to be buffered but are intermittently incapable of resisting sharp price rises, in accordance with the evidence. For cartelized commodities the subsequent price falls after the sudden price spikes may be muted.

2. - The Costs of Income Variability

The cost of risk can be estimated if we are prepared to accept the normative version of the *Expected Utility Hypothesis* (Newbery and Stiglitz [16]). According to this hypothesis, there is no difference in the present value of utility of a stream of consumption, c_t, which varies in a predictable way, and one which takes the same values at each date, but whose values were not known initially. There is, however, an important difference between two identical but variable income streams, y_t, one known in advance, and the other unknown. If income is predictable, then it is possible to compute its present value, and to determine the optimum time path of consumption permitted by this certain value and the opportunities available for lending and borrowing. If income is uncertain, then such precise consumption smoothing is not possible, and the achievable time path of consumption will have lower value than in the former case (4).

With this in mind, consider the problem of calculating the cost of risk for a country that has economically unresponsive production ("zero supply elasticity") and which seeks to maximize the expected utility of its representative consumer:

$$(1) \qquad\qquad V_t = \sum_{t=0}^{\infty} \beta^t U(c_t)$$

where E is the expectations operator, c_t is consumption in period t, and U is utility, concave in consumption. The rate at which utility is discounted is r, where $\beta = 1/(1+r)$. Using standard formulas for the

(4) The psychological costs of uncertainty as opposed to variability may not be so small, for a variety of reasons, not least of which is the frequent failure of the expected utility theory to predict behaviour by failing to accurately model perceptions of risk. Whether these costs are real or based on mis-perception is of course the key issue in determining the welfare basis of the expected utility hypothesis (*EUH*). The maintained hypothesis here is that these psychological costs are based on mis-perceptions, and that the *EUH* properly measures the actual welfare costs.

cost of risk (Newbery and Stiglitz [16]), if the coefficient of (partial) relative risk is R (defined for annual variations in consumption), and if the coefficient of variation (CV) of consumption σ_c, then the annual cost of risk, ρ, is defined implicity by $U(\bar{c}-\rho)=EU(c_t)$, where a bar over a variable indicates its expected value, and the relative cost, $\rho/\bar{c}$, is approximately $\frac{1}{2} R\sigma_c^2$.

Consider what these formulas imply for the magnitudes of the costs of market risk by consumers and the benefits of risk reduction. Newbery [20] updated earlier estimates of the variability of 7 *soft* commodities, and found that price variability had increased some-what when comparing the period 1970-1986 with the period 1950-1969. The unweighted average coefficient of variation (CV) of prices was estimated to be 22% (5). The cost of price instability increases as the *square* of the CV, which means that a consumer completely specialised in production of jute with a 12% and with no output uncertainty and no variable inputs, has a CV of income of 12%. If income is entirely consumed each period, the cost of risk to this consumer, assuming a coefficient of relative risk aversion $R=2$, is about 1.4% of income. Were the product coffee, with a CV of 24%, the cost of risk is four times as high, that is around 6%, not twice as costly, as the figure for the CV might tend to suggest. If the coffee export had a mean share α of consumer's income, the rest of which was essentially deterministic, the cost would be a $6\alpha^2$%. We can explore the practical magnitudes of the cost of risk and its reduction in four countries highly dependent on a single primary export, using the data in Table 6.

The exercise answers the following question. What would be the effect on the variability of commodity export revenue and of total export revenue, assuming that the price of the commodity received by the country was equal to a price stabilised at a weighted average of the current and previous four year's real world price level, with linearly declining weights? The levels of export are assumed to be unchanged, and the export unit values are assumed to change in line with commodity prices. The scheme might have an international

---

(5) Calculated as the root mean square of the average of the squared percentage deviations form the centred five year moving average of prices.

TABLE 6

EFFECTS OF STABILIZING COMMODITY PRICES, 1961-1988

Country/commodity	Average share of commodity in GDP (1)	exp. (2)	Coefficients of variation commodity revenue/total exp. unstab (3)	stab (4)	unstab (5)	stab (6)	Risk benefit of stabilisation income from: com. (7)	exp. (8)
Copper exporters								
Chile	14	62	18	9	17	13	2.4	1.2
Zambia	34	91	21	11	22	15	3.2	2.6
Coffee exporters								
Brazil	4	26	22	14	14	13	2.9	0.3
Colombia	7	58	15	14	10	9	0.3	0.2

Legend:
(1) 1984 share of commodity exports in GDP
(2) is the unweighted average of the annual shares of commodity exports in total export revenue
(3) is the SD of percentage deviations from centred 5-yr MA commodity export value
(4) is the SD of percentage deviations from 5-yr MA commodity export revenue valuing the exports at prices stabilised at their backward 5-yr MA level
(5) as for (3) but for total export revenue
(6) as for (5) but assuming commodities are sold at stabilised prices
(7) $\frac{1}{2}R\Delta\sigma^2$, where $\Delta\sigma^2$ is the change in the CV^2 from cols (3) and (4), and $R=2$.
(8) As (7) but from cols (5) and (6).
Source: IMF, World Bank Commodities Division for commodity price data, 1991.

commodity stabilisation manager who would first calculate the stabilised price from the available data. The difference between the stabilised and spot price would be transferred to the country (rather as is done under Stabex but not as a loan, and with the contractual implication that if the spot price exceeded the stabilised price the country would transfer money to the stabilisation manager). The crucial feature of this stabilization scheme is that it can be implemented using observed data. Whether it would be feasible raises questions of default risk, considered below.

Table 6 shows that stabilizing the price of copper halves the variability of copper export revenue (and thus lowers the cost of that variability to one-quarter), and has a somewhat smaller effect on the variability of total export revenue. (Variability in this case is measured as the standard deviation (*SD*) of percentage deviations from the

GRAPH 7

STABILIZING ZAMBIA'S COPPER PRICE
PERCENT DEVIATION FROM 5 YR MA (*)

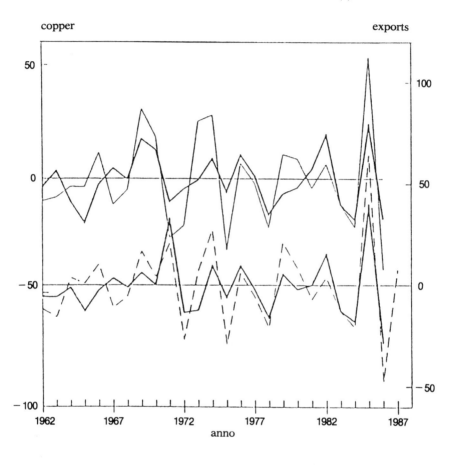

exports RHS   exports stabilised
copper Rev LHS   copper stabilised

(*) Deflated by MUV.

GRAPH 8

STABILIZING BRAZIL'S COFFEE PRICE
PERCENT DEVIATION FROM 5 YR MA (*)

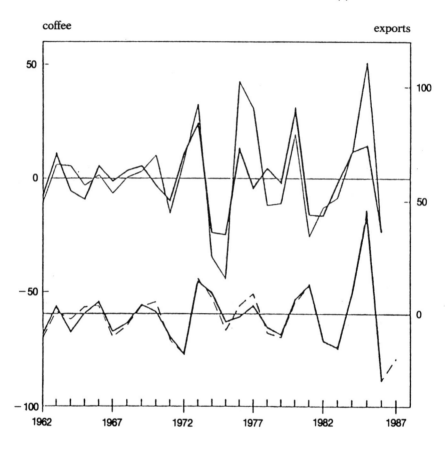

coffee   exports

- -   exports RHS   ——— exports stabilised
———   coffee Rev LHS   ——— coffee stabilised

(*) Deflated by MUV.

centred five year real moving average export revenue (effectively the *CV*). It is an *ex post* measure of the welfare benefits). Graphs 7 and 8 show the effect of stabilizing the price of copper for Zambia and coffee for Brazil. (The former is an extreme example of a country heavily dependent on one primary commodity, the latter shows the large effect of spreading the risk over all exports). The graphs give the percentage deviations from the centred 5 year moving average, and the graphs of deviations of commodity exports and total exports are displaced vertically to make it easier to see what is going on — commodity deviations are shown on the left-hand scale and total exports are on the right — hand scale. The graphs have been scaled to be directly comparable, and the prices have been deflated by the index of manufactured unit value of exports to LDCs. Powell [22] comes to a similar conclusion that price stabilisation has a rather smaller effect than might be expected for Zambia.

Stabilizing the price of coffee reduces the variability of Brazil's coffee export revenue by one third (and almost halves the cost) but has a rather small effect on the variability of Colombia's coffee revenue. It has a smaller effect still on the variability of total export revenue for both countries (though the levels of total export variability are not particularly high in any case). The final two columns give the *ex post* risk benefits of this stabilisation policy, relative to commodity revenue and total export revenue, for a value of R of 2. They are surprisingly small. Col 1 gives the share of the commodity in total GDP, and if stabilisation had no effect on the other components of GDP (a strong assumption), then spreading commodity price risks evenly over the whole economy would greatly reduce their cost (to between 1 and 10% of the values of col 7). However, for various reasons we do not observe full domestic diversification, and for heavily indebted countries, we are interested in the benefits of stabilizing imports. We therefore look for other solutions.

3. - Remedies for Price Instability

Kletzer, Newbery and Wright [14] considered the problem of a consumer choosing an intertemporal consumption plan to maximise

(1). In the special case of quadratic utility in which the consumer can freely lend and borrow at the same rate of interest, r, as he discounts future utility they showed that the optimal consumption at date t, c_t, satisfied:

$$(2) \qquad\qquad c_t = r\,\beta(D_t + y_t) + \beta\,E_t y_{t+1}$$

where D_t is the bank balance at the start of period t, and $\beta = 1/(1+r)$. If $D_0 = 0$, this equation can be written:

$$(3) \qquad c_t = \beta\,E_t\,y_{t+1} + r\beta\left(\sum_{i=0}^{t-1}(y_{t-i} - E_{t-i-1}\,y_{t-i}) + y_0\right)$$

Thus consumption varies directly with accumulated balances, which follow a martingale process. If output stable and commodity prices followed a stationary i.i.d. process, then so would income, and the optimal consumption path would be one of constant consumption:

$$(4) \quad c_{t+i} = E_{t+i-1}\,y_{t-i} = E_t\,y_{t+1} = c_t, \qquad i = 0,\,1,\,2,\,3,\,...$$

But what if y is serially correlated? In the extreme case of a random walk, no such intertemporal tradeoff can be anticipated. The standard argument (e.g. Hall [12]; Davidson *et Al.* [4]) is that consumption should follow a random walk if there are no adjustment costs, and this would seem to be the implication of *(3)*. For such cases, lending and borrowings are of little apparent use.

Kletzer, Newbery and Wright [14] point out that if both lenders and borrowers could commit themselves fully to any future pattern of transfers, and if lenders were risk-neutral, then even in the case of commodity prices following a pure random walk, it would be possible to transfer all the risk to the lending country, and to completely stabilise consumption at its initial level, $c_o = y_o$. The commodity producer would need to agree to transfer to the lender full title to future income streams from the commodity, in return for a constant income stream of y_o. The two income streams would have the same expected present value of y_o/r at date 0. Full commitment by both parties is necessary, as the present value of the commodity sales in any subsequent year will be y_t / r which will almost surely differ from the initial present value of the contract y_0 / r, giving one side or the other an incentive to renegotiate. A series of one-periods loans allows parties to renegotiate each period, and so cannot replicate the stabilisation properties of full commitment. Normal lending and borrowing are thus unable to achieve optimal consumption smoothing if commodity prices are serially correlated.

Of course, it is hard to imagine a contract of the type considered above, in which the lender effectively nationalises the commodity export, as it violates the sovereignty of the commodity exporter. It does, however, point to the potentially large benefits from full contractual commitment, and suggest that any proposed stabilisation scheme should be checked to see if it makes unreasonable assumptions about commitment possibilities between sovereign nations, or between nationals in different jurisdictions. In this context, consider the possibility of using futures markets to smooth consumption, for the moment making the assumption that both parties to the futures contract can commit themselves to satisfactory contract performance. Whether this is reasonable will be considered once the form of the optimal hedging contract has been derived.

3.1 *Hedging Commodity Price Risks on Futures Markets*

For a discussion of future contracts, it is useful to begin defining some notation. Let p_t be the spot price at harvest in year t; $F_{t,j}$ be the futures price for delivery after harvest in year t at date $j \le t$; $b_t = p_t - F_{t,t}$ be the contemporaneous basis; $f_t \equiv F_{t,t-1}$ be the futures price at start of year t; and $f_{t+1} - f_t$ be the intertemporal basis. Trading in future markets exposes producers to two different kinds of risk, both confusingly called basis risk. Contemporaneous basis risk arises because the producer who has sold futures to hedge output typically liquidates this by buying them back in the terminal month, and selling his output. If the terminal futures price were equal to the spot price there would be no risk; but in general this is not true, so *ex ante* the producer faces the risk that the two prices will not be the same that is, he faces basis risk. Wile this basis is the stuff on which futures markets survive or perish, the risk involved is small compared to the risk of not hedging for most producers (i.e. those for which the futures market offers an appropriate contract). For countries exporting primary commodities, many are selling on forward contracts that are linked to terminal future prices, for which there is clearly no such basis risk. We shall therefore ignore this type of risk, and assume that $b_t = 0$, or $F_{t,t} = p_t$. We shall also adopt the convention that $Ex_t \equiv E_{t-1}x_t$, and assume that the futures market is unbiased, so that $f_t \equiv E_{t-1}p_t$. As we are assuming no output uncertainty, with credible commitment on both sides, full smoothing is achieved by selling all production forward one period. If the hedging is starting *de novo* in year t, this full smoothing starts in year $t+1$. If prices are i.i.d. then futures prices at the start of the year will always be the same and full consumption stabilisation results, as with lending and borrowing.

Commodity prices, as argued above, are strongly serially correlated, while futures markets only extend forward about a year, so simple hedging would not stabilise consumption from year to year and runs into the same problems as lending and borrowing. Is it possible to do better?

Suppose prices follow the following simple autorepressive scheme:

$$(5) \qquad\qquad p_t = \alpha p_{t-1} + (1-\alpha)\,\bar{p} + \bar{u}$$

where $\tilde{u}_t$ is i.i.d. with zero mean, and is the forecast error at the start of year t. Given our assumptions on the futures price, this can be written as

$$p_t = f_t + \tilde{u}_t, \qquad f_t = E_{t-1}p_t + (1-\alpha)\,\bar{p}$$

Notice that the "intertemporal basis", $f_{t+1} - f_t = \alpha(p_t - p_{t-1})$, now becomes significant because it will fluctuate from year to year, possibly substantially. Even if futures markets extend only one year ahead and incur transactions cost, it is possible to roll over hedges to provide additional income smoothing to that achievable within the crop year. The appendix shows how to construct a sequence of roll-over hedges in the futures market that provides considerable risk reduction and insurance against this basis risk.

The way the roll-over works is to sell more futures initially than needed for one-period hedging, and then use the surplus futures sales to finance the next year's futures transactions. This is not perfect, for the amount of hedging required next year will depend on production, and that will depend on the futures price prevailing next year, not as yet known. Consequently, despite the absence of production risk, future output cannot be perfectly hedged, and there remains some residual risk (as there would be if there were output risk). Nevertheless, because the cost of risk increases with the square of the deviation, reducing the risk by a given fraction reduces the cost of risk by more than that fraction and can be worthwhile.

The appendix shows how to construct a rolling n-period hedge for the special case of no output risk, but with supply responsive to futures prices. The model has a linear supply schedule (linear in the futures price, which is the action certainty equivalent price in the absence of output risk). In year t, production q_t is planned, and at the start of the year $q_t [1 + \alpha\beta + \ldots + (\alpha\beta)^{n-1}]$ hedges are sold on the futures market. Hedging for longer periods reduces risk, but requires additional purchases of hedges, but higher transactions costs. The formula for the marginal benefit/cost ratio in increasing the period of hedging from $n-1$ to n (and the number of hedges by $(\alpha\beta)^{n-1}$), when each extra futures contract costs μ is:

$$\frac{(\alpha\beta)^{n-1}(1 + \alpha\beta)R\sigma^2}{(1+\beta)(1-\alpha\beta)\mu}$$

The optimal length of the hedge, n, is given by:

$$n = 1 + 1n\left(\frac{\mu(1+\beta)(1-\alpha\beta)}{(1+\alpha\beta)R\sigma^2}\right) / 1n(\alpha\beta)$$

Clearly, as the time horizon of the hedge increases, the marginal benefit also falls. Table 7 relates optimal hedge length to the value of the serial correlation coefficient, α, the rate of interest, r, and the

TABLE 7

OPTIMAL HEDGE LENGTH

σ	0.1		0.15	
r % pa	5	10	5	10
σ	Optimal hedge length (years)			
0.1	1	1	1	1
0.3	1	1	2	2
0.5	3	2	4	3
0.7	6	5	8	7
0.8	10	8	13	11
0.9	21	15	26	19
0.95..................	36	22	44	28

forecast error, σ, when the coefficient of relative risk aversion is 1, and the transaction costs as a fraction of the value of the hedge is 0.3 of 1% — a figure taken from Gardner [11]. The table shows that if $\alpha = 0.7$, $\sigma = 0.10$, and $r = 10\%$, then it would be worth setting $n = 5$, and at $\alpha = 0.8$, n should be 8. But is clear that the value of such hedging (on the favourable assumption of no output risk) is quite low, as transaction costs are low and the benefit-cost ratio is in terms of these transaction costs. Higher transactions costs would shorten the horizon over which hedging was cost-effective.

The other point to make is that the number of hedges rises with the horizon, which would increase the risk of performance default if the contracts did not require payment of margin calls as the future price changes, to cover any change in the value of the contract. The transaction costs calculated by Gardner include the foregone interest rate differential on the money left on deposit to cover margin calls, and this can be thought of as ensuring contract performance. A two-period version of this arrangement would be in effect a commodity bond, a combination of a futures hedge and a loan on the proceeds. The loan would be used as a performance bond to ensure that the hedger delivers on the contract, were the latter not liquidated by the offsetting trade. But this just shifts the commitment issue back one step. What ensures repayment of the loan? Until recently, the financial literature on commodity bonds (Brennan and Schwartz [2]; Schwartz [24]; O'Hara [21]; Priovolos and Duncan [23] chapters 2-7) like the literature on futures markets, has neglected the commitment issue; but that is central to the discussion of intertemporal international transactions.

Kletzer, Newbery and Wright [14] examine the case of smoothing the consumption of a sovereign less developed primary commodity exporter (LDC). If the LDC borrows and lends to smooth consumption, then its debt may rise to the point that it would be more attractive to default on the debt than to continue to enjoy access to the developed country capital markets that offer these smoothing services. Knowing this, lenders will be unwilling to make unqualified loans in states in which the risk of default is non-zero. They derive the optimal state-contingent contract of loan and repayments subject to the borrowing country finding it unattractive to default. They consider the case of pure price uncertainty with income $y = p\bar{q}$, where $\bar{q}$ is fixed output. The exporter is tempted to default whenever her expected utility from consuming her income in the current and every future period (after she observes the current price) exceeds the utility she expects to receive from maintaining access to consumption-smoothing by paying her creditors. Since the borrower is risk-averse, she will be willing to pay more to preserve access to consumption-smoothing from abroad when her income is high than when it is low. In equilibrium, the borrower is willing to pay nothing in the lowest income state to avoid permanent exclusion from credit markets, but in the equilibrium smoothing relationship she is never expected to do so. As her income rises, her willingness to pay increases, so that in this sense the costs of default increase with income. But so does the temptation to default. The high-income states are the states in which she is expected to pay for the smoothing she receives in lower states.

They show that if the price process follows a Markov chain, and satisfies certain first-order stochastic dominance conditions (both of which would be satisfied by the mean-reverting autoregressive scheme of *(5)*), then consumption levels will be allowed to gradually ratchet up to some long-run sustainable level, and will therefore not in general completely smoothed. They also show that how to construct a commodity bond from a one-period simple loan and a put option for the exporter, that can achieve smoothing qualitatively similar to, but less efficient than the (in practice less liquid) constrained optimal state-contingent contract for Markovian price processes.

4. - International Stabilization Schemes

The dramatic price falls in the mid-1970s, and the evident success of OPEC in raising oil price (both shown in the graphs) lead to rewened calls for international action to stabilise commodity prices at "fair" levels. The Integrated Program for Commodities (IPC) was to set up buffer stocks to stabilise prices by storage. What is the case for such coordinated international action? In a world of well-informed, rational, risk-neutral and competitive agents, the competitive level of storage undertaken in response to profitable arbitrage opportunities would provide the efficient level of price stabilization, in the absence of any macro-economic externalities (Newbery [19]). Indeed, an earlier section argued for the importance of private storage in accounting for the characteristic shape of commodity price time series, while the prevalence of futures markets for these commodities does much to disseminate information and reduce risk (especially in storage, where it is likely to be most damaging), making the world more closely approximate the ideal required for the efficiency of private storage.

If many primary exporters are debt constrained and unable to buffer their income fluctuations it no longer follows that a competitive storage market and set of futures markets will provide the efficient level of consumption smoothing to these exporters. Is there a case for international price stabilisation as a surrogate for a decentralised market solution in this case? Private lenders would not be willing to lend as much as might be needed to prevent consumption falling in periods of low commodity prices, as the temptation to default is greater in such periods. There would therefore seem to be a *prima facie* case for additional buffering or lending in these periods. The first point to note is that the IMF does lend on concessional terms to countries when commodity prices are low (via the Compensatory

Financial Facility or CFF), though such loans are presumably not available if the country is in default to the IMF. One possible response might be to make the CFF take the form of a non-repayable grant to poor countries whenever the commodity price falls below some pre-determined real level.

This might be cheaper than the alternative of attempting to increase the degree of price stabilisation by subsidising storage, though the costs of the two should be compared. (Note that providing storage subsidies but leaving storage in the private sector should be cheaper than the alternative of setting up an international buffer stock scheme, as if it were to achieve greater price stabilisation than the free market it would have to make private storage unprofitable, in which case all private stocks wuold be effectively transferred into public ownership. This would almost certainly raise the cost of achieving even the original level of storage, and reduce the efficiency of intervention by the wrong choice of intervention rule. See Newbery and Stiglitz ([16], ch. 30). Subsidising storage has the potential attraction that some of the extra stocks would be sold during periods of high prices at a profit, partially offsetting the costs of greater storage during periods of low prices. The extra storage would almost certainly change the average price received, possibly to the detriment of exporters. The direct costs of the storage subsidy would be the subsidy per unit stored times the new (average) total equilibrium level of storage. The direct cost of CFF grants can similarly be readily calculated. Their impact will be definitely to lower the average commodity price through reducing the risk of adverse outcomes, thereby raising the average return to producing the commodity and increasing supply. The degree of consumption smoothing could also be calculated, though the calculation would have to take account of the optimal policy for the LDC given the chosen form of intervention. The costs of the schemes can therefore be compared with the risk benefits (of consumption smoothing), taking account of any transfers of revenue caused by changes in average prices realised.

The market failure justifying this form of international intervention derives from the inability of countries to commit themselves to long-term financial contracts. There are additional market failures that might also justify international intervention. One, considered by

Newbery and Stiglitz ([16], ch. 30), is the absence of an adequate set of insurance markets. It is difficult to argue that this is quantitatively serious, given the existence of futures markets, though if access to futures markets is denied because of debt constraints, then the market failure is subsumed under the problem of commitment, discussed above. The more serious one is that of macro-economic disequilibrium precipitated by the income and demand fluctuations caused by commodity price instability. Kaldor [13] provided an early example for a "North-South" model of macro-economic interactions. He supposed that the South specialised in primary commodities while the North specialised in manufactures. If commodity prices fell, so would income in the South, and with it demand for manufactures. The fall in demand would not result in a new equilibrium set of market clearing prices being established, because it was argued that (real) manufactured price were sticky (presumably ultimately because of the stickiness of real wages in the North), and instead output would fall with demand, creating Keynesian unemployment. Conversely, if commodity prices rose excessively, there would be inflationary (wage) pressure in the North, inducing governments there to respond with tight monetary and fiscal policy, also creating unemployment. If commodity prices could be stabilised, then developed countries could maintain full(er) employment, average demand for primary commodities would be higher, and both North and South would benefit from higher average incomes. The micro-economic deadweight losses associated with price fluctuations are typically small triangles, and are unlikely to exceed 1% of GDP, whereas output fluctuations could easily amount to average output being 3-5% below full capacity.

Kaldor's argument raises several questions — was this ever a good description of North-South trade and macroeconomic instability, and is it now? Is it feasible to buffer the kind of instabilities that have large macro costs? There is certainly an element of plausibility in noting that the depression of 1930s led to dramatic falls in primary commodity prices, which, together with the possibly induced protectionism, caused a collapse of trade that magnified the consequences of the depression. By 1989, however, the share of primary commodities in world imports has fallen to 27%, of which about one third is petroleum (World Bank, 1991) (6). There is no doubt that large changes in the price of oil can and did have large macro-economic effects, but no other single commodity comes close to oil in importance. Thus, if we take 1982-1984 average world export values, timber and wheat at $ 16 billion each are the two largest after oil, while sugar and coffee are next with about $ 10 billion each, out of world exports of $ 1,225 billion, and oil exports of $ 241 billion (World Bank, 1988). Thus the larger non-oil primary products amount to about 1% of total world trade.

As oil is the largest commodity, it is worth asking whether oil shocks might have been alleviated by international agreements. It is hard to see how these would have evolved given the acute geo-political and strategic nature of oil trade, well summarised in Yergin [27]. Whether the importing countries acting in consort through the IEA with controlled releases from strategic oil reserves would be able to prevent major disruptions in the future remains untested, as the IEA programme, which requires a shortfall of 5% to be triggered, has not yet been invoked. The more serious problem would seem to be that as an exhaustive resource, the price of oil depends heavily on expectations of future scarcity, so that sudden changes in expectations can have quite long-term impacts on the price level, and lead to considerable persistence of price shocks, as revealed by Graph 6. The natural mechanism for dealing with short-run fluctuations, namely borrowing and running trade deficits, worked well in the short run in 1974-1975, but rapidly lead to debt problems for LDCs as the price proved more persistent than expected. Kaldor's macro-economic costs of resisting the inflationary impact of oil prices were very evident in OECD countries.

It is hard to think of other primary commodities for which price rises might have anything like the same magnitude, if only because price spikes are typically far less persistent, and hence can better be buffered by borrowing. To the extent that they are caused by excess demand (as in the Korean war boom) the consequent macro-

---

(6) The share of primary commodities in world trade for 1984 was 38% of which just over half was petroleum, showing again the effects of oil and other price changes (World Bank, 1988).

economic adjustments are less induced by the price rise than the underlying excess demand, and buffering the prices would not cure this problem (though it might reduce its severity somewhat).

Do commodity price falls have adverse effects on the North by leading to a fall in demand for manufactured goods by LDCs? Certainly, most commodity prices have been historically low for the past decade, but again, there is a problem of disentangling cause and effect. LDC demand for manufactures can be sustained by lending, provided LDCs are not too heavily indebted. The problem of the past decade is primarily the problem of the LDC debt burden, which has been made worse by the fall in LDC earnings resulting from the fall in commodity prices. Indeed, by forcing countries to increase exports, the debt problem may have encouraged LDCs to increase primary exports excessively, further driving down their prices. In 1989, LDCs' share of primary commodities in total merchandise exports was 47% (Table 1), and interest payments on debt were 10.8% (World Bank, 1991). If primary commodity prices were 25% below "normal" (7), the loss of income implied by this shortfall is about 16% of total exports, or substantially greater than the currently high interest payments. The figures for the "severely indebted countries" identified by the World Bank would be a loss of income of 19% compared to interest payments of 16.3% of exports. Ignoring oil, the figures might be halved, but still very substantial.

The costs of placing sufficient commodity into buffer stocks to drive the prices up by the 33% needed to restore "normality" if the price elasticity of demand were as low as -0.3 would of course be huge. 10% of exports would need to be kept off the market (placed into store or destroyed) each year for the duration of the "abnormal" trough — perhaps 5-10 years. If the real interest rate were as low as 5%, and the average time to liquidation were 10 years, then the average cost would be about 63% of the amount put into store, or the equivalent 6.3% of exports. Confining stocks to just non-oil commodities, where their share is 27% of LDC exports, the annual cost would be 1.7% of LDC exports, equivalent to forgiving them 16% of their total interest payments. (Of course, this is a deadweight cost,

(7) See GRILLI - YANG [8], Fig. 4, p. 14, which suggests that this a plausible reading of the evidence, though their emphasis is on longer term secular declines.

whereas forgiveness would be a transfer. Put another way, in order to transfer increased income to LDCs equal to 9% of exports (by raising the price of non-oil primary commodity exports by 33%), the deadweight loss would be 1.7% of exports, or 19% of the transfer. This is large, and together with the implied sizeable revenue transfers, might be just as difficult to sell as substantial debt forgiveness.

Conclusions

Primary commodity prices exhibit considerable instability together with substantial persistence or serial correlation. The characteristic time series shape is one of periodic but randomly occurring upward spikes, most simply· explained by stockouts, and longer periods in which prices bump along in the trough, possibly because storage prevents sharp downward falls. Looking at logarithmic plots, the percentage price increases and decreases look more symmetrically distributed. Storage thus exercises a profound influence on commodity price series, being on the one hand forward looking, and on the other, non-negative and hence prone to stockouts.

If prices were not so strongly serially correlated, the instabilities could be more readily buffered using futures markets and/or lending and borrowing, but serial correlation makes both strategies problematic for LDCs who are debt constrained, though there are financial instruments that can go some way to improving consumption smoothing. Problems of contract enforcement for sovereign nations makes complete smoothing infeasible, and strengthens the case for international stabilisation, either of prices, or of incomes by grants when prices are unreasonably low. Macro-economic costs arising from debt burdens that may be caused or magnified by low commodity prices further strenghen the case for international action, though the persistence of price shocks makes further storage potentially very expensive, and arguably as difficult to achieve as debt forgiveness which would also solve the problem (though perhaps by ignoring the incentive effects of hard budget constraints). There would therefore seem to be no easy solutions to the problems of primary commodity price instability.

BIBLIOGRAPHY

[1] ASLAKSEN I. - BJERKHOLT O.: «Certainty Equivalent Procedures in the Macro-Economic Planning of an Oil Economy», Chapter 12 in BJERKHOLT O. - OFFERDAL E. (eds.): *Macroeconomic Prospects for a Small Oil Exporting Country*, Dordrecht, Martinus Nijhoff, 1985.

[2] BRENNAN M.J. - SCHWARTZ E.S.: «Analyzing Commodity Bonds», *J. Finan. Quant. Anal.*, n. 15, 1980, pp. 907-29.

[3] CUDDINGTON J.T. - URZUA C.M.: *Trends and Cycles in Primary Commodity Prices*, Washington (DC), Economics Department, Georgetown University, mimeo, 1987.

[4] DAVIDSON J.H. - SRBA D.F. - YOO S.: «Econometric Modelling of the Aggregate Time-Series Relationship between Consumption, Expenditure and Income in the UK», *Economic Journal*, n. 88, 1978, pp. 661-92.

[5] DEATON A.S. - LAROQUE G.: «On the Behaviour of Commodity Prices», Princeton, Woodrow Wilson School, *Discussion Paper*, n. 145, 1989.

[6] — — — —: «On the Behaviour of Commodity Prices», *Review of Economic Studies*, n. 59, 1992, pp. 1-24.

[7] GRILLI E.R. - YANG M.C.: «Long-Term Movements of Non-Fuel Commodity Prices: 1900-86», Washington (DC), World Bank International Economics Department, *Working Paper*, Processed 1987.

[8] — — — —: «Primary Commodity Prices, Manufactured Goods Prices, and the Terms of Trade of Developing Countries: What the Long Run Shows», *World Bank Economic Review*, n. 2 (1), 1988, pp. 1-48.

[9] GUSTAFSON R.L.: «Carryover Levels for Grains», US Department of Agriculture, *Technical Bulletin*, n. 1178, 1958.

[10] GREEN E. - PORTER R.: «Non-Cooperative Collusion Under Imperfect Price Information», *Econometrica*, n. 52, 1984, pp. 87-100.

[11] GARDNER B.L.: «Rollover Hedging and Missing Long-Term Futures Markets», *Amer. J. Agr. Econ.*, n. 71, 1989, pp. 311-8.

[12] HALL R.E.: «Stochastic Implications of the Life Cycle Permanent Income Hypothesis: Theory and Evidence», *Journal of Political Economy*, n. 86, 1978, pp. 971-87.

[13] KALDOR N.: «Inflation and Recesion in the World Economy, *Economic Journal*, n. 86, 1976, pp. 703-14.

[14] KLETZER K. - NEWBERY D.M. - WRIGHT B.D.: «Smoothing Primary exporters' Price Risks: Commodity Bonds, Futures, Options and Insurance», *Oxford Economic Papers*, Forthcoming, 1992.

[15] NEWBERY D.M.: «Commodity Price Stabilization», in LAL D. - SCOTT M.F.G. (eds.): *Public Policy and Economic Development*, Oxford, Clarendon Press, 1990, pp. 80-108.

[16] NEWBERY D.M. - STIGLITZ J.E.: *The Theory of Commodity Price Stabilization*, Oxford, Oxford University Press, 1981.

[17] — — — —: «Optimal Commodity Stock-Piling Rules», *Oxford Economic Papers*, n. 34 (3), 1982, pp. 403-27.

[18] NEWBERY D.M.: «Commodity Price Stabilization in Imperfect or Cartelized Markets», *Econometrica*, May 1984, pp. 563-78.

[19] NEWBERY D.M.: «Missing Markets: Consequences and Remedies», in HAHN F.H. (ed.): *Economics of Missing Markets*, Information, and Games, Chapter 10, Oxford, Clarendon Press, 1989, pp. 211-42.

[20] — —: «Commodity Price Stabilization», in LAL D. - SCOTT M.F.G.: (eds.): *Public Policy and Economic Development*, Chapter V, Oxford Clarendon Press, 1990, pp. 80-108.

[21] O'HARA M.: «Commodity Bonds and Consumption Risks, *Journal of Finance*, n. 39, 1984, pp. 193-206.

[22] POWELL A.: «Options to Alleviate the Costs of Uncertainty and Instability: A Case Study of Zambia», in PHLIPS L. (ed.): *Commodity Futures and Financial Markets*, Dordrecht (Netherlands), Kluwer Academic Publishers, 1990.

[23] PRIOVOLOS T. - DUNCAN R.C. (eds.): *Commodity Risk Management and Finance*, Oxford, Oxford University Press, 1991.

[24] SCHWARTZ E.S.: «The Pricing of Commodity-Linked Bonds», *Journal of Finance*, n. 37, 1982, pp. 525-41.

[25] WILLIAMS J.C. - WRIGHT B.D.: *Storage and Commodity Markets*, New York, Cambridge University Press, 1991.

[26] WRIGHT B. - NEWBERY D.M.: «Financial Instruments for Consumption Smoothing by Commodity-Dependent Exporters», in PRIOVOLOS T. - DUNCAN R.C. (eds.): *Commodity Risk Management and Finance*, published for the World Bank, Oxford, Oxford University Press, Chapter 9, 1991, pp. 124-33; Published in ROUMASSET J.A. - BARR S. (eds.): *The Economics of Cooperation: East Asian Development and the Case for Pro-Market Intervention*, Chapter 3, Oxford, Westriew Press, Bouldez, 1992, pp. 39-50.

[27] YERGIN D.: *The Prize*, Simon Schuster, 1992.

A Dynamic Analysis
of a North–South Trade Model (*)

Massimo Di Matteo
Università di Siena

In general the theory of international trade is concerned with the case of a single small country or of two similar countries, i.e. countries that are different enough to trade with each other but not structurally different. They can differ in the technology used to produce the goods (as in the Ricardian analysis), in the relative endowment of resources (as in the Heckscher-Ohlin theory), in demand patterns, in size (1).

One can also construct a general equilibrium model of international trade but such models are in a sense too rich in comparative statics results and encompass many possible outcomes. Appropriate model specifications are therefore needed to tackle real issues.

On the other hand here is a strand of literature that focuses on the existence of two (groups of) countries that are structurally different from each other, the so-called North-South (*N-S*) models. The two countries are different in respects other and beyond those necessary for reciprocal trade.

In the economic literature these two classes of model are separate

(*) The paper is a revised version of the lecture I gave to the Summer School, *Issues in International Economics*, in July 1992 in Siena. To a certain extent it reflects the didactic character of the occasion. I am grateful to G. Chichilnisky and G. Heal for endless discussions about the paper and great encouragement. Very warm thanks for extremely helpful suggestions go to M. Caminati and P.M. Pacini.

I am indebted to Italy's Ministry of Scientific Research (60% funds) and the CNR (*Nato Fellowship* programme) for financial support.

(1) See the analysis put forwards by CAVES [4] and FINDLAY [9] respectively.

(*) *N.B.:* The numbers in square brackets refer to the Bibliography at the end of the paper.

and no easy comparison can be made between then, because the General Equilibrium (GE) approach is static whereas North-South models are typically dynamic. Moreover the GE approach is in favour of free trade which it demonstrates to be superior to autarky (under conditions), whereas the other approach is radical in character and generally suspicious of the theoretical and practical relevance of this result, being more inclined to blame trade itself (and other factors) for the South's backwardness.

At the same time there has been a huge amount of empirical research on the connection between exports and growth in the South. No firm conclusion can be drawn from these findings though some of the studies failed to find a positive correlation between growth and exports in the South.

GE analysis can therefore be applied to see under what circumstances in the South exports and capital accumulation are negatively related both in a static and in a dynamic framework. Here we use a model that Graciela Chichilnisky produced some years ago (Chichilnisky [5]).

In what follows I will review and discuss her static model (Section 1), present a dynamic version of it (Section 2) and relate the latter to the results obtained with other *N-S* models (Section 3).

1. - There are two (groups of) countries, the North (*N*) and the South (*S*), that trade with each other. There is no specialization so that each country produces both the basic good (*B*) and the industrial good (*I*), using two resources, labour (*L*) and capital (*K*), with no intermediate inputs. For each good, the technique of production is different in each country and has fixed coefficients. It is assumed that the supply of resources depends on its reward. It is well known that the supply of labour can be a negative function of the real wage when the latter is sufficiently high. This possibility is ruled out by Chichilnisky: a justification could be that the values of the real wages for which this may occur are not feasible in the model.

In equilibrium prices equal costs, demand for each good is equal to supply and the same is true for resources. In addition trade is assumed to the balanced, namely the value of exports equals the value of imports for each country.

The model can be cast in formal terms (we keep to the original notation as much as we can). All parameters are assumed to be positive.

Let us consider the South starting from the no (extra) profits relation:

(1.1) $P_B = a_1 w + c_1 v$

(1.2) $P_I = a_2 w + c_2 v$

where: $P_B (P_I)$ is the price of the basic (industrial) good, w is the wage rate, v is the price of the services of capital and $a_i (c_i)$ are the labour and capital coefficients in the i-th sector ($1 =$ basic, $2 =$ industrial) (2).

Following Chichilnisky we assume that:

$$D = a_1 c_2 - a_2 c_1 > 0$$

This implies that the basic sector is more labour intensive than the industrial sector.

Labour supply (L^S) is an increasing function of the real wage:

(1.3) $L^S = \alpha w / p_B + L_0$ where: $L_0 > 0$

Differing from Chichilnisky's original analysis we assume that the constant term is positive so that the elasticity of the labour supply with respect to the real wage varies together with the parameter α (3).

We also define a supply of capital (K^S) as an increasing function of v (4):

(1.4) $K^S = \beta v + K_0$ where: $K_0 > 0$

---

(2) For simplicity we neglect depreciation.
(3) Indeed it is true that:
$$\frac{\partial \eta}{\partial \alpha} = (L_0 w / P_B) / (\alpha w / P_B + L_0)^2$$
where η is the elasticity of the labour supply with respect to the real wage.
(4) The assumption is palatable in so far as there is an alternative use for capital.

Then we have the demand functions for capital (K^D) and labour (L^D):

(1.5) $K^D = B^S c_1 + I^S c_2$

(1.6) $L^D = B^S a_1 + I^S a_2$

where: $B^S (I^S)$ is the supply of basic (industrial) goods.
    The equality between demand and supply for resources is

(1.7) $L^D = L^S$

(1.8) $K^D = K^S$

It is assumed that the South will export (import) the basic (industrial) good. This can always be sustained by a suitable choice of I^D and $I^D (N)$ (5). Exports of the South, are:

(1.9) $B^S - B^D = X_B^S$

and imports: X_I^D

(1.10) $I^D - I^S = X_I^D$

where $I^D [B^D]$ is the demand for industrial (basic) goods in the South.
    We now come to the trade balance condition, the value of exports equals the value of imports:

(1.11) $p_B X_B^S = p_I X_I^D$

Equations for the North are similar [with a (N) added] except for different parameters and different values of the exogenous variables and for the fact that the North exports (imports) industrial (basic) goods: therefore imports [exports] are:

$$[X_B^D (N)] \; [X_I^S (N)].$$

---

(5) See infra for their definition and Graph 1 for illustration.

Finally there are other self explanatory conditions to be fulfilled in the international equilibrium with immobile resources:

$$(1.12) \qquad\qquad p_I = p_I(N)$$

$$(1.13) \qquad\qquad p_B = p_B(N)$$

$$(1.14) \qquad\qquad X_B^S = X_B^D(N)$$

$$(1.15) \qquad\qquad X_I^D = X_I^S(N)$$

The last relation however, is not independent of the other equations of the system. It is automatically satisfied when *(1.11)* is satisfied in both countries together with *(1.12)*, *(1.13)* and *(1.14)*.

Finally we have to choose the numeraire:

$$(1.16) \qquad\qquad P_I = 1$$

Therefore in the equation defining the supply of labour, w/p_B can be taken as a measure of the real wage.

There are 11 equations for each country (from *(1.1)* to *(1.11)*), in addition to *(1.12)*, *(1.13)*, *(1.14)*, *(1.16)* making 26 equations altogether. Variables to be determined are 14 in each country:

$$K^S, \ L^S, \ K^D, \ L^D, \ B^S, \ I^S, \ B^D, \ I^D, \ P_B, \ P_I, \ v, \ w, \ X_B^S, \ X_I^D$$

The latter two for the North are: $X_I^S(N)$, $X_B^D(N)$.

There are two degrees of freedom. To make the model determinate we need two more equations representing demand conditions, either those for the industrial good or those for the basic good, or finally those for exports. Following Chichilnisky's original presentation we choose to close the model by assuming (6):

$$(1.17) \qquad\qquad I^D = I_0^D$$

$$(1.18) \qquad\qquad I^D(N) = I_0^D(N)$$

---

(6) Alternative closures are considered in CHICHILNISKY [5], with little change in results.

It is also true that in equilibrium Walras' Law holds. In the South it takes the following form:

$$(1.19) \qquad p_B B^D + p_I I^S = p_B (B^S - X_B^S) + p_I (I^S + X_I^D) =$$
$$= p_B B^S + p_I I^S = wL + vK = Y$$

where Y is income. In this way we see how in equilibrium the demand for basic goods is also determined in each country.

It turns out that the model can be reduced to one quadratic equation in P_B, the terms of trade of the South. Starting from:

$$X_I^D = X_I^S(N)$$

and substituting where necessary we get:

$$(1.20) \qquad [A + A(N)]\, p_B^2 + \gamma p_B - [V + V(N)] = 0$$

where:

$$A = \beta a_1\, a_2 / D^2 > 0$$
$$V = \alpha c_1^2 / D^2 > 0$$
$$\gamma = I_0^D + I_0^D(N) + C + C(N)$$
$$C = [1/D]\{c_1 L_0 - a_1 K_0 + [\alpha c_1 c_2 - \beta a_1^2]/D\} > 0 \ (7)$$

are for the South $[A(N), V(N), C(N), D(N)$ are the corresponding expressions for the North].

Clearly *(1.20)* has one positive solution. Once it is known all the other endogenous variables can be computed.

The model can be illustrated with a simple diagram representing the demand and supply conditions of the industrial good in the two countries.

The dotted lines represent the equilibrium values of P_B in autarky where demand equals production. After trade is open, the terms of trade will be at a value such that the export of industrial goods from

---

(7) When α in the South is very large, see infra 1.1.

GRAPH 1

A DYNAMIC ANALYSIS OF A NORTH-SOUTH TRADE MODEL

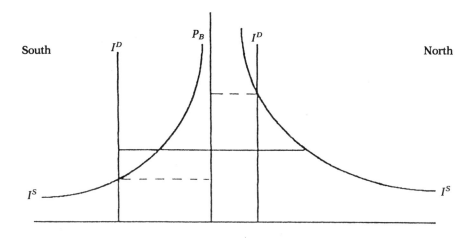

the North equals the imports of industrial goods from the South (see the continuous line).

1.1 Having described the model in general terms it is now time to introduce the appropriate specifications mentioned in Section 1. Chichilnisky argues that the South is characterized by two features conveniently summarized as:

assumption a: a highly responsive supply of labour
assumption b: dual technology.

The first states that the labour supply is very responsive indeed to the real wage: in the model this is expressed as a very large value of α. It is precisely to accomodate this feature that the model has variable factor supplies. This assumption is a bit less extreme than that elaborated by Lewis [15] in that the latter requires the elasticity of the labour supply to the real wage to be infinite. With the second assumption we describe a situation in which the labor/capital ratio is much higher in the basic than in the industrial sector: in the model this is reflected by a high value of D for the South. The precise condition for obtaining the results given below is $c_2/D < 2w/P_B$ which is assumed to be satisfied by a large D.

Four main results can be derived from the model specified by these two assumptions; in parenthesis we indicate the assumption(s) sufficient for each result to be true:

result (i): inverse relationship between demand for industrial goods in the North (South) and P_B, the terms of trade (a)

result (ii): inverse relationship between terms of trade and exports in the South (a, b)

result (iii): positive relationship between terms of trade and demand for basics in the South (a)

result (iv): positive relationship between terms of trade and export revenues in the South (a, b).

Results (ii) and (iv) are reversed if b does not hold. However it must be borne in mind that a) and b) are also sufficient for ensuring stability of the equilibrium (8).

In economic terms the chain (ii) - (iv) means that a decrease in the terms of trade (triggered by a change in the North's demand for the industrial good or by other factors) is associated with an increase in exports, a fall in the welfare of the South (the consumption of the industrial good being fixed) and a decrease in the export revenues (9). Therefore a reduction in the value of world commerce is not beneficial to the South (under conditions) and the opening up of trade is beneficial to the South in that the terms of trade increase (compare the continuous line in the left part of Graph 1 with the dotted line). It is also true however that in the South an increase in the quantity of exports is associated with a decrease in export revenues: hence the critique of export-led policies that Chichilnisky derives from her analysis in the paper.

In my opinion the label "export-led policies" is inappropriate because it traditionally refers to a growth model of the Keynesian type (Beckerman, Lamfalussy, etc.). It remains true that in this model an

---

(8) For a thorough analysis of the latter see also HEAL-McLEOD [11].

(9) Here welfare is measured by the total amount of the consumption goods. A more precise analysis should consider the consumption per capita.

equilibrium with a higher volume of exports is associated with a fall in export revenues and in welfare in the South.

An intuitive explanation of (*ii*), along the lines of Arrow's interpretation quoted in Chichilnisky [5] can be given as follows. Assume that an increase in the exports of the South is associated with an increase in the terms of trade. Exports are highly labour intensive (assumption *b*) and therefore in the reallocation of production an increase in the real wage is necessary. At the same time labour supply also is highly responsive to the real wage (assumption *a*). The consequent increase in the wage income is absorbed by the demand for the basic good since the demand for the industrial good is fixed. As a consequence the increased internal demand for the basic good would be in contrast with the assumed increase in exports. Therefore the terms of trade have to fall to ensure the increase in exports.

What is the situation of the North after a fall in P_B? If we could show that the demand for basic goods had increased then there would be a clear case of conflict between the two (groups of) countries. Since the North imports basic goods its demand is the sum of domestic production $[B^S(N)]$ and of imports from the South $[X_B^D(N)]$: the first is a positive function of the terms of trade, P_B, but the second is a negative one (recall that the North's imports are the South's exports and result (*ii*). Therefore we cannot say whether demand for basics is larger or smaller after a fall in the terms of trade.

We can show however that the demand for basics in the North increases with a fall of the terms of trade

  1) the higher the volume of exports of the North
or:
  2) the lower α in the North (10).

The second condition can be reasonably accepted and the former, when true, can be taken as an indicator of the dependency of the South on the North.

We notice *en passant* that the increase in $I^D(N)$, by lowering P_B [result (*i*)], has lowered the real wage in both countries and increased

---

(10) Other conditions can be found in CHICHILNISHY [5], proposition 5.

the price of the service of capital. This can be seen on solving the subsystem formed by *(1.1)* and *(1.2)* in w/P_B and v as function of P_B:

(1.21)

$$w = -\frac{c_1}{D} + \frac{c_2}{D} P_B$$

$$v = \frac{a_1}{D} - \frac{a_2}{D} P_B$$

Therefore the generalized Stolper-Samuelson theorem does hold in this model, since when P_B falls, for example, there is an increase in the unit reward of the owners of the factor (capital) intensively used in the expanding industry (the manufacturing one). It is also true that the welfare of the workers decreases since the real wage and employment fall, and the welfare of the owners of capital goes up since v and K increase, again as in the Stolper-Samuelson theorem which is also valid in this case of variable factor supplies. So not only are there conflicts between countries but also within each country.

2. - The static model is ill-suited for answering questions emerging from a proper comparison with the North-South literature, and also those connected with the relationship between exports and accumulation of capital.

I therefore make the model dynamic. I start from the observation that by putting $\beta = 0$ (i.e. if we consider the capital stock to be given [namely K_0] at the beginning of the period), the results reported in 1.1 are unaffected in qualitative terms, as long as P_B is positive. Indeed when $\beta = 0$ the resolvent equation is no longer a quadratic as in *(1.20)* but a linear one:

(2.1)
$$P_B = \frac{V + V(N)}{I_0^D + I_0^D(N) + C' + C'(N)}$$

where:

$$C' = (1/D) \left[c_1 L_0 - a_1 K_0 + \frac{\alpha c_1 c_2}{D} \right]$$

and $C'(N)$ is the corresponding term for the North.

It is immediate to check that there are values of the capital stocks that make the equilibrium terms of trade negative. In the sequel we will assume that the terms of trade are always positive. This can be sustained with an appropriate choice of the exogenous values of the demand for industrial goods.

We therefore reinterpret the static model of Section 1 and 1.1 as a uniperiodal model with a given stock of capital in each country. With respect to the latter and to the conditions of demand for industrial goods, we are able to define the equilibrium terms of trade and the equilibrium values for any other variable of the model, including income. At the end of each period everything that has been produced is demanded but part of the goods (according to a rule to be specified) are not properly consumed but are transformed, via an implicit production function (11), into capital that is available at the beginning of next period. In this second period with a new level of capital stock in both countries a new equilibrium level of the terms of trade is reached and of the endogenous variables as well. In this way the dynamics are built according to the method recommended by Pareto at the beginning of this century (12).

The simplest rule of accumulation, which is consistent with a class of utility functions (13), is that a fixed share of income will be transformed into capital next period. We can write the following dynamical expression for the South, taking explicit account of depreciation:

$$K_{t+1} - K_t + \delta K_t = \sigma Y_t$$

where δ, $\sigma > 0$ are the depreciation rate and the share of savings in income respectively (Y is derived from *(1.19)*).

This formulation leads to a dynamical system of the form:

$$K_{t+1} - K_t = F[K_t, K(N)_t]$$

$$K(N)_{t+1} - K(N)_t = G[K_t, K(N)_t]$$

---

(11) One can imagine that a third factor (say public infrastructure capital), whose price is given, produces the capital good in cooperation whit the amount of the industrial and basic goods that are not properly consumed.

(12) The method was given an extremely interesting application by the Italian economist La Volpe in 1936 (LA VOLPE [14]).

(13) See e.g. MORISHIMA [17].

since in each period Y is a function of the terms of trade, that are in turn a function of the two capital stocks (for any level of the demand for industrial goods).

However to study such a system is rather difficult since $F(G)$ function (s) have a complicated form. Following the analysis by Lewis [15], it can be argued that in the South capital accumulation depends on (part of the) profit income, rather than on total income. This assumption greatly simplifies the analysis if it can be extended to the North as well, thus leading to the following system:

$$K_{t+1} - K_t = -\delta K_t + \sigma v_t\, K_t$$

$$K(N)_{t+1} - K(N)_t = -\delta_n\, K(N)_t + \sigma_n\, v(N)_t\, K(N)_t$$

where $v K$ is the income of the owners of the capital which depends on the terms of trade and therefore on the capital stocks (for any given level of the demand for industrial goods).

We can switch to the differential version which is easier to handle and we then divide both sides of each equation by its own capital stock to obtain:

$$\dot{K}/K = -\delta + \sigma v(K, K_N)$$

$$\dot{K}_N/K_N = -\delta_N + \sigma_N v_N(K, K_N)$$

where for simplifying the notation the terms referring to the South are without subscript, and those referring to the North have the subscript N.

We now determine the stationary point (s), where the rate of growth of each capital stock is zero, namely:

$$\delta = \sigma v$$

$$\delta_N = \sigma_N v_N$$

However within each period of time the price of the services of capital depends of the terms of trade in this way (see *(1.21)*) and we have:

(2.2) $$\delta = \sigma a_1 / D - P_B \sigma a_2 / D$$

$$\delta_N = \sigma_N (a_1 / D)_N - P_B \sigma_N (a_2 / D)_N$$

It is clear that unless a well specified relation exists between the various parameters, the system does not have a solution for which the capital stock of both countries are stationary at the same time (14).

To appreciate this situation better, let us insert in *(2.2)* the value of the equilibrium terms of trade within each period as derived from the static model (see *(2.1)*). We get:

(2.3) $$\frac{D}{a_1} \left\{ C'' + C''(N) + [V + V(N)] \left(\frac{\sigma a_2}{\delta D - \sigma a_1} \right) - \left(\frac{a_1}{D} \right)_N K_N \right\} = K$$

$$\frac{D}{a_1} \left\{ C'' + C''(N) + [V + V(N)] \left(\frac{\sigma_N a_{2N}}{\delta_N D_N - \sigma_N a_{1N}} \right) - \left(\frac{a_1}{D} \right)_N K_N \right\} = K$$

where:

$$C'' = I_0^D + (1 / D) (c_1 L_0 + a c_1 c_2 / D)$$

and $C''(N)$ is the corresponding term for the North.

The first equation describes all the combinations of K and K_N such that K is stationary, whereas the second equation describes all the combinations of K and K_N such that K_N is stationary. We immediately see that in both cases K is a linear function of K_N so that all the combinations that have the property that the capital stock does not change for each country lie on a segment in the (K, K_N) plane. It is also clear that the two are parallel segments and that if D is much bigger than D_N the two curves can be represented as follows:

---

(14) Other ways of analyzing the system are possible, but the following seems to be the most interesting.

GRAPH 2

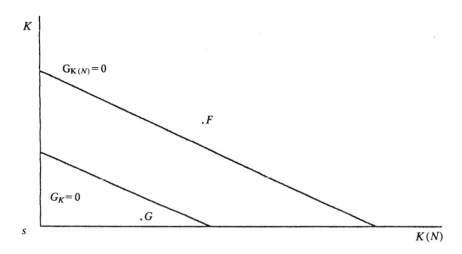

where G_K ($G_{K(N)}$) is the rate of growth of the capital stock in the South (North).

Along each curve we have exactly the level of the price of the services of capital and therefore exactly the level of the terms of trade such that savings are just sufficient to replace the capital stock that depreciates. We stipulate that the assumption *b*, namely technological dualism implies that $D > D_N$.

We now have to consider what happens when the system finds itself at a point like *F*. Here capital stocks in both countries are greater than the values for which the rate of capital accumulation of the North and the South is zero. There is a positive association between the level of each capital stock and the terms of trade derived from *(2.1)*:

$$(2.4) \qquad \frac{\partial P_B}{\partial K} = \frac{(a_1 / D) [V + V(N)]}{[C' + C'(N) + I_0^D(S) + I_0^D(N)]^2}$$

therefore in *F* the terms of trade will exceed the value they take when associated with the stationary solution in each country. In other words in *F* the price of the services of capital will fall short of the value that guarantees an unchanged net capital stock in both countries and therefore the stock of capital in the South and in the North will fall, so that the point will move *SW*. The same argument in reverse applies for points, like *G* that lie below the $G_K=0$ line: in this case the capital stock of both the North and the South will increase, the point travelling *NE*.

It is now time consider what happens when the initial conditions of the capital stocks are such that the representative point lies between the two curves. In this situation, in which the technological dualism assumption holds. the capital stock of the North will increase and that of the South will decrease, the representative point travelling *SE*. In the limit, if nothing new happens, the capital stock of the South will be annihilated.

This is a very bleak perspective for the South. The North and the South can grow together for a period of time (eg if they start from a point like *G*); however as soon as the South reaches the point at which the capital stock is unchanged, growth of the North drives the South to ruin. When the initial conditions insert the system in the region between the two stationary lines, the two countries are totally opposed to each other.

We can now appreciate the special case in which the two curves overlap: this requires that the parameters in *(2.2)* be related in a special way. In this special case the two countries either grow or decay together depending on the initial conditions, but it is not possible that one grows and the other decays or viceversa.

We now briefly describe the dynamic evolution of the system, starting from the point *G*. Terms of trade will increase as we have already noticed and this is accompanied [result *(iv)*] by an increase in the value of exports of the South or, which amounts to the same thing, an increase in the value of imports of industrial goods. At the same time during the process of growth, exports from the South fall in physical terms [result *(ii)*]. Hence the growth process in the South, when there is one, is accompanied by a decrease in the quantity of exports. On the contrary for the North growth is matched by an increase in the physical quantity of exports (via result *(iv)* and *(1.16)*).

It is somewhat more difficult to say what happens when the system enters the intermediate zone between the two stationary lines:

capital stocks are changing in opposite direction and this exerts contradictory influences on the terms of trade. Recalling *(2.4)* we notice that if technological dualism holds [i.e. if $D > D_N$] the effect of Northern capital is greater than that exerted by Southern capital so that the terms of trade will actually increase as Northern capital is increasing. So even in this region the same pattern will prevail as below the $G_K = 0$ line.

We conclude by noting that during the process of capital accumulation the real wage is increasing in both countries since it is directly linked to the terms of trade as is clear from *(1.21)*: at the same time the price of the services of capital is falling in both countries. This is an important aspect crucial to the dynamics. This fall comes out of the working of the whole model which exhibits constants return to scale in the production of both goods. This shows that no endogenous growth is possible in the model as it now stands; as there is no expanding external force (like population growth or technical progress) it is only too natural that growth is deemed die out (15).

However it is interesting to see whether the model can be modified to include the case of an increasing price of the services of capital (and hence the *possibility* of endogeous growth). Before doing so let me speculate how the picture will change if we postulate that savings are out of income rather than profits.

To answer this question one has to consider how income is linked to the terms of trade. It turns out that the sign of the relation depends on the absolute value of the capital stocks (16). If the latter are sufficiently small, income is positively related to the terms of trade; beyond a certain critical value income is, like the price of the services of capital, negatively associated with the tems of trade. As a conse-

---

(15) We are abstracting from the oldest case of endogenous growth, the Harrodian analysis: for some comments see DI MATTEO [7].

(16) The exact formula is:

$$\frac{\partial Y}{\partial P_B} = \alpha \frac{c_2^2 - c_1^2 P_B^{-2}}{D^2} + \frac{c_2 L_0 - a_2 K_0}{D} +$$

$$\alpha_N \left(\frac{c_2^2 - c_1^2 P_B^{-2}}{D} \right)_N + \frac{c_2 L_0(N) - a_2 K_0(N)}{D(N)}$$

and for small values of the capital stocks, the sign is determined by the sign of the term multiplying α. The latter is positive to ensure that the real wage is positive.

quence there can be an unstable region for small values of the capital stocks. This means that if the capital stock is very small the country cannot but decay, which makes sense; otherwise the former analysis remains valid from a qualitative point of view.

Let us now come back to the behaviour of v. The negative relation between the price of the services of capital and the terms of trade results from the fact that P_B is the price of the labour intensive good. Should the basic good be the capital intensive good then the relation would be a positive one. Does this entail a change in the proposition of our dynamic model? The answer is no. If the basic good is the capital intensive good, D is negative contrary to our assumption. In this case the derivate *(2.4)* would be negative so that an increase in the capital stock would lead to a fall in the terms of trade, however the slope of the two stationary lines (see *(2.3)*) would be unchanged. A point above both lines, such as point F, would have terms of trade below the level that guarantees the stationary level. The value of v would be lower than that associated with the stationary level and therefore the stock of capital would be decreasing: again as in the previous case.

We continue to suppose that the South exports B, now the capital intensive good. Starting from the point where a process of growth is possible, the terms of trade will fall and export will decrease again (17). Hence in both cases there seems to be an association between capital accumulation and decrease in the physical quantity of exports of the South: with the present model rather than Chichilnisky's we can properly answer the questions raised by "export-led policies".

Coming back to the question of how the South can prevent a fall in v so that accumulation can be sustained, it is immediately evident that changes in I^D and c_2 will do the trick. First let us take the case of an increase in the demand for the industrial good that we have kept fixed as in Chichilnisky's original model. It is very likely however that

---

(17) When $\beta = 0$ we have:

$$\frac{\partial X_B^S}{\partial P_B} = \frac{\alpha c_1}{D^2 P_B^2}\left(\frac{2 c_1}{P_B} - c_2\right) + \frac{a_1 K - c_1 L_0}{D^2 P_B^2} - \frac{I_0^D(S)}{P_B^2}.$$

The sign is positive since it is determined by the term in α and the expression in parenthesis has be positive in order to ensure the positivity of the real wage in the case of $D < 0$ (see *(1.1)*).

as the process of growth unfolds the amount of that good demanded will increase too. In each period this will exert a negative influence on the terms of trade (see result *(i)*) and therefore a positive one on v and accumulation. This will also be true if the demand for the industrial good increases in the North: in this very specific sense the North can help accumulation in the South.

On the other hand technical progress in the South leading to a fall in c_2, i.e. a fall in the capital coefficient of the capital intensive sector, will exert a positive influence on v for any level of the terms of trade and this again will boost the accumulation process. The possibility of a reduction in c_2 could be derived from Arrow's analysis of the "learning by doing process" (Arrow [1]). As the accumulation of capital goes on, the level of technology evolves (remember that the North produces both goods) leading to a reduction in the various technical coefficients: in this model the most *uniformly* efficacious method of enhancing growth is the reduction of c_2, though reduction in the others will also have some effect.

These two examples show that the very pessimistic conclusion drawn from the analysis of the dynamic system can be mitigated and point to an effective role for policies aimed at increasing the level of I^D and at favouring technical progress.

There are some final remarks on the limitations of the analysis. It is proposed a dynamic extension of Chichilnisky's model that leaves the original structure of the model substantially unaltered. In this new context, the negative association between volume of exports and capital accumulation found is the theoretical counterpart of the results reached at the static level. However it is apparent that some of the peculiar results of the model (eg the lack of a global stationary solution) depend on the symmetry it displays in the rules of accumulation that in both countries make investments depend on capital income. However other solution implying an asymmetric accumulation rule would have greatly complicated the analysis and have therefore not been considered.

3. - The next step is to compare very briefly the results of the model just presented with those reached in the North-South literature.

In the latter the following assumption are widely held:

a) the rate of growth of population in the North is exogenous (18);

b) there is complete specialization: each country produces just one good (19);

c) the capital good needed by the South to produce the only good is totally imported (20).

Neither of these three assumptions were made in the present dynamic model. Population or rather the supply of labour is endogenously determined, being a function of the real wage; each country produces both goods and there is no intermediate input to produce each good in the two countries.

Other assumptions of many North-South models are derived from Lewis [15] namely a very large pool of labour in the South (Findlay [10]) and the fact that workers do not save. Some models also embody the assumption, that appears to be supported by empirical evidence (21), that the good exported by the South is less capital intensive that the one exported by the North. All these three assumptions are part of the present model.

In the North-South literature, the North is either represented by a neoclassical growth model *à la* Solow (Findlay [10]) or is shaped according to a Neokeynesian approach (Taylor [19]) (22). Findlay [10] shows that the South's growth rate is equal to the exogenously given population growth in the North. His model is stable under conditions analogous to those known as Marshall-Lerner's. These are traditional results that trade is the engine of growth in the South, which is dependent on the North. Findlay assumes *inter alia* that the demand for the two goods are unit elastic with respect to income.

A Keynes-Lewis model shows again that the South's growth depends on growth in the North but via *animal spirits* rather than exogenously given population growth and in this way an expansion in the North benefits the South.

---

(18) See eg. FINDLAY [10].
(19) See eg. FINDLAY [10] and TAYLOR [19].
(20) See eg. FINDLAY [10].
(21) See eg. BELASSA [3] and KRUEGER [13].
(22) There are also some Kaldor-inspired models such as MOLANA-VINES [16] and CONWAY-DARITY [6].

In comparison the present dynamic model shows under what conditions there can be simultaneous growth in both countries (though in our model there is not a steady state common to both countries) and under what conditions the negative association between growth and (the physical amount of) exports from the South remains valid. We have also shown how the dynamics can be constructed when the rate of growth is not exogenously given.

The next step will be to espress our model in a way similar to that emerging from the new literature on endogenous growth, since we have already shown a possible link (23).

4 - The three aims of this paper were 1) to present and discuss the North-South model elaborated by Chichilnisky in a static context; 2) to elaborate a dynamic version of it and check whether one of its main results was confirmed; 3) to compare the differences in modelling and results between this dynamic model and other North-South dynamic models.

On the first point we confirmed the results reached by Chichilnisky even in the case when capital supply is not linked to the price of the services of capital. On the second point we interpreted the static model as a uniperiodal model and built a dynamic model in which each period is linked to the previous via the accumulation of capital, the labour supply being endogenously determined. On the third point we have shown that the general result of the literature, namely that the North can be a driving force for the South, may be invalid and that the favourable link between exports and the process of capital accumulation can also be invalid when the South is characterized by a labour supply extremely responsive to the real wage and by dual technology.

---

(23) For an extremely terse and lucid exposition of this recent analysis see SOLOW [18].

BIBLIOGRAPHY

[1] ARROW K.J.: «The Economic Implications of Learning by Doing», *Review of Economic Studies*, n. 29, 1962, pp. 155-73.

[2] BELASSA B.: «Exports and Economic Growth», *Journal of Development Economies*, n. 5, 1978, pp. 181-9.

[3] — — : *The Newly Industrializing Countries in the World Economy*, New York, Pergamon Press, 1981.

[4] CAVES R.: *Trade and Economic Structure*, Cambridge, Harvard University Press, 1960.

[5] CHICHILNISKY G.: «General Equilibrium Theory of North-South Trade», in HELLER-STARR-STARRETT (eds.): *Essays in Honour of K. Arrow*, vol. II, Cambridge, CUP, 1986.

[6] CONWAY P. - DARITY W.A.: «Growth and Trade with Asymmetric Returns to Scale: a Model for Nicholas Kaldor», *Southern Economic Journal*, n. 57, 1991, pp. 745-59.

[7] DI MATTEO M.: «Warranted, Natural, and Actual Rates of Growth: Reflections of a Perplex», Università di Siena, *Quaderni dell'istituto di economia*, n. 68, 1987.

[8] — — : «Forms of Trade Control in an Equilibrium North-South Model: A Comparative Evaluation», *Rivista internazionale di scienze economiche e commerciali*, n. 40, 1993, pp. 63-74.

[9] FINDLAY R.: *Trade and Specialization*, Harmondsworth, Penguin Books, 1970.

[10] — — : «The Terms of Trade and Equilibrium Growth in the World Economy», *American Economic Review*, n. 70, 1980, pp. 291-9.

[11] HEAL G. - McLEOD D.: «Gains from Trade, Stability and Profits», *Journal of Development Economics*, n. 15, 1984, pp. 117-30.

[12] KRUEGER A.: *Liberalization: Attempts and Consequences*, New York NBER, 1978.

[13] — — : *Trade and Employment in Developing Countries*, vol. III, Chicago, Chicago UP, 1983.

[14] LA VOLPE G.: *Studies in the Theory of General Dynamic Economic Equilibrium*, Introduction by Morishima M. - Di Matteo M., London Macmillan, 1993.

[15] LEWIS A.: «Economic Development with Unlimited Supplies of Labour», *Manchester School of Economic and Social Studies*, n. 22, 1954, pp. 139-91.

[16] MOLANA H. - VINES D.: «North-South Growth and the Terms of Trade: a Model on Kaldorian Lines», *Economic Journal*, n. 99, 1989, pp. 443-53.

[17] MORISHIMA M.: *Theory of Economic Growth*, Oxford, Oxford University Press, 1969.

[18] SOLOW R.M.: *Siena Lectures on Endogenous Growth Theory*, in SORDI S. (ed.), mimeo, 1992 (forthcoming at La Nuova Italia Scientifica).

[19] TAYLOR L.: *Structuralist Macroeconomics*, New York, Basic Books, 1983.

Index